PRAISE FOR *The Once and Future Lake*

"A moving tribute. The soul of our state and its beating heart is Great Salt Lake. Gathered here are some of the voices who have known and loved the lake through generations and others who are meeting the lake for the first time. If you haven't spent time there, read this book and then GO! Or better yet, take this book with you and read it while you look for snowy plover and Wilson's phalarope."

—ANNE HOLMAN, The King's English Bookshop

"A thoughtfully compiled collection. It is something bigger, deeper, and wilder than could be imagined—a collective story tinged delicately by hope that may only be realized in its being shared."

—NOAH BASKETT, Salt Lake City Public Library

"Great Salt Lake is one of the strangest, most wondrous, and mysterious places on the planet. It has been revered and abused. Its immensity often obliterates attempts to capture it in text or in art and words can be woefully inadequate in the face of its sublimity. And yet, this poignant and heartfelt collection of essays and poems brings Great Salt Lake to life for its readers."

—JONATHAN P. THOMPSON, *Sagebrush Empire*

"A buoyant collection and a pressing call to action. Like the rivers of the Great Basin, these essays, poems, and stories pour past city lawns and alfalfa fields toward the unassuming Great Salt Lake, begging us to see its beauty and recognize its many inhabitants—before it's too late."

—ZAK PODMORE, *Life After Dead Pool*

"Contributors to *The Once and Future Lake* invite us to their beloved lake so we can all envision a healthier future for her—and for the rest of the more-than-human world, too."

—LAURA PASKUS, editor of *Water Bodies*

"*The Once and Future Lake* is a demonstration of love for Great Salt Lake. Read it to learn and be inspired. Read it for solace and hope. Read it to find the connections between us and the lake."

—DEEDA SEED, Senior Utah Campaigner,
Center for Biological Diversity

THE ONCE AND FUTURE LAKE

EDITED BY
MICHAEL MCLANE

TORREY HOUSE PRESS

Salt Lake City • Torrey

First Torrey House Press Edition, June 2026

Published by Torrey House Press
Salt Lake City, Utah
www.torreyhouse.org

International Standard Book Number: 979-8-89092-009-6
E-book ISBN: 979-8-89092-010-2
Library of Congress Control Number: 2023952237

Cover design by Kathleen Metcalf
Interior design by Eryon Shondíín Greenburg
Distributed to the trade by Consortium Book Sales and Distribution

Torrey House Press offices in Salt Lake City sit on the homelands of Ute, Goshute, Shoshone, and Paiute nations. Offices in Torrey are on the homelands of Southern Paiute, Ute, and Navajo nations.

CONTENTS

Introduction

Michael McLane

I

Nearly every day of my life has been spent in close proximity to Great Salt Lake. As a child growing up in the Wasatch foothills, I could see its glimmer in the distance from our front porch, the wavering limit of my imagination at sunset. This thin ribbon holding the valley together was impossible to reconcile with the alien landscapes I took in from the rear-facing back seat of my parents' Buick station wagon—causeways and salt pools, derelict dance halls, basin and range upside-down and glassy in the inches-deep and endless sea. As I got older, I seemed only to gravitate closer and closer to Great Salt Lake, both literally and intellectually, my address always moving north and west, my mind immersed in the waterways that fed and feed it, in the military-industrial complex that threatens it. From the cityscape of downtown Salt Lake City, it was rarely visible, but ever-present. Wind brought the smell of salt and lake effect snow in winter and the smell of beached death in late summer. There were the shadows of countless birds against the desert sky. I circumnavigated Great Salt Lake in long, exhausting days, and brief episodic bursts—Warm Springs and Kelton, *Sun Tunnels* and Stansbury, *Spiral Jetty* and Thiokol, bird refuge and bombing range. What might seem empty is an evolving ecotone, a massive palimpsest of change and danger and life.

But life takes curious turns and I have now lived away from

Great Salt Lake for nearly six years. I've lived just out of sight of the ocean most of that time. I know it's there, and if I strain just so or walk into the hills near our home, I can see the edge of the world and smell deep, deep waters on the southerlies that scour town. I drive to the beach some days just for orientation or a little humility. But the water is different, as is the salt and the wind. Like the Great Basin, it is sublime, but almost inverse. Most days, I still feel I have yet to get my bearings. It is easy to forget how the bodies of water we belong to shape our way through the world. This is all the more true in places where water is scarce.

The notions of *whakapapa* and *pepeha* are crucial to Māori peoples where I live now, in Aotearoa/New Zealand. The former encompasses ideas of genealogy, lineage as well as ancestral and geographical inheritance while the latter is a way of providing your *whakapapa* in social situations by way of your ties to family and place. The first lines of a pepeha typically identify a person's *maunga* (mountain) and *awa/roto* (river/lake):

My mountain is Olympus
My lake is Great Salt Lake

These words are meant to depict relationship, not ownership. They orient me, even all these many miles away. I miss my mountain. I miss my lake. It is why I jumped at the chance when Torrey House Press asked me to edit this volume. I wanted to feel the love of a place that often seems too easy to overlook, to forget, to distract us from while it is subjugated. While the ominous headlines about Great Salt Lake accumulated, there were still so many people doing the hard work of activism, or community building, of hope. We wanted to hear their voices.

II

In 1849, under the auspices of the US Army Corps of Topographical Engineers, Captain Howard Stansbury set out on a two-year expedition to the Great Basin to survey and study a wide range of topics—the Mormon settlements there, Native American communities in the region, as well as the viability of a military post somewhere in the wide, desolate, and largely unmapped expanse. Primary amongst his tasks was a survey of Great Salt Lake, its waterways, and their navigability. Their to-do list was monumental, though Stansbury and his coterie proved to be up to the task.

Stansbury was hardly the first to see, or to send word of, the strange, desert lake. Frontiersman Jim Bridger observed Great Salt Lake in 1824, John C. Frémont's expedition offered a survey of Great Salt Lake Valley in a more abbreviated form in 1843 and 1845, and the ill-fated Donner Party traversed the valley and the salt flats in 1846. Two days after their July 1847 arrival in the Great Salt Lake Valley with Brigham Young's first Mormon settler party, Thomas Bullock and others set out to explore the network of geothermal springs that contributed to the network of wetlands around Great Salt Lake. Writing about the area of Warm Springs, near what is now Beck Street in Salt Lake City, Bullock wrote "we returned to the nearest hot spring and bathed in it . . . it was very warm and smelt very bad." It was the first record of the new arrivals taking to the waters that make up the lake's ecosystem, and Bullock's ambivalence would prove an enduring quality of the interactions to come.

But it was Stansbury's survey, which involved a month-long circumnavigation of the lake by land, that was the most sustained, immersive interaction with Great Salt Lake by non-Indigenous peoples to that point. To a large degree, Stansbury was not impressed. He wrote of his surprise to find "although so near a body of the saltiest water, none of that feeling of invigorating freshness which is always experienced when in the vicinity of the ocean." He was unsettled by Great Salt Lake's "bleak and naked shores, without a single tree to relieve the eye." It was "a scene so different from what I pictured in my imagination of the beauties of this far-famed spot, that my disappointment was extreme."

None of this deterred the armchair explorers and tourists whose imaginations continued to run wild amid such descriptions. This was amplified by a concerted effort from Young and other Mormon leaders to maintain a correlation between their new homeland and more Biblical environs—a "dead" saline sea in a vast desert, a persecuted people wandering the wilds in search of a new homeland. Young understood that such metaphors not only tightened the bonds amongst the Mormon faithful, but also offered a means by which to navigate the inevitable encroachment of the outside world upon their isolation. Jared Farmer writes, "Where else could you find a mysterious religious capital alongside a sulfurous warm spring and briny inland sea." Travelers were already intrigued by Young's "Kingdom of Deseret," ascribing to it an "Asiatic" quality that was reinforced by the idiolect of the Mormons with words such as Zion and Jordan figuring prominently into their geography and mythos. Their polygamous families were compared to Turkish harems. It was a curious place with a curious people and an enormous dead sea all too similar to that of the Holy Land. Likewise, Great Salt Lake and the hot springs that fed into it offered both medical and recreational opportunities at a time when the practice of medical geography and the curative properties of particular places was at its peak. Writers and marketing men were happy to take up this theme. Geographer and explorer Richard Burton compared the confluence of fresh and salt water, as well as hot and cold water, in the valley to that of the Middle East. He describes "These springs, together with the fresh-water lake and the Jordan, are held to be more purifying than Abana and Pharphar, rivers of Damascus."

Such accounts, and the tourism they drove to the city, fed an already burgeoning recreational industry based upon Great Salt Lake and the surrounding waterways. Resorts sprouted up all along the periphery of the lake—Black Rock, Garfield Beach, Saltair, Warm Springs, Beck's Hot Springs, Lagoon. At one time, one could take a boat from the now-extinct Hot Spring Lake down a short tributary to the Jordan River and on to Great Salt Lake. For the less seafaring, a dedicated "pleasure train" ran multiple times a day from Black Rock around the southeast shores of the lake and north to Lagoon. Swimmers bobbed in the waters of the lake at each resort and danced in grand pavilions. Great Salt Lake was the focal point of leisure for Salt Lake City, and a draw for tourists from around the nation and around the world.

This heyday was bright, but brief. In the first half of the twentieth century, it seemed that Great Salt Lake was destined to shift from medical geography to forgotten geography, from the valley's heart to a kind of amputated limb, a blank space in the landscape. By the early 1900s, many of the resorts were floundering. Fires and disinterest combined with an increasing interest in the recreational opportunities offered by the surrounding mountains took a toll. The Great Depression, bookended by two world wars, forced austerity and muted tourism everywhere. By the end of World War II, Saltair and Warm Springs were essentially the only pleasure palaces left standing, and both were in disrepair. The blossoming ski and alpine recreation industry continued to draw visitors away from Great Salt Lake (a great irony given Great Salt Lake's crucial role in the ski industry on the Wasatch Front) even as increasing automobile usage should have made visitation easier. Meanwhile, the network of industries that were coalescing into the American military-industrial complex had already taken over vast swaths of lake shore and wetlands, taking advantage of not only the resources available in and around the lake, but also the transportation corridors that run along its eastern edge and traverse its waters. It seemed the lake had entered its senescence, its timing perfect for those who sought to take more than memories from their time there.

That is not to say that everyone viewed Great Salt Lake with the same kind of disappointment Stansbury felt in 1849. There were still voices more akin to that of Alfred Lambourne, the painter who homesteaded on Gunnison Island in the 1860s, and who painted and wrote with great love and awe of Great Salt Lake and the island, describing them as "deeper than all imagining" and "the savage poem around me." Sometimes, it takes a poet. In 1934, Gertrude Stein undertook a nationwide tour of the United States, during which she felt a deep affinity for the Great Basin, and the salt flats and Great Salt Lake in particular, writing to Alice B. Toklas that "it is a satisfaction to know that an ocean is interesting even if there is no water in it," and writing again in a later text that "there is the land which nobody can see because there is the sea, and yet there is the land in America, there is the land salt lake land where there is no sea." In 1949, Dale Morgan published The Great Salt Lake, what was the most extensive study of Great Salt Lake to date and, in terms of its treatment of the cultural history, particularly that of Indigenous peoples, remains so to this day (though several volumes are in development, including a wide-ranging series from University of Utah Press). The opening passages of the book make room for both the disappointment of Stansbury's experience and the sublime of Lambourne's. He writes:

> Great Salt Lake is unique among American lakes, arresting in its name, yet least known. Its name itself has an aura of the strange and mysterious, but it resists those who would know it. Lake of paradoxes, in a country where water is life itself and land has little value without it, Great Salt Lake is an ironical joke of nature—water that is itself more desert than a desert.

Despite the scope of Morgan's project, and his enduring affection for the topic, it is perhaps more telling of disinterest in Great Salt Lake over much of the past seventy-five years that the book is currently unavailable and its last printing was in 2002. Nonetheless, Morgan paved the way for so many of the writers in the anthology you are now reading, even if his book now often feels as forgotten as the lake itself. The agency Morgan grants Great Salt Lake was rare in the literary history of the lake to that point. He acknowledges Great Salt Lake on its own terms, even dropping the "The" used in most accounts as well as his book's own title. This was no small gesture, and the notions of agency, personhood, and inalienable rights for Great Salt Lake have been taken up by numerous subsequent writers and activists. If the current activism and conversations around Great Salt Lake are any indication, it is an idea whose time has finally come. Legal precedent granting rights and/or personhood to rivers, mountains, and forests have arisen in Ecuador, Aotearoa/New Zealand, Brazil, and even the United States, to name a few.

Few individuals have done or written more to drive a rethinking of our relationship to Great Salt Lake and point to the dangers of human-driven destruction of Great Salt Lake's ecosystem than Terry Tempest Williams. In 1991, she published *Refuge: An Unnatural History of Family and Place*, a book that defied genre and convention, weaving seamlessly between natural history, genealogy, Mormon history, and lyric essay with Great Salt Lake always as its wild and breaking heart. It is a chronicle of the winter and spring of 1982/1983 when a combination of heavy snowpack and unseasonable early warming caused Great Salt Lake, which had largely been in recession for decades, to flood out into the wetlands, the bird refuges and even the city beyond. It is a book full of powerful currents and undercurrents: the history of Mormon stewardship and activism in the West, a history at times both hypocritical and seemingly irreconcilable; the myriad love letters to the birds of Great Salt Lake, both itinerant and permanent; the relentless damage enacted upon female bodies and all things feminine. The raw and formidable lyricism of Williams' prose, alongside the confluence of science, history, and family with a lifetime of both careful observation and love of place, drove a generation of readers not only to new ways of writing, but to a whole new experience of Great Salt Lake.

It is not a stretch to say that, without Williams, *Refuge*, and her myriad other essays and works dealing with Great Salt Lake, the book you now hold would not exist, or at least it would be radically different. Her influence can be viewed directly or indirectly in the majority of work in this anthology. Some mention her by name while others studied with her or with teachers she taught. Others have taken up the call to action around Great Salt Lake and do the day-to-day work of pursuing rights and protections for Great Salt Lake and all who call her home. It is work that has largely gone unrecognized until very recently. Despite the enormous influence of *Refuge*, Great Salt Lake again began to recede both literally as drought conditions increased and figuratively from the literary record and public consciousness. Great Salt Lake makes cameos in poems and stories, a temporary backdrop in films. Even the repair of the causeway and reopening of Antelope Island State Park, which drastically increased visitation to Great Salt Lake, did little to shift its overall reputation as Utah's most prominent example of forgotten geography.

III

That brings us to the work in and of this anthology. The authors included here cover a wide range of disciplines, genres, and backgrounds. They are scientists and historians, poets and essayists and novelists, activists and skiers. Many are more than one of these things. Most are residents of the Wasatch Front, or were for some time, though others live further afar—on the peripheries of the ancient inland sea, be it near Sevier Lake, Great Salt Lake's endorheic sister to the south, or not far from Red Rock Pass, where the last great breach of Lake Bonneville occurred.

I was not prescriptive in my invitations to authors. I wanted to hear what aspect of Great Salt Lake or the larger lake ecosystem resonated with them most. Our relationship to Great Salt Lake is complex—from spirituality and recreation to industry and economics. Even when recreational interest shifted from Great Salt Lake to the mountains, the burgeoning ski industry's reliance on lake effect snow only further reinforced this relationship. We have "taken the waters" in ways literal and figurative from the moment the first Mormon wagon party arrived in the valley. Paiute, Ute, Shoshone, and earlier peoples did so in other ways for thousands of years before that. While it was convenient and beneficial to industry for interests to shift elsewhere, the death of Great Salt Lake spells disaster for industrial interests as well.

The range of what arrived in the authors' responses reflected all these complexities and more. Whether lyric or academic, they did not disappoint. All viewpoints are needed in this effort. Odes to brine flies (Joel Long)? Meditations on the literary luminaries who passed along Great Salt Lake's edge (Andy Hofmann)? Love stories and ghost dogs amid the military-industrial shadows of the salt flats (Sarah Fox)? Yes, yes and yes. The fiction pieces are few but fierce, with Alyssa Quinn and Charles Waugh offering studies of human violence on or in Great Salt Lake that bookend the history of settler societies on its shores. Calls for personhood for Great Salt Lake arrive in many forms, from Willy Palomo's ghazal to Brooke Williams' cantos and Nan Seymour retelling of ancient myth. Scott Morris' expansive study of the "Last Great Bison Hunt" on Antelope Island illustrates how complex the conversations around Great Salt Lake and conservation have been for over a century. Sarah

May's poems juxtapose issues of bodily autonomy and sexual assault against violence perpetrated against Great Salt Lake in heartrending lyricism.

The above list speaks to only a portion of the contributors included here. Their experiences of Great Salt Lake range from the ecstatic to the most visceral fear of what the loss of Great Salt Lake means for us going forward. What is consistent in all of them is a deep-seated love of place and recognition that the urban space in which they dwell is neither separate from Great Salt Lake nor possible without the abundance its presence and its greater ecosystem offer.

The repercussions of Great Salt Lake's potential death are hard to fathom. For all the pressure put on non-human communities in and around Great Salt Lake, which are discussed in detail in this volume, the hundreds of thousands of humans living on the lake's periphery will likewise be at risk. We depend upon Great Salt Lake in myriad ways. While the more abstract benefits of wild places and unique ecosystems are harder to quantify, Great Salt Lake is inextricable from our economic, industrial, and recreational health in ways that are measurable in jobs and dollars. Snowpack provides recreation dollars as well as drinking water and is imperative to Salt Lake's ability to remain a livable city. Moreover, Great Salt Lake's most beneficent role in human life at its edges only truly comes into focus as the waters recede. Great Salt Lake has for decades absorbed the waste and the byproducts of our development: from petroleum refining to magnesium, copper, and salt extraction to brine shrimp fishing. The heavy metals of our industry lodged themselves in the lakebed, ostensibly contained and forgettable, affecting only the non-human residents who swam and ate and bred amongst them. But as with Owens Lake and the Aral Sea before, when the waters recede and the ground dries, these poisons are weaponized by wind, spread across the land, deposited in the lungs of everyone who breathes. There are precedents for such disasters.

They can be quantified in human lives and suffering. Salt Lake City and much of Utah was born of a people who believed themselves exceptional, who wandered far into the wilderness in exodus and whose myths tell of "making the desert bloom." But we know how these water stories end. We can only be exceptional in our capacity for both empathy and change. Our myths cannot save us this time. The only persecution here we have brought upon ourselves. We have a brief window to shift this trajectory, and it is imperative we are honest about the equality of sacrifice and changes necessary to achieve it. Some groups are rising to that challenge. In recent months, the Mormon church has relinquished water rights along the Bear River, a small but consequential gesture, as their influence on developers and on the state legislature (itself made up of an outsized proportion of developers) is significant. Darren Parry and the Northern Shoshone people are restoring riparian habitat on lands purchased by the Tribe while working with their neighbors in hopes they will do the same.

There is a critical mass that has formed around protection, conservation and revitalization of Great Salt Lake. At times, it can feel as if it is something new, a mass awakening. But that ignores decades of work done by individuals too numerous to count here. While some of the authors included here, such as Nan Seymour, Darren Parry, and Brooke Williams, have been at the forefront of those efforts for many years, most of us are the beneficiaries of their work and sacrifices. Of course, the work of artists and activists do not arise or exist in a vacuum either. A wide spectrum of scientists, journalists, community activists, and nonprofit organizations made all of our work possible. We owe an enormous debt to the work of countless geologists, hydrologists, naturalists, ornithologists, and recreationalists whose experience and knowledge feed us all. The efforts of groups such as FRIENDS of Great Salt Lake, Great Salt Lake Institute at Westminster College, Great Salt Lake Collective, and the *Salt*

Lake Tribune, and recreational groups like Ducks Unlimited, are inseparable from the efforts now taking shape to save Great Salt Lake. The inter-agency effort led by Brigham Young University that produced the 2022 report referenced several times in this anthology, and that so pointedly raised the alarm, was for many the impetus for action. With a lot of sacrifice and a little luck, that report may have come just in the nick of time. This has always been a collective effort, and we are more numerous now than ever. The word is out and the world is watching.

The Parable of the Pelicans

Terry Tempest Williams

They say St. Francis preached to the birds. At Great Salt Lake, the birds are preaching to us. In the spring of 2023, Utah state biologists counted five thousand white pelicans on Gunnison Island. On June 29, 2023, scientists saw no adult white pelicans on Gunnison Island. None. They observed "a few *dozen* juvenile birds, too young to fly, hiding in some rock outcroppings."

Why did they disappear?

Will they return?

Since 2016, Great Salt Lake has been receding creating land bridges to islands normally protected by water. Predators such as coyotes and foxes have found access to Gunnison Island which means entrée to one of the largest white pelican sanctuaries in North America, home at one time to as many as twenty thousand individuals, 20 percent of the total population in the lower forty-eight states.

No doubt predation has occurred, coyotes spooking juvenile pelicans into the air when they are not strong enough to fly the long distances with the adult birds, sometimes as far as one hundred miles a day to locate fresh water where fish can be found. The young birds would find themselves stranded, starving, weak and dying from fatigue and thirst.

Biologists initially said it could be avian flu or parasites, but when they tested bodies found dead on the island, results came back negative. Many questions remain. They will continue their investigation as to why the pelicans disappeared.

But there is another factor. There is an 11.8-mile-long causeway built in 1959 that divides Great Salt Lake in two—now known as the south arm and the north arm. Most of the mining industry resides in the south arm, which is also where the brine shrimpers operate, alongside recreation. The north arm is wilder, more remote where Gunnison Island is located. On February 3, 2023, Governor Spencer J. Cox signed an executive order to raise the causeway five feet higher with no flow to the north arm. The reason: There was concern over the health of the brine shrimp surviving the high salinity rate, close to 19 percent, the upper reaches of what brine shrimp can endure.

It was a gamble. Call it a game of poker: *I'll raise you five; I'll raise you another five.* Which is exactly what happened. Within a matter of months after the causeway was raised five feet, record snowfall fell in the Salt Lake Valley, as a result, the south arm rose five feet; the north arm, barely a foot. A five-foot rise in the north arm would have made Gunnison Island an island again.

The pelicans lost. They left.

In the spring of 1984, I flew over Gunnison Island with the Utah Division of Wildlife Resources for a bird count. On that trip, Great Salt Lake was in the process of rising to its historic high. The stark, rocky island was engulfed by water, but even so, the pelicans were flourishing. The landscape from above looked like white-beaded buckskin there were so many pelicans nesting. Ten thousand white pelicans in the middle of Great Salt Lake.

It felt miraculous.

It felt right.

We shared a common place in proximity to Great Salt Lake.

■ ■ ■

In 1948, Dr. William H. Behle, the distinguished ornithologist at the University of Utah, wrote his opus, "The Bird Life of Great Salt Lake." It was the first comprehensive survey of colony nesters on the islands of Great Salt Lake focusing on the populations of California gulls, double-crested cormorants, great blue herons, and white pelicans.

Behle notes the cyclic nature of Great Salt Lake, how it rises and falls, and each time the colony nesters become more vulnerable. He recounts in vivid detail the harshness of the drought in 1935, how he watched pelicans in flight and witnessed some of the members so weary from lack of food that they dropped out of formation and fell from the sky to their deaths; he saw dozens and dozens of dead pelican bodies piled up against the causeway; and other bodies made immobile by salt encrustations heavy on the wings of the birds, making it impossible to fly, now dead from starvation. But still, the population of white pelicans has always bounced back.

"Forecasting the future of Great Salt Lake bird colonies is, of course, a difficult thing," Behle writes, "but if current trends continue, there is danger that the islands of Great Salt Lake will be entirely abandoned by the colonial birds…Pelicans faced a critical condition in 1935 and seem to be slowly recovering, but still their existence is precarious."

Seventy-five years later, Dr. William H. Behle's prediction has come true: the pelicans have disappeared. Their existence is indeed precarious.

What do the pelicans know that we do not?

What might the parable of the pelicans offer us?

Pelicans embody thirty million years of evolutionary perfection on the planet—that's how long they have inhabited Earth. There is speculation by some ornithologists that the ancestors of Great Salt Lake's white pelicans inhabited islands like these during the Pleistocene, including Lake Lahontan, 12,700 years ago. Their bodily structures have changed very little. With a wingspan up to twelve feet, they are angels among us. They glide along Great Salt Lake with barely an inch between their bodies and the body of water; they can fly one hundred miles to freshwater to fish communally, corralling their prey in a circle where they scoop up the fish into their great pouches, returning to their young who await fresh food; and they have been seen spiraling the Grand Teton above 14,000 feet offering up their prehistoric cries for the sheer joy and pleasure of flight.

In 2023, white pelicans chose to leave their ancestral home of Great Salt Lake. What were the clues and cues given by the great white birds whereby one pelican followed another pelican and another and another, until Gunnison Island was left empty of their vibrant and peculiar presence of mind?

▪ ▪ ▪

In medieval times, it was thought the pelican fearing her young were starving would peck at her breast so violently that blood would rain down into the open mouths of the baby birds. Through her sacrifice, her kin were spared. Research librarian Emily Baren describes a "vulning pelican" as described in the sixteenth century:

> The term vulning comes from the Latin verb "vulno" which means "to wound." When pelicans feed their young, the mother macerates fish in the large sack in her beak then feeds it to her babies by lowering her beak to her chest to transfer the regurgitated fish more easily. The observation of this feeding practice led to the mistaken descriptions of female pelicans pecking their breasts and spilling blood onto their babies to provide sustenance.

The red water I see now is the blood of pelicans.

The blood of pelicans is on our hands.

They left. We remain. And now, an inconsolable loneliness enters my bloodstream.

A fundamental part of me feels lost, adrift, without bearings.

What will we do to repair the rupture we have caused by withholding water, holy water from our Mother Lake that touches all the lives she sustains? There is no more sacrament, only sacrifice.

What do we know of sacrifice when all we want is more of everything at the expense of other lives? We want more water from Great Salt Lake, water that protects the lives of pelicans. They leave. We stay and hardly notice their absence. We water our fields and lawns and brush our teeth while leaving our taps on, believing there is no end to water.

But the white pelicans know.

■ ■ ■

To wound. This is what we have done. *To harm*. This is what we continue to do without thought by caring only about ourselves. Great Salt Lake is suffering. White pelicans are suffering. We are sacrificing Wilson's phalaropes and eared grebes, brine flies and brine shrimp and the entire Great Salt Lake ecosystem by allowing Great Salt Lake to disappear and die.

For what?

What we know about sacrifice is that we are forfeiting the wild lives that surround us for our own gain. Our behavior as humans in the epoch of the Anthropocene is a sacrilege. A sacrilege is an act that violates and wounds the sacred; sacred comes from the Old French *sacrer*—to consecrate, to anoint, to dedicate. In Latin, the source root of sacred is *sacrare*: to hold sacred, to make holy, immortalize; set apart, sanctify. We are not honoring, worshipping, or respecting creation—we are destroying it.

The roots of our language can create a path of return. We can come to the receding shores of Great Salt Lake as pilgrims who see this water body as holy. We can humble ourselves in supplication to this venerable presence who is a reflection of beauty and change. We can change our behavior by changing how we see Great Salt Lake and her inhabitants, making prayers to pelicans that they might return as we consecrate their lives through our devotion. We can make holy what we are now sacrificing if we will commit to something so much larger and wiser than ourselves.

Pelicans through time have become symbolically aligned with Jesus Christ, as like beings who understand sacrifice. Just as the son of God was willing to give up his blood on the cross to save those souls that would come after him, so too, was the pelican willing to bear the wounds of love.

What does it mean to wound another and bear the wounds of those we love simultaneously?

What are we willing to sacrifice? Please let it not be the birds. The sacrifices we make on behalf of Great Salt Lake begin with our own conscience and consciousness, our will to give back what we have taken without thought: Water. Our commitment to bringing back water to Great Salt Lake is our commitment to the sanctity of white pelicans.

The parable of the pelican is our future foretold. Just as the pelicans of Great Salt Lake were vulnerable and left. We are vulnerable, another linguistic turn of *vulno.* Will we too be forced to leave an untenable situation, in our case, the dusting of our bodies in arsenic? The pelicans are showing us the way forward. We can show them the way back by bringing forth the waters to a whole and holy Great Salt Lake—now.

Welcome to Great Salt Lake

Holly Simonsen and Lynn de Freitas

Great Salt Lake is composite, and as such often defies description. The intensity of the sun setting along the western shore will sear your eyes, before transforming into deep autumnal hues that render a skilled painter's palette dull and the most advanced camera's capture seem technologically saturated. Often described as a "dead sea," Great Salt Lake is teeming with life. Salinity levels fluctuate between eight and ten times saltier than any ocean; this salt erodes boats, destroys dock pilings and railway trestles, while simultaneously preserving bird carcasses, essential habitats, and the livelihoods of all who live along the Wasatch Front. Great Salt Lake is as harsh as it is welcoming, as wild and free as it is constrained by perception and policy. These binaries allow us to deconstruct them: Great Salt Lake is all of the above—a biological and cultural ecotone, wherein all who live along its shores are richer and more diverse in both species and heritage because of it.

Great Salt Lake was once part of a vast inland sea known as Lake Bonneville, which covered much of western Utah, southern Idaho, and northeastern Nevada. Over fifteen thousand years ago, Lake Bonneville breached Red Rock Pass in Southern Idaho, which dropped the level of the lake by more than three hundred feet. As the climate continued to warm, Lake Bonneville further receded, eventually leaving behind Great Salt Lake as a mere puddle. Even as a remnant of its ancient predecessor, Great Salt Lake is the largest saline lake in the Western Hemisphere and the eighth largest terminal lake in the world sitting at the bottom of a twenty-one thousand-square-mile watershed.

Located in the second most arid state in the nation, Great Salt Lake is fed by the Bear, Weber, and Jordan Rivers. The Lake is relatively shallow—only thirteen feet deep on average, and thirty-five feet at most. Due to its terminal nature, fluctuations in the Lake's surface area are historically common, with the optimal range being 4,198 to 4,205 feet. Over the last decade, however, water diversions due to population increase and climate change have depleted Great Salt Lake to its historic low: 4,188 feet, recorded in November 2022. Prior to 2022, the previous record low was set in October 1963, with an elevation of 4,191.

In contrast, robust winters and unseasonably warm springs spurred a dramatic melting of the snowpack during the early 1980s. Great Salt Lake reached its historic high of 3,300 square miles and an elevation of 4,211 in 1986, prompting the state of Utah to install a massive pump system to relocate Great Salt Lake's water to the west desert where it would then evaporate. The city streets flooded as the rivers, creeks, and canals that fed Great Salt Lake reached levels far beyond capacity. Many Salt Lake City residents can recall being called out of Sunday services to volunteer filling sandbags, as the city's major urban thoroughfare, State Street, became a "river."

If we were to see similar dramatic inflows in the future, water diversions, reservoir management, and advanced infrastructure would make this type of flooding highly implausible. While Great Salt Lake is unlikely to breach any boundary that influences human development or commerce, that doesn't mean building around Great Salt Lake is feasible.

Along the shores of Great Salt Lake, you won't find lake cottages or quaint bed-and-breakfasts, a fact that always eludes visitors. However, less than three miles (as the crow flies) from the shoreline, you will find the Utah State Correctional Facility, which can house up to 3,600 incarcerated people and whose construction in 2022 came in 42 percent over budget as a result of structural difficulties due in part to the region's high water table and inconsistent soil makeup.

At Great Salt Lake, there are no fish to catch and traditional watersports like powerboating or waterskiing are too dangerous due to the extreme density of the water—falling into the Lake at those speeds would be like falling on concrete. But you will find one of the nation's first and longest running yacht clubs. Great Salt Lake Yacht Club, established in 1877, boasts "the saltiest sailors on earth," both in terms of salt-encrusted equipment and attitude. Sailing on Great Salt Lake is also an exercise in contrasts: The water can be a sheet of glass one minute and the next full of wave swells due to the Lake's shallow nature, which can topple even the most experienced crew. We have yet to meet a sailor who hasn't had to be rescued by the harbor master.

You'll also find a Hawaiian Outrigger Canoe Club, Hui Paoakalani, run by members of Utah's robust Pacific Islander Community. You'll find rowers and stand-up paddleboarders. You'll see curious tourists testing the waters—indeed buoyant and floating like corks—then you'll see members of the Great Salt Lake Open Water Swim Club slathering themselves with a mixture of Vaseline and lanolin they dub "the grease" to prevent the salty water from corroding their skin. During winter, you'll hear shots from waterfowlers, hunting the Lake's impressive population of ducks. This is all to say, housing and recreation abound at Great Salt Lake, but not always in the way one expects.

Two landfills, the Salt Lake Valley Landfill and the Promontory Point Landfill, sit dangerously close to the lakeshore on Promontory Peninsula. FRIENDS of Great Salt Lake (FRIENDS) aggressively fought (and succeeded for now) against propositions to open Promontory Point Landfill to Class V hazardous waste. There are tailings ponds from copper mines, evidence of Utah's proposed new Inland Port (railyards and warehouses currently being constructed). Adjacent to all this human pollution, you'll also find Utah's highest concentrations of active wetlands.

In Utah only 1 percent of our total area is wetlands, and 75 percent of those wetlands are located on and around Great Salt Lake. In addition to providing important habitat, wetlands control flooding, reduce erosion, and act as filters that improve water quality. Wetlands in Utah have declined from 1.2 million acres in the 1950s to approximately 400,000 acres today. Encroachment remains a significant factor, but Great Salt Lake also deals with invasive phragmites. The plant not only sucks up water from Great Salt Lake but also degrades important bird and wildlife habitat.

Of course, humans have successfully been living along the shores of Great Salt Lake for thousands of years. Indigenous peoples managed water and utilized the unique ecosystem for their benefit, even mining and trading salt, long before European expansion. Primary Indigenous communities include the Shoshone, Ute, Goshute, Paiute, and earlier peoples. Many Tribal members and leaders continue to be voices of restoration, reparation, and continued advocacy for Great Salt Lake issues. As more Tribal members achieve their rightful voices in policy-making spaces, we remain encouraged that Indigenous wisdom will continue to shape Great Salt Lake policy in new or underrealized ways. True collaborations among all knowledge systems are needed in order to enact creative solutions for Great Salt Lake protections.

Among the first Europeans to arrive at Great Salt Lake was the John C. Frémont expedition of 1843. Frémont, an explorer and US Army officer, mapped parts of the western United States and provided some of the earliest detailed accounts of the region, including Great Salt Lake. On Frémont's heels was Howard Stansbury, who was explicitly dispatched by the United States Army Corps of Engineers to survey Great Salt Lake, and whose most telling account is *Exploring The Great Salt Lake: The Stansbury Expedition of 1849-50.*

Simultaneously, Mormon Pioneers, led by Brigham Young,

arrived at Great Salt Lake on July 24, 1847. Their arrival marked the beginning of a significant migration and settlement effort in the region, perhaps most notably by creating permanently farmed crops and agricultural infrastructure. They achieved their mandate to "make the desert bloom." Today's agricultural operations often come under scrutiny for water-usage and potential water-waste, though some of Utah's contemporary farmers largely understand the responsibilities that come with their cultural heritage and are offering innovative solutions to keep both their farms and Great Salt Lake viable.

Shortly after the arrival of Mormon Pioneers, the transcontinental railroad connected east and west with Utah's famous "Golden Spike" in 1869. The importance of the railroad cannot be overlooked in terms of the industrial development of the United States. Often overlooked are the effects of the Lucin Cutoff, which bisected Great Salt Lake from Lucin to Ogden. Built in 1902 as an alternate route from the original rail line north of the Lake through Promontory, the Lucin Cutoff saved forty-four miles in length and hundreds of feet in grade, and dramatically altered Great Salt Lake's ecosystem.

Over time, the Lucin Cutoff's original wooden bridge was replaced with a rock-filled causeway, which included two culverts that allowed water to flow freely; however, the slow settling of the causeway into the lakebed eventually cut off flow between the north and south arms—essentially creating two distinct ecosystems, and the arresting color variations depicted in this volume's cover art.

The color differences are due to pinkish-orange algae (*Dunaliella salina*) and violet-pinkish halophiles that live in the North Arm of the Lake, and green algae (chlorophytes), such as *Dunaliella viridis*, and blue-green algae (cyanophytes) in the South. Halophiles are extreme salt-loving microorganisms that have a unique pigment, giving the water its peculiar pinkish color. These extremophiles have contributed much to scientific literature, including projects funded by NASA to study potential life on Mars.

In 2016, the causeway was breached to restore some flow between the north and south arms. The breach is currently managed (raised and lowered) by the Utah Division of Water Resources, with the goal of maintaining viable salinity levels for the organisms that live within each ecosystem.

Those of us who study Great Salt Lake know that every day on and around Great Salt Lake is different. The Lake is dynamic and abundant with life, an oasis at the bottom of the Great Basin. Essential to this life are microbialites—calcium carbonate structures that function as Great Salt Lake's coral reefs. They carpet much of the lakebed and are essential for brine fly production.

As we've witnessed during the past few years, brine flies function as harbingers for the Lake's health. A vital food source for birds, brine flies are high in protein and break down organic matter that would otherwise accumulate in and around the ecosystem. When we're at risk of losing the flies, we know we'll eventually lose the birds, and this is what scientists mean when they suggest that Great Salt Lake is at risk for a full ecosystem collapse.

Great Salt Lake's hallmark species is artemia, or brine shrimp, or "sea monkeys" for anyone who ever ordered these pets from the pages of an old catalog. Brine shrimp, and particularly their harvested cysts, are an immense part of the world's aquaculture and are used to sustain fish hatcheries around the world, which in turn sustain human diets. Brine shrimp are also an important food source to the region's extraordinary migratory birds.

Great Salt Lake's birds elevate the region to a global scale of importance, as over ten million migratory birds rely on Great Salt Lake for food and habitat. Three hundred thirty-eight species come here for resting, staging, and nesting as they make their migratory journey through the Western Hemisphere. The impressive flock includes: Wilson's Phalarope, 340,000 annually, which is the largest staging concentration in the world; American Avocet, 250,000 annually—many times higher than any other wetland in the Pacific Flyway; Snowy Plover—nearly a quarter of the continental population; American White Pelican—Great Salt Lake is one of the top five breeding populations in North America; more than 500 wintering Bald Eagles—one of the top ten winter populations in the lower forty-eight states; and millions of Eared Grebes.

Reduced water coming to Great Salt Lake results in a higher concentration of salts. While organisms of Great Salt Lake's South Arm are adapting to tolerate higher levels of salinity than most, they do have limits. When the Lake's microbialites are exposed, or the algae and bacteria clinging to them reach their salinity thresholds, there are fewer flies and shrimp for the birds to eat. Two primary species rely on brine flies and brine shrimp: eared grebes and Wilson's phalaropes. Grebes visit Great Salt Lake each fall by the millions. Adult birds will spend three to five months molting their feathers and building energy reserves feeding mainly on brine shrimp. During this time, their bodies expand while their muscles atrophy leaving them flightless and especially vulnerable to changing environmental conditions. Hundreds of thousands of Wilson's phalaropes come to Great Salt Lake each year mainly to feed on brine flies. It remains important to monitor salinity, brine fly production, and brine shrimp viability for the sake of these important species.

All of this biological abundance has not fully quelled the cultural misconceptions about Great Salt Lake. Many people who call this place home fail to appreciate Great Salt Lake for its economic impact. Perceptions abound that this landscape is a barren wasteland. These misconceptions have filtered their way into Utah's policy decisions, most importantly Utah's water law. It's no secret that water in the West will always be a contested issue.

The history here is anchored in an archaic notion that "beneficial use" was narrowly defined as fresh water to support human consumption or agricultural needs. Thereby, historically, every drop of water to reach Great Salt Lake via canal, river, or reclamation was considered "wasted." Utah water law is primarily governed by the principle of prior appropriation, which means that water rights are granted based on the first person to divert and beneficially use the water. This system plays a significant role in managing the water resources that flow into Great Salt Lake. Utah formally recognized Great Salt Lake as a beneficial use in 2022 when the Utah State Legislature passed House Bill 33, which aimed to clarify that Great Salt Lake is considered a beneficial use for purposes of protecting and preserving its environmental and ecological benefits. This legislation was a significant step toward recognizing the Lake's importance not only for its ecological functions but also for air quality and other societal benefits, paving the way for more comprehensive water management strategies focused on sustainability and conservation.

Great Salt Lake contributes to Salt Lake City's air quality, which is often among some of the worst in the nation, and also Utah's ski industry and its famously dubbed "The Greatest Snow on Earth". The drying lakebed and exposed playa are vulnerable to windstorms wherein dust is kicked up and lingers in the atmosphere. The dust contains dangerous levels of arsenic and methylated mercury. In contrast, a healthy Great Salt Lake's lake-effect snowstorms add significantly to the region's snowpack and outdoor winter recreation, notably supporting the 2002 Salt Lake City Winter Olympics and the promise of the upcoming 2034 Winter Olympics.

Today, Great Salt Lake sustains several industries, among them mineral and salt extractive companies that harvest salts and essential minerals from Great Salt Lake, and Great Salt Lake Brine Shrimp Cooperative, Inc., which harvests and exports brine shrimp cysts. Great Salt Lake's specific industries contribute over 1.9 billion dollars to our local economy. It sounds impressive and it is—commensurate with tourism income from all five of Utah's National Parks and an entire year of visitors to our major ski resorts. Still, Great Salt Lake's contributions sit quietly in the background.

It's no surprise that artists working with and advocating on behalf of Great Salt Lake have always been ahead of the curve. Since Alfred Lambourne departed to homestead Gunnison Island in 1895, where he penned some of the most evocative prose about Great Salt Lake, artists have been translating the wonder and mystery of Great Salt Lake. FRIENDS of Great Salt Lake celebrates the relationship between artists and Great Salt Lake in our annual Alfred Lambourne Arts Prize, which has honored many of the writers in this volume.

We haven't even begun to scratch the surface of Great Salt Lake's history and cultural wonders. There's the Great Saltair resort and dance hall, built in 1893, which was once dubbed the "Coney Island of the West." At the height of the resort's popularity in the 1920s, Saltair was a bustling place where young people came to dance and feel free. Three major fires coupled with the economic effects of the Great Depression and WWII left the resort abandoned until it was renovated to its current state in 1992. Today's scene is decidedly different, with Charleston Era swings replaced with electronic dance music, but people still congregate at Saltair to enjoy this unique venue. Consider Frémont Island, where Kit Carson carved his iconic cross onto a rock outcropping and which Frémont himself nicknamed "desolation island." Later Brigham Young designated it as a penal colony for one prisoner in particular, the grave robber, Jean Baptiste who, according to lore, purportedly escaped by swimming over five miles to the mainland. Wildly, during our recent low-water years, you could walk to Frémont Island without even getting your shoes wet. Then there's Antelope Island State Park, just ninety minutes from the Salt Lake City International Airport, where you'll see bison, bighorn sheep, bobcats, coyotes, and foxes, not to mention hundreds of thousands of birds—species that will be on every birder's life list.

It's often difficult to understand why Great Salt Lake isn't heralded for its cultural, economic, and ecological wonder, and upon reading this volume, you may be curious as to how you can help spur its protection and preservation. First, please visit. If you live in the vicinity, it's a no-brainer, and if you don't live nearby, it's worth a trip. Spend an afternoon at Great Salt Lake Marina State Park, Black Rock, and the Gilmore Sanctuary. Spend the day birding at Farmington Bay or Bear River Migratory Bird Refuge. Visit Rosel Point to see the tar seeps and Robert Smithson's iconic earthwork, *Spiral Jetty*. Build your own relationship with the Lake.

Great Salt Lake is a touchstone to Utah's future and the West's heritage. When Great Salt Lake reached its historic low in 2022, many people began to understand, some for the first time, its importance. Whether you are a long-time Lake lover or are just being introduced to Great Salt Lake via this anthology, welcome. There is a place for you here and we need your voice. At times, Great Salt Lake is a place of mourning; equally, it is a place of celebration. Most importantly, it is a place of reflection, both literally and figuratively, as the writers in this volume demonstrate. The Lake will show us who we are as searingly as it will show us what it is. It remains our responsibility to look at that reflection, to see ourselves and our human impacts, then see the truth of Great Salt Lake reflected back at us. We then must respond accordingly to preserve and protect Great Salt Lake in perpetuity.

Still-Life with Ghosts

Rob Carney

Our house is built on a seabed.
Count back far enough, and almost everyone's is:

First, fire; and then water;
then the two of them combining into air,

plus buckling some deep-down rock
so it can rise, click together into continents.

What's next depends on your timeline.
And even then, the dead might disagree,

like the voices I hear when no one else is home.
Not in this room, or that room either,

not the radio on, no people on the sidewalk,
but voices—*something* talking—somewhere near.

Nothing stays silent, I guess. Look at me,
tossing words across Great Salt Lake.

It used to be an Inland Sea.
I used to be young.

Lake Woman Leaving

after the Inuit legend of Fox Woman

Nan Seymour

Born of water, this story came while walking along the receding shoreline of Great Salt Lake on the ancestral and unceded homelands of the Shoshone, Goshute, Paiute, and Ute Peoples.

Once upon a time, there was an angler who lived all alone in a small cabin at the top of a canyon in a high mountain range. They tended a simple garden and speckled trout were abundant in the river nearby. The Angler did not often go hungry, but sometimes they were lonely.

One early summer evening the Angler returned from a long day on the river to find a fire already lit in the hearth. They looked around and saw no one. Had they left the morning's fire untended? No matter, they cooked the trout they had caught and each bite was more delicious than the last.

The next morning, they set out for another day on the river. Once again, when they returned there was a fire in the hearth. This time a savory fish and potato stew simmered in the cauldron. Upon tasting, they found it sublimely seasoned, with just the right amount of salt.

The next day, the Angler left early as usual. Instead of heading to the river, they quietly circled back, determined to learn the source of their recent comforts. Through the window, they saw the figure of a woman flowing about the room.

They were astonished by her beauty and enchanted by the

ever-changing colors of her tresses. As they marveled, shimmering pink became magenta, and tumultuous green shifted into gradient shades of blue. Locks of slate gray alchemized into silver and then molten gold. Colors appeared that they did not know how to name.

Yellow-bellied, blue-headed swallows circled the air above her head, an ever-singing crown. A vast cloak of gossamer and waves trailed behind her, receding and swelling like a tide. She smelled richly of petrichor, saline waters, and microbial life. This was Lake Woman.

Hesitantly, the Angler opened the door and crossed over the threshold. Without words, the two stood across the room and drank each other in. The whole house trembled like a sky ready to release a hard rain, the trusses crackled like a storm cloud gathering lightning.

For three days and nights, the two scarcely ate and barely slept. They thundered and stormed. They sighed and smiled and laughed and howled and loved. The full Flower Moon spilled through the window, their singular witness.

It was as if the two had always been together, days became weeks, and their lives grew playful and tender. The couple fell into a pleasant rhythm: fishing and weaving, strolling, cooking, and mending. In the evenings, they danced by lamplight. Every meal they shared was seasoned with just enough salt to make it sing.

Wherever Lake Woman went, even in the house, she was followed by birds, and not only swallows, but also herons, eared grebes and avocets, prairie falcons, and snowy egrets.

There was seemingly no end to the variety of birds she conspired with.

On rare occasions she went into town and the birds went along. As she walked down the streets and into shops, people turned their backs and whispered. Lake Woman remained unperturbed, but the whispers of the villagers became rumors which made their way back to the Angler who felt ashamed.

As weeks became months, the Angler began to notice that Lake Woman took up a great deal of space in their bed. And although she hung her wide cloak in the hall, the garment gave off a fecund smell that troubled them. They began to be bothered by the birds... but they loved Lake Woman dearly and did not wish to complain.

As the months went on, their judgments festered. They grew resentful and impatient. One morning, on their way out the door they turned to face her. Your cloak, they said... that smell, they said... and all the space you take in the bed... feathers everywhere, the cacophony...their words echoed the accusations of the villagers and their voice was steeped in disdain.

Lake Woman listened without speaking. If the Angler had only paused to listen in return, they would have heard a terrible whisper, the faint sound of water receding.

All day long the Angler brooded on the river and did not catch a single fish. When they returned, Lake Woman was gone. Every bird had departed with her. No one left to catch the light or stir the currents. The hearth was cold and empty. The tiny cabin felt cavernous.

Only two traces of Lake Woman remained: the outline of a great body imprinted in the bed and a fine dust hanging in the air, ubiquitous. They cried out into the night, pleading for her to come back. Their pleas would go unanswered. They were too late, and it was not enough.

The Angler still lives all alone at the top of the canyon, forever yearning for the sight of their beloved. To this day, they can be found peering down every path. Even now they are wiping the dust from their brow, searching an empty sky for any sign.

Naming Creatures

Katharine Coles

From a plane into Salt Lake City, Great Salt Lake's smooth surface flashes silver or pink, tinted by beta-carotene-producing algae, its shoreline crusted white with salt. Your mental picture may include photos of Robert Smithson's *Spiral Jetty* taken from the air, through which the Jetty, so bound to place, travels to exhibitions on both coasts, in fly-over country, abroad. Given flight paths, most of us—except white pelicans, commuting nests-to-feeding grounds—never get a bird's-eye view, but if you drive to the remote shoreline at Rozel Point, you can take an angled eyeful of its 1,500-foot unwinding from a nearby bluff.

When the lake cooperates, *Spiral Jetty* exerts charisma from air or earth, as Smithson intended, black basalt stones salt-laced, rolling through a sheet of water glinting pale to electric rose, its winding wanting walking. Riding it out from shore, you travel into liminal space. Are you on land or lake? Will the surface hold? You divide your attention between your feet, finding their precarious way among the rocks, and the water, unnaturally smooth, its colors inviting you into the strange.

At its farthest point, the spiral turns you left, curving inward until you dead end dead center, no longer on the edge but absorbed and bounded.

Go back the way you came. No shortcuts.

Where are you now?

■ ■ ■

January 2019: I am in an airplane flying from New York back to Salt Lake, not thinking about the lake and earthwork lying under darkness a thousand miles ahead.

I am reading my friend Lee Bricetti's *Blue Guide*, whose title and mention of columbine set a piece of my mind to work on the idea of *blue, blueness, bluenesses.* Her poem "*Face of North America*" chronicles her journey west in 1976, declaring its commitment to hard science by taking title and some lines from geologist Peter Farb. Where she quotes, "*youthful river expands its energies cutting downward in its bed. . . mature river widens its banks,*" youthful Lee scrawls "*true!*"

I jot, "You won't find consolation," cross it out. Lee's "sunburnt crust of ice-flow" floats alongside a glimmer of something I read about how deer, eyes lacking our ultraviolet filter,

see blue

Better than we do, a blue

I am not consoled

Lives beyond me.

"You won't find consolation" and blue envy got me to deer. "I am not consoled" tells me I elegize. My deer drink from an alpine lake so blue it must be glacier-fed.

I cut "vanishing/In your lifetime," put it back.

Farb noted Glacier National Park's "*retreating ice*" in 1963.

Now, meaning a summer afternoon in 2022, I realize the time has passed when I might unselfconsciously write into a poem a memory of kneeling beside my childhood friend Robin in a glacier high in Wyoming's Wind Rivers Range as we wash our long hair in the stream running through the ice. Halfway through a grueling two-week backpack circuit: maybe twelve, wanting clean hair to toss in the sun I shiver now, remembering water so cold my head echoed with its ache, ice numbing my knees.

Is it still there?

▪ ▪ ▪

In 2019, violinist Hasse Borup asked me to join the wildly interdisciplinary group Artivism4Earth to create an earth day event. I told him I wasn't a nature poet, unless you spell 'Nature' with a capital N, meaning *reality*.

As a student, I'd learned to distrust nature writing from the best: Wordsworth in "I Wandered Lonely as a Cloud," celebrating himself alone, or projecting himself onto Mount Snowdon, to worship "the perfect image of [his] mighty mind"; Thoreau obsessively measuring, extracting morals to justify his own unpleasantness. Each makes nature his mirror, and preens. I recognize their *greatness*, but loving them, like wearing shorts in winter, is a young man's game, inheritors of our long Romantic age *using* nature to lever themselves through radiant epiphanies, while the reader, wanting a little of what *they're* having, breathlessly watches what should be a private event.

Keats called it the "egotistical sublime," and instead vanished into a sparrow, "[Taking] part in its existence and pick[ing] about the gravel," "informing and filling some other body" to become "the most unpoetical of any thing in existence."

The "unpoetical" Dickinson names herself "Nobody" and invites her reader to join her in "zero-at-the-bone," often whimsy-tinged encounters with nature, which change her, nature not at all.

"I started Early/Took my Dog" sends up the Wordsworthian day hike: not lonely, Dickinson's speaker takes Carlo, a Newfoundland larger than she, to make a "visit" to the sea, where she's observed by unimpressed "Mermaids" and "Hempen-hand[ed]. . . Frigates." Her detour into the fantastic shrinks her to a "mouse," humble and surely more comic than Keats' sparrow.

Keats' voice settles in self-erasure; his inability to "see what flowers are at [his] feet" reduces him to invisibility and restores him to hearing, where he loses self to bird through song.

The sea, being *the sea*, overwhelms Dickinson, rising over "belt" and "Boddice," threatening to engulf (or strip) her entirely. "Unmoved" until the sea physically moves her, she's too busy not drowning for epiphany, retreating lest water "eat [her] up"—presumably to rejoin Carlo, who, being a dog, neither belabors nor is transfixed by tides. Unlike us, he knows none of this is about him.

■ ■ ■

Sunrise, May 2020. *Good morning*, in spite of all we've caused. I step onto the upstairs deck and whistle as I put out feeders, offering seed for lazuli buntings and finches, already racketing impatience; hummingbird nectar; grape jelly and oranges for the clackering orioles. Winged bodies rise then fall back into treetops—dinosaurs whose ancestors, small, quick, and bright, survived the last catastrophe, as some may survive ours. Our bird populations explode and collapse: one year Steller's jays jockey at the feeders; the next, tanagers flutter in from nowhere, all yellow bellies and cherry-red heads; we have too many quail to count or fifty-odd wild turkeys milling in the driveway before they settle to roost in the oakwood between house and street. Predators follow: Cooper's and red-tailed hawks, egg-loving raccoons, weasels, foxes, a lone bobcat who visits for a few days and leaves behind dismembered squirrel tails and piles of feathers like dresses stepped out of after a party and left crumpled on the ground.

My world home-sized by lockdown, with nothing to pull me inside except coffee, I gaze west over the city and north into the canyon named City Creek. Watching sun and cloud play over mountains and valley, I linger: chickadees call (*Ding-dong, I am here, here, are you?*), and I whistle back (*Ding-dong, right here*).

Twenty miles west the lake shines like the edge of a nickel between glimmering buildings and the mountaintop now called Stansbury Island because it rises from water, as Ensign Peak across the canyon once floated in Lake Bonneville, its ancient shoreline now marked by a trail we hike.

I keep photographing it every day, now for three years. It took me months to realize I was documenting its vanishing.

■ ■ ■

Before it became a lake, it was a sea, covering western Utah and parts of Idaho and Nevada for twenty thousand square miles. We call the freshwater lake that still covered the valley and beyond when the sea receded Lake Bonneville. Our trail, which we access up the street, marks high water from thirty thousand years ago when the lake was spilling through the Red Rock Pass north into Idaho and flowing down the Snake and Columbia rivers to the Pacific. A glacier running all the way down to the mouth of Big Cottonwood Canyon calved regularly into waters where neighborhoods now mark the city's highest rim. Back then, when none of these names existed, we might have had lakefront property.

Now, tide's out hundreds of miles, the lake, like the ice on Anvers Island, having reached its lowest point. In January 2022, Utah State Legislators performed their newfound concern by flying in helicopters over its shrinking. Their video shows sand flats still sheened in places with water, Stansbury Island heart-stopping in silver mist. The politicians, realtors and alfalfa farmers, see for themselves Antelope Island no longer entire of itself. Antelope Peak. Winds we haven't seen before, not this strong or this often, pick up dust from the exposed lakebed and ravage the city with fallout.

▪▪▪

Though the iconic photos present *Spiral Jetty* at its showy best, just two years after Smithson constructed it in 1970, when a white man could still take a bulldozer onto public land and build a magnificent question mark, Utah had a long, wet spell, and it went under. A scant year later, Smithson died in a plane crash in Texas. For most of thirty years, you could neither see the jetty, even from the air, nor walk it. It became a suggestion rippling just out of sight, a memory we couldn't recover.

Utah's problem with the lake then was what to do with all that water flooding marina and pleasure palace. We joked about renaming it Lake Bonneville. In 1987, as the current drought began, the government built a set of giant pumps in the west desert to send water over there. Now, they hulk on the sand in case we need them again, more than ten miles from shore.

▪ ▪ ▪

In 2002, *Spiral Jetty* resurfaced for good.

In 2005, before we all carried GPS in our pockets, I got hopelessly lost with my friends Guy and Jackie in the maze of deep-rutted, ill-mapped dirt roads meandering the northern shore of the lake—roads meant not to carry curious poets from highway to earthwork, but to get cattle and ranchers from one scant patch of forage to another. Finally, after many random turns, we saw a man in a cowboy hat leaning beside his horse, chest-high against the other side of a barb-wire fence. In three steps and the time it took to roll the window half down, the cowboy flowed up and over the fence and alighted on our side, the long fringes of his chaps billowing around him—no kidding—like the clouds of myth.

"Light like a bird," Calvino says, quoting Valery, "and not like a feather".

I don't tell you about that aerodynamic cowboy to stop your hearts as he stopped ours, though any of us might have climbed out to ask him for a two-step. His flight becomes a reason to say yes when Elisabet Curbelo, an Artivism4Earth composer, asks if I will write a poem about the lake for her to set. The cowboy, like my grandfather, stands (or flies) in my imagination as figure, story, sign of romance and Anthropocene. Water law being law out west, every drop is spoken for before it exists, human "use" its only value: iphoned off as snow melts and flows down from the mountains, it is allocated in "use-it-or-lose-it" shares for farmers and water parks and the profligate, unmetered watering of lawns, the desert blossoming, as Brigham Young exhorted, "like a rose." For generations, that cowboy's family has diverted water before it reaches the lake to grow alfalfa and beef, crops with heavy thirst that has no business slaking itself in the desert; like any man of his time or, now, behind it, he takes from the land what has been made his business to take, as before him it was his father's and grandfather's.

No man can make chap-fringe dance that way who wasn't born to it.

■ ■ ■

A couple of times a year, Chris and I drive out to visit birds on Antelope Island or at the Bear River Migratory Bird Refuge, both on one of the world's major migratory routes. Though the refuge is visibly drying—and audibly too, as bird cacophony diminishes—we watch golden eagles by the scores in winter; rafts of white pelicans drifting like icebergs on water too salty to freeze (the pelicans eerily silent, except when grunting in sex or aggression or peeping embryonic complaints about the temperature inside their eggs); shore birds (herons, egrets, avocets, stilts, plovers and godwits and the long-billed dowitchers) wading the shallows, dunking heads, coming up fed. The lake being too salty for fish, birds feed on algae-grazing brine shrimp or on the brine flies the shrimp also feed, at least for now.

For years, a flamingo amused regular birders, who named him Pink Floyd. Nobody knew how he had come so far north—blown here by storm, or smuggled in by some human who knew the lake would provide carotenoids to keep him a pink that looked ordinary at home and here, in a place he must have found bone cold and lonely, was exotic beyond measure.

In one day during the 2002 fall migration, just as *Spiral Jetty* was reasserting itself, half-a-million Wilson's phalaropes were counted, a third of the world's population.

▪ ▪ ▪

In the dry summer of 2022, as she was beginning her composition, Elizabet and I drove washboard roads to see: *Spiral Jetty* now spinning over a shimmering bed of salt. While we walked the labyrinth, a white helicopter circled then landed on the lakebed, disgorging a woman, also in white, impossibly pristine. She snapped photos while Elisabet captured water-sound from a puddle, then me reading at the heart of the spiral.

I stepped off the *Jetty* onto the lakebed and followed a single set of footprints to a sunburnt Windsor chair positioned on the long salt mile stretching between sculpture and water. I sat looking over the spiral toward shore, bluff, ghostly helicopter: a view I couldn't have imagined twenty years ago.

A human put the chair there, making an elegy for the *Jetty*, though time and gravity will take me far sooner than it.

▪ ▪ ▪

Later, while Elisabet recorded me reading again on shore, a flock of pelicans beat the air around us into sound.

That week, the last boats stranded at the marina were craned out of what water's left.

A miracle of bird marsh and blue shimmer, reducing then—almost?—to the point of no return.

▪ ▪ ▪

What consoles me?

Geologic time.

Farb says "*all species change the world, but the Earth cannot keep up with us—*". Or is it the other way? In earth's time, we occupy a twitch of crust that can obliterate us, and will.

For Elisabet I read to the accompaniment of wings, and

how could we object? who bulldoze shorelines, turn aside rivers, waylay all we come by—driving hard, pulling dust clouds behind us, looking for an exit. *Where are you?* Like me, the sculptor flew, looking down; like Icarus, he fell to earth, he sank and rose. Can this keep? Now, his maze lies high, winding us over an old seafloor dreaming of time. Parch, thinking of it. Look:

Not dead. Brine shrimp feed flies; birds dive-gorge; from brush the lark still sings herself into being: *I am right here,* sings answer, and from cover the owl calls present, haunting. Phalaropes swim the sky—still hundreds-of-thousands swarm—then settle on water. One spins himself a whirlpool and eats whatever turns up, speaking himself, *Here.* Along this new old shoreline, wind lifts veils we almost see through: bird bodies evaporated to dust, salt, metals. *Breathe* or not. Each body for now a world remaking others, the dead winding into me, you—deep time losing nothing.

Around us, voices remind us: *We are*, and *Here.*

For now, we answer.

Appearance of Beak

Sarah May

Along the bank of the river
pia okwai
I drink of your water
before it reaches your salt bed
surprised to see the dark gray-blue
reflecting the same look
I have seen in your eyes
when clouds cover the sky
and the wind moves your waves

There is a gentleness
in this body of water leading to yours.
the water here moves steady and smooth
with the curves of the earth
coots and mallards dance together
in the river bends
beavers carry cottonwood bark as offerings
cutthroat trout sunbathe in shallow waters
a quiet current moves duckweed and grass
growing underneath the surface
reflecting and absorbing the sky
as the river brings the water that feeds you

All I have ever known of men is what they took
from me
I wonder if the kindness of men ever reached you

I wonder if we will ever see their pain not turn to
cruelty

I see the sacred masculine
molded and shaped by his wounds
drained before he can
reach your source
the sacred father guiding and protecting
mother and father hand in hand
palms touching in shared knowing
appe ma'ai pii

He teaches me to look at what I cannot face
to let my grief and sadness pass through me
held by the water

I stand at the riverbed
unearthing my roots from the soil
cold mud building underneath my fingernails
hitting rock after rock
throwing them into the water
covering my body with mud and clay
until I am so cold I feel nothing

You show me how your waters
lake and river
become one
the source of different lifetimes
choosing to be one together
this divide the essence of my power
embracing duality
greeting fear as an old friend at the end of a long
day
making peace with what I cannot see

I plant seeds in my ears
and wait for them to bloom in the spring,
nightshade and reeds wrapping around my arms
connecting me to your waters

My roots pushing the rocks out of the soil
braiding my words into sweet grass,
our ancestors burning into the night
transforming our words into sacred smoke.
nawaiti.

A Morning at the Inlet

Teri Harman

On the morning of March 2, 2025, the sound of stampeding water pulled me across Saratoga Springs Inlet Park. Camera ready, I walked down a boat ramp and splashed into the upper channel of the Utah Lake-Jordan River Inlet. Boots firmly lodged in slick mud, I faced triplet flow gates framed by a concrete structure. These wide, silver rectangles rule the gravitational outflow of Utah Lake. The eastern gate hovered open, lake water escaping in a frothy, giddy churn. The early morning sun burned my eyes as I took photos and videos of 70,000 acre feet of water leaving Utah Lake to travel fifty-one miles north through Jordan River to help quench the desperate thirst of Great Salt Lake. The water curving around my ankles transformed from lake to river, destined to be lake again. Now managed by human engineering, this confluence claims ancient origins, created 14,000 years ago after the draining of Lake Bonneville.

The knowledge of this watershed connection has drifted outside of collective memory. Many Utah residents don't know that Utah Lake is connected to Great Salt Lake through the Jordan River. This forgetting is a well-established pattern in recent history. The confusion started with a mapping mistake in 1844 recorded by American surveyor John C. Frémont and cartographer Charles Preuss. During two expeditions to the Great Basin, Frémont visited portions of Great Salt Lake and Utah Lake but not the land between. He assumed the two were one large lake with a saltwater end and a freshwater end connected by a short, narrow channel. He missed the long, linking river completely, then called Pia Okwai. An embarrassing error—one he was ridiculed for for years—easily avoided by a conversation with the Timpanogos and Ute of Utah Valley who lived there.

Frémont's incorrect map and accompanying reports of Northern Utah landed in the hands of Joseph Smith and Brigham Young, founding leaders of the Mormon (LDS) church. Desperate to flee persecution that included Smith's assassination and to protect the faith's controversial practices, Young dedicated significant efforts to moving the Mormons west. Frémont praised the abundance of the Wasatch Front, especially that of Utah Valley. Utah Lake offered everything Young wanted for his irrigated and grazed Zion far from the reach of the federal government. In 1845, he pointed to Utah Lake on Frémont's map and ordered an overland exodus.

Plans shifted slightly north to the Salt Lake Valley a short time later. Because of the generous watershed, Utah Valley had a dense population of Native Peoples—the largest in the Great Basin at that time. Young decided to create some space between his group and the Timpanogos and Utes until he better understood the area. Mormons arrived in the Salt Lake Valley in 1847. Immediately, they discovered Frémont's mapping error and, recognizing the similarities to the Dead Sea and Sea of Galilee system near Jerusalem, re-named Pia Okwai the Jordan River in honor of the biblical echo. Within a few short years, the settlers engaged in irrigation projects that launched a new version of forgetting and a nearly complete decoupling of Utah Lake and Great Salt Lake.

Eager to get as close as possible to the open flow gate, I scrambled over the steep boulder-enforced embankment to the concrete frame and squatted at the water's edge. The flow's rumble cut off all other sounds. Water surged against the rocks, splattering my thighs and face. I was tempted to jump in, to feel the press of that driving urgency against my body, but instead I watched the spray ricochet sunlight. Recording video, I tracked the movement downstream to the pump station catch basin. A blend of historic and modern structures, the pump complex sits slightly north-east of the gates. Six hump-backed pipes drop off the back of the main building into a pond that collects water before sending it northward into the Jordan River meander.

In 1859, Mormon settlers built the first dam structure here at the Utah Lake-Jordan River Inlet. The work transformed the widespread riparian junction into a dredged channel and native wetland plants were cleared. A second dam followed in 1872 farther north at The Narrows in Salt Lake Valley, near present day Bluffdale. Both dams served to re-direct Jordan River's flow to irrigation canals and mill races in Salt Lake County. After a devastating drought at the turn of the century, a group of mill owners met with Salt Lake City officials to plan a massive pump station at the Inlet. The first pump was installed in 1902 and by 1913 seven more were pulling water from Utah Lake to guarantee Salt Lake water needs. At full capacity, the eight pumps delivered 700 million gallons of water every twenty-four hours, the largest pumping plant in the world at that time. Modernized a couple of more times over the years, the pump station still controls the inlet today. Jordan River is the only outflow for Utah Lake and so the dams and pumps essentially converted Utah Lake into a storage reservoir for human purposes.

Great Salt Lake evolved to depend on freshwater inflows from all directions: Jordan River from the south, Bear River from the north, and Weber River from the east. Before Mormon settlement, Great Salt Lake enjoyed the majority of Utah Lake's outflow. Early damming efforts ignored maintaining any dedicated water from Utah Lake to Great Salt Lake and contributed to tributary reduction across Northern Utah. Much like John C. Frémont's mapping mistake, human diversions essentially erased the southern connection. The current outflow from Utah Lake to Jordan River varies year to year but the median is 216,000 acre feet, and nearly all of that is promised to irrigation and industrial water rights in both valleys. Some return flows do come back into the river and end up in Great Salt Lake, so in a round-about way a little of Utah Lake reaches its saltwater sibling. But Great Salt Lake does not *own* a designated portion of Utah Lake's water. This is especially consequential because Great Salt Lake's continued survival depends on consistent *annual* freshwater flow from all the rivers to balance the saline ecosystem. Under modern management parameters, Utah Lake only shares large contributions with Great Salt Lake, if there is *extra* water in the system, or more water than is needed to fulfill water rights. Offloading this water also prevents shoreline flooding in Utah Valley.

The 70,000 acre feet released in early March was one of these circumstantial gifts. Thanks to plentiful snowfall of the previous two winters, Utah Lake had extra water. These supplemental releases feel bittersweet. Though the aid headed to Great Salt Lake is a relief, it's also an uncomfortable reminder that Utah Lake doesn't supply a significant annual offering. It presents a stark example of the precarious limits of the current system. If extra water depends wholly on generous winters, which grow more erratic with each climate-changed year, and not careful, consistent conservation, then scarcity rules. Northern Utah, also known as the Wasatch Oasis, is not a desert. Water scarcity here is created mostly by water use decisions.

Most years, the Inlet gates and pumps don't start distribution until Utah Lake is swollen with spring snowmelt in late April or early May. When the gates open, I always visit the watersmeet, but this March release drew me in early. I wanted to witness and document; I wanted to breathe in the joyous spray of Utah Lake briefly reclaiming its right to play a crucial role in Great Salt Lake's survival. Leaving the flow gates, I walked along the channel to the Saratoga Road pedestrian bridge. From the perch of the steel bridge, I captured photos of the center pump building reflected in a wedge of truffle brown water. The six pumps dropping off the structure looked lavender under the blaze of sun. Gulls sliced in and out of frame. I heard a fish jump but didn't see it. The roar of tumbling water was replaced by the buzz of cars on the road bridge behind me. Like all modern waterways, the Inlet is a layered, hybrid space. The wild layered with the engineered, the human interacting with the nonhuman. The past echoed in the present. Culture interacting with ecology. Confluence embracing confluence.

I followed the water and crossed Saratoga Road, walked down another boat ramp, and stood in Jordan River. The water lay perfectly still, cradled in the first bend. Several winter-naked cottonwood trees stood watch, roots bathing in riverbank nutrients. On the mental map of my mind, I tracked a fast-forward journey of the Utah Lake release. Moving out of Saratoga Springs, the water passed National Guard units at Camp Williams to reach the five distribution canals at The Narrows dam. Shuttled into the correct canal by the sophisticated workings, the water continued north into South Jordan, passing through East River Front Park, not far from the LDS Jordan River Temple.

Next, the shops at Gardner Village, site of the historic flour mill, once owned by Archibald Gardner who first suggested the pump station. The water continued into Taylorsville and West Valley, streaming through neglected areas clogged with invasive phragmites reeds and dumped trash. Then past the Salt Lake Valley Detention Center and Tracy Aviary's Nature Center at Pia Okwai. Sometimes the channel was wide and luxurious, other times cramped and narrow. Creeks and streams from the Wasatch and Oquirrh mountains emptied their contributions along the way. People met friends to walk the Jordan River Parkway Trail, the longest paved urban trail in the United States. Others fished on the banks or rested to the soundtrack of moving water. Kids threw rocks or played in the mud.

All along the course, the water intertwined with the riparian web. It carried fish: Utah suckers, Bonneville cutthroat trout, and common carp. Birds of prey dropped in to hunt the fish, and also mice and voles on the banks. Songbirds and waterfowl arrived to eat, drink, and swim. Muskrats, beavers, raccoons, skunks, bats, coyotes, foxes, and deer moved in and out. Trees, wildflowers, bullrushes, and grasses—some native and restored, some invasive and problematic. Hidden in the plants were frogs and snakes, midges and spiders.

The Utah Lake-Jordan River water passed under traffic on I-215 and I-80, to bend around the Salt Lake International Airport. Then finally, the release into the Jordan River Delta, a small patch of wetlands connected to Farmington Bay on the southeast arm of Great Salt Lake. Fifty-one miles, lake to lake. Utah Valley through Salt Lake Valley. Freshwater to saltwater.

I ended my Inlet morning with a loop back past the open flow gate and around the hot springs to stand shin-deep in the water of Utah Lake. Gazing over the hazy blue swath of my home lake, I considered power and priorities. A pump station is a powerful tool, but the distribution of that potential depends on cultural values. Since construction of the first Jordan River dam, Utah has largely commodified flow and forgotten natural connections. Great Salt Lake cannot survive without a committed, annual release from Utah Lake. Though this change alone can't solve the problem—more annual flow is needed from *all* tributaries—rehabilitating this life-blood connection is a compelling challenge. When nearly every drop of Utah Lake's water is already claimed, committing yearly acre feet compels a redistribution of power and priorities. Promising to restore the wild-made interrelation of these two lakes requires conservation and adjustment. It also courageously declares that this confluence matters to Utah's past, present, and future.

Before heading back to my car, I knelt down and put my hand in Utah Lake. I swirled the icy water into spirals and scooped it into the air to watch it trickle back down. All at once I touched snow, lake, river, and future lake. When I lifted my head, two coots slipped by, black spots on the glassy shine of water. I raised my camera and took their portrait.

Return of Water

Rachel White

I

Every city has its own light—

and mine has Great Salt Lake
like a mirror placed to peer around a corner,
it brings
back to me rays from the
sun below the horizon,
embers in magenta,
smoldering purple above a
burning
rosy orange glow far
away behind lavender
mountains, range after
range draped in beaded
curtains
of indigo rain that
evaporate before they hit
the ground, ethereal virga
in reflected radiance
mysterious, the Great Basin
version of Northern Lights,
semblance of some other,
more perfect plane, a realm

beyond us, who have barely
begun to understand
the resonance of our existence.

II

Perhaps, if we return a part

of what belongs to the land,
in thanks, start to recognize
we live—as do all things
alive—in relation,

rain will return, replenish
the reservoir of deep time,
waters that connect us
to the people of the past,
millennia upon millennia
of intercontinental
migrations like great rivers
converging in the flyways
of millions to this vestige
of prehistoric lakes,
ancient tracks across a marsh, microbialites,
salt reefs that transform light
—an ongoing miracle
like the parable of loaves and fish—
into masses of brine flies
and shrimp that feed the famished birds,
who rest to keep flying on.

The Silent Sibling

Ayja Bounous

I was born at the base of Little Cottonwood Canyon in the Wasatch Mountain Range of Utah. I grew up on the ancient shoreline of an inland sea we now refer to as Lake Bonneville. Just over a mile from where my childhood home sits used to be the terminus of a glacier that carved Little Cottonwood Canyon from the spine of the Wasatch between thirty thousand and ten thousand years ago. Twelve miles long—the longest in the Wasatch range—the glacier transported materials from glacier head to canyon base, where it met Lake Bonneville. Boulders ripped from their original resting place and deposited at the glacier's end are easily still seen today at the mouth of the canyon, where they'll sit until the next major geographical upheaval. Snow that fell in the upper reaches of the canyon compressed into glacial ice in the accumulation zone and slid slowly along the glacial pathway into the ablation zone, where it's believed the glacier calved into the lake. Icebergs the shade of sapphires would have floated above the current cities of Sandy, Draper, and Cottonwood Heights.

I was a geology-obsessed child. With parents and grandparents who skied and worked at Snowbird Ski Resort up Little Cottonwood Canyon, I spent much of my childhood in the canyon. I'd fantasize about the magnitude of that glacier often. I'd imagine what it would have been like to sit on the shoreline near my house and witness ice calving into the frigid depths of the lake below. I'd stand with my father on top of a steep chute at Snowbird, and amid my terror of skiing it, I'd think about the erosion that sculpted this chute. At my hesitation, my father would coax me to breathe—*inhale, exhale*. On the exhale, I'd push myself over the precipice. My ski tips would follow the fall line, the same path water would have taken as it made its way down onto the glacier below and beyond into the lake.

The transfer of materials from peak to lake looks different today. Snow that falls in Little Cottonwood Canyon has a longer distance to travel, about twenty-seven miles, before reaching the shores of what remains of Lake Bonneville—Great Salt Lake. From a seasonal standpoint, the lake seems little more than the West Desert's lung. With each full swing around the sun, the lung completes a single breath. Inhaling as the snow melts off the mountains, swelling rivers and shorelines. Exhaling as the sun breaks hydrogen and oxygen bonds and the water retreats into the arid sky. With no outlet, the only escape from Great Salt Lake is up.

Shallow enough to be a mirror laid flat on sand, the lake is a game of tug-of-war between evaporation and precipitation, a steady march across the desert: one step forward, one step back. With the combined threats of climate change and water mismanagement, it's one step forward, three steps back. The once enormous body of water is currently at risk of receding into crystals of salt and arsenic. In an exhale of evaporation, that arid lung shrinks as more water is lost to the desert air, becoming a lung unable to take a full breath.

Though the relationship between Little Cottonwood Canyon and Great Salt Lake might not be as direct as a glacier calving into a lake anymore, there is still a symbiotic push and pull between the two. Every spring, the snowpack melts and the lake begins to reach into the surrounding marshlands, providing habitat for brine shrimp and birds. In the winter, the lake gives some of this moisture back to the mountains.

To a skier or snowboarder living along the Wasatch Front, one of the most exciting phrases to hear during a winter storm is "lake effect." It's a phenomenon that works in the opposite direction of gravity and snowmelt—molecules of water lifted from the lake to the mountains. Sometimes, when the conditions are right, a storm rolling in from the northwest will gather more moisture as it passes over the lake, depositing another few inches of unanticipated snow as the storm gets caught in the mountains. You'll hear the phrase passed around the Snowbird tram during a storm as a predicted twelve inches of snow becomes sixteen inches. The locals will whoop, "Lake effect!" as they push themselves into the powder, praising the relationship between the lake and mountains that make the Wasatch so unique. There's even a cocktail bar in Salt Lake City named after the phenomenon.

It seems so romantic, a cyclical give and receive between lake and mountains. And we—the humans residing along the Wasatch Front—are the idle benefactors of this beautiful cycle.

The reality is not so romantic. We are not idle benefactors, we are disruptors of this cycle, the creators of a darker, more sinister cycle. We divert moisture en route to the lake, sucking it up through farms and emerald lawns, siphoning the water before it can reach the brine shrimp and the millions of migratory birds dependent on the shrimp. We allow toxins to enter our waterways. We are slowly suffocating the lake, slowly suffocating the organisms that rely on it.

Though I grew up on the shoreline of Lake Bonneville and spent my childhood imagining glaciers and icebergs, I never once during my upbringing walked along the shores of the lake in its current form. The closest I ever came was when our airplanes would take off and land at the SLC International Airport, circling over wetlands and islands. For all of the countless hours I spent frolicking in the snow, I had never once dipped my toes into the water that those snowflakes ended their hydrologic journey in, their final resting place before escaping into the sky. Never once had I actually visited what gives the city I live in—

Salt Lake City—its name.

Over the years Utahns have created clever little catch phrases to use in marketing plots to draw people, and therefore profit, to our state. Most are centered around the mountains and snow. *Life Elevated* is painted on billboards, welcoming drivers along the roadside borders. *The Greatest Snow on Earth* famously became the subject of an unsuccessful lawsuit pressed by the traveling circus with a nearly identical name. As far as I know, there is no catchy slogan inviting tourists to visit *The Greatest Salt on Earth*, or any marketing that promotes visiting the largest natural lake west of the Mississippi, the largest saltwater lake in the Western Hemisphere, or the eighth largest terminal lake in the world.

It was a sunny Saturday in October, during the fourth decade of my life, when I finally waded into Great Salt Lake and felt its cool grip around my ankles. At my feet, bird bones lay still in the salty shallows. The water stretched endlessly toward the horizon, blending with a cerulean sky. It was undeniably peaceful. Afterwards, I sat in the sand next to a poet who gestured at the mountains and said, "The slogan, *Life Elevated*, makes us, as a culture, believe that everything worth caring about is *up*, at the higher elevations." She shifted her gaze to the birds wheeling over our heads, to the serene water at our side. "We aren't taught to value the lowest point of the valley."

I exhaled sharply at her words. I had spent my life loving the mountains, yet never Great Salt Lake, their silent sibling. For all the times I had praised "lake effect," I had never praised the lake itself. I once hiked along Antelope Island, the lake's largest island, and even then my eyes were drawn to the reflections of the mountains on the water, rather than the water itself. My attention had always been on the mountains, on the snow, never the lake. Never the feature that might define my home even more than the mountains. Never the feature that might hold the future to the snow I so cherish.

Those winter recreationists who call in sick on powder days to drive up glacial canyons might not see the similarities they share with brine shrimp, avocets, or white pelicans, but there are plenty. The same water that sustains life in the marshlands of the lake is necessary for the survival of the snowpack into the future. It's the same water that is necessary for the survival of our health as a community in northern Utah.

If we continue to block the natural passage of water from mountains to lakes, it won't be long before the lake will reciprocate the abuse. The dry and salty playa bed left behind as the lake's shorelines recede is full of the toxins we've allowed to accumulate. Winds and storms that once gathered moisture will instead gather what's left behind when the water recedes. Arsenic, mercury, copper, and lead could become part of the new "lake effect"—a phenomenon of toxic dust storms.

One of the greatest threats to snow in the American West is dust. The darker particles absorb sun rays that would normally be reflected by the facets of snow crystals, causing the snow to melt quicker. If Great Salt Lake continues to shrink, winter recreationists will watch helplessly at the early deterioration of our precious snowpack. As our lungs and mountains fill with dust, we will see the empty stretch of land that was once a mirror laid flat on sand and wish we had had the foresight to save it sooner. Abused and ignored for too long, the lake will take its revenge.

Inhale and exhale. Evaporation and precipitation. Give and receive. Steal and suffocate.

We are all downstream of Great Salt Lake. Unlike most waterways, which only carry materials in one direction, we are being held accountable for how we treat the lake's tributaries. Toxins that wind up in our riparian zones are, in fact, upstream. Today's water policies will directly impact the health of our community in the coming decades. We are upstream of the lake and downstream of ourselves. When those northwest winds that bring the snowstorms blow, we are also downwind of our toxins, our choices. We exhale, and the lake inhales what we breathe into it. The lake exhales and we inhale our own decisions and policies, our toxins and dust. That arid lung is our lung. If we choose to breathe life into the lake, allowing water to fill its shorelines, the lake will in turn breathe life into us.

Inhale, exhale.

Walking the Bear

Star Coulbrooke

I walk on water, take the river
from its high Uintas
down Utah's cascades,
wander Wyoming's meanders,
Montpelier's meadows,
to Soda's hair-pin curve
where thirty-thousand years ago
lava turned the Bear
away from Blackfoot's Snake
and sent it down to Grace.

Doubling back from Gem Valley
to Cache, I walk the river's cobbled bed
where tributaries surge, rowdy Cub,
Little Bear, Beaver-headed Logan,
six-tined fork of Blacksmith.

Down the length of floodplains
I pass, through wetlands
of cattails and bulrushes,
to bottomlands leveled and drained,
where the river silts in, slows down,
its honeyed pace tamed for grain.

On the river's gliding current
I travel miles each step,

a dreamlike passage
through cedar and cottonwood,
hawthorn and chokecherry,
lifting like a heron over dams
and sluggish lakes
that halt the river's breath.

I walk the Bear all summer
as it builds strength again,
widens into marshes, joins
in lush bird-heavy congress
with the great peculiar Salt,
a lake that would surely die
if not for this river, this path,
this milk and honey

Self-Portrait as Beehive

Adam O. Davis

Then their lung gave out,
                                        their canary
told a lie,
                their livelihood became lore.

Their blood long cooped in the cells
of themselves begat copper
                                        until they,
metaled with earth,
                              grew rich, went
forgotten,
                settled like knives in the ribs
of that mountain.

                              I was that mountain.

I was that canary.

                              I was that copper
in the lung,
                              that sagebrush in
                                        the blood,
those clouds that hung
                                        & hummed
like hives in the skies that men
had built

without safety equipment.

I was the world as the world
had been built:
on loan from loam
& leashed
to that knowledge—
no better
than bee
or bush
or bullet
in the breast
of a man who wanted nothing
other than to die,
no better
than anything pushed from the dirt
that drank his blood
& housed
those dead men
who did dead man things
as I drove past the prison,
past Provo,
past Levan,
severe
river through Scipio
& into Cedar City
whose streets stood quiet
as uranium
in the summer dusk
& where no one
dared ask what I meant
by my being.

I was all
that the dirt had given me.

Ancestral Waters

Danielle Beazer Dubrasky

Along old US Route 91—the frontage road between Cedar City and Kanarraville—a sign set up by the Utah State Commission marks Lake Bonneville's southern rim. It reads: "The low ridge of the south end of this valley forms the south rim of the Great Basin which in prehistoric times was the bed of a vast body of water now referred to as Lake Bonneville.... Lying at the lowest part of the lakebed, and having no outlet, Great Salt Lake became the 'dead sea' of the western hemisphere." Maps show that this southernmost part of the lake was diverted from its main body into a long bay, covering what is now Milford and extending its shores beyond Old Irontown, an iron mine ghost town west of Cedar City. A Pleistocene freshwater lake once teeming with fish and reptiles, the Ice Age lake was as old as thirty thousand years, covering twenty thousand square miles over Southern Idaho, Eastern Nevada, and Western Utah.

I have lived in the south rim of the Great Basin for over thirty years, a transplant from the Piedmont Valley east of the Blue Ridge Mountains. When I first moved here, I carried images of the dogwood blossom as a talisman to remember my hometown. Each spring the "petals" open into four bracts—modified leaves surrounding a greenish pistol—splashing pink and white against woods of maple and oak trees. The palm-sized flora was a vibrant thing through which I could imaginatively return home. But after three decades, the desert has crept into my blood. My talisman has transformed from the ephemeral flower to the durable ammonite fossil. My collection sits on my dresser, roughhewn or polished, or manifested in pottery pieces, a glass dish, an amulet on a leather string. When I pick up one of the smooth fossils, its curled center gives me a touchstone to this landscape's past.

One September afternoon, to get a sense of that ancient lake and the fossil's original home, I drove west on State Route 56 over the Harmony Mountains toward Newcastle and Beryl Junction. The lake was shallow here. No dramatic shorelines follow the mountains' edge compared to the Wasatch Front. On my drive, I keep thinking about the title of a poetry book by Natalie Young: *All of this Was Once Under Water.* The poems imagine a sea monster that roamed Lake Bonneville and its thousand-foot depths. I imagine her monster swimming this far south, feeding on mottled sculpin, chubs, and trout—Late Pleistocene fishes that still swim in this century's waters—until it abandons these southern shores to follow the diminishing sea north and thrash against its shrinking home, near the lights of Salt Lake's ever-expanding city. We all have our reasons for leaving. In my case, the death of a parent and domino effect: a childhood home sold, a migration from the coast to the desert, a living blossom traded for the mineralized past. For the ancient lake, it was another kind of death. Climate change—the gradual warming of the temperatures and lack of rainfall. The waters receded, away from the Harmony Mountains and dormant volcanoes that once were islands, to leave behind only fossils.

At the Junction, I go north along Beryl Highway and pass a few houses until the road cuts a straight line for miles through sagebrush and sand, finally curving along the railroad tracks for Union Pacific trains. A light dust-haze ripples along the valley edge as if a bay laps the base of the mountains. They look like prehistoric reptiles warming themselves in the sun, their brown jagged backbones descending into low ridges of leathery tails. I turn around before sunset and drive back east on 56, paying more attention to where the highway rises and dips, imagining that "all of this was once under water." I drive over the summit toward home and marvel at the brilliant blue sky against red rock hills flanking Cedar City. But my pleasure in the scenic vista is naive. The more azure blue the sky, the less moisture in the air. I have lived back east where a comparable blue happens only after a storm sweeps out weeks-long gray humid skies. Now I live in one of the driest counties in Utah. Yet, Iron County uses up three times the amount of water compared to the national trend.

The first Utah Mormon inhabitants to settle this territory Welsh and Scottish miners and farmers. They left behind oppressive politics and landscapes abundant with bodies of water to settle in land-locked arid valleys where they could set up their own politics. In establishing their new homes, they displaced the Indigenous Paiute people who had been seasonally migrating through the Great Basin since 1000 CE, setting up homes along what is now called Coal Creek that runs through Cedar City to empty into the western valley. Winter conditions would send them south. Generations of Indigenous people passed throughout this land for almost nine hundred years, before pioneers arrived in 1851 and permanently disrupted the wayfarers' cyclical journeys.

A year ago, this area, along with the rest of the state, suffered a megadrought. We woke up each morning to one stunning blue and cloudless day after another, only vaguely aware of how this paradise was slowly thirsting us to death. At the end of that summer in 2022, Governor Cox asked Utahns to pray for rain. Although an environmental agency back in Washington requested (somewhat bemusedly) a more comprehensive conservation plan, the prayers seem to have worked—for now. In the winter of 2023, La Niña sent storm after storm that replenished the snowpack, filled reservoirs, revived dry lakes, and saved Great Salt Lake from the brink of death. Coal Creek, a mile east from my house, roiled all winter like a wild animal released out of its cage. But I suspect the anomalous amount of snow only postponed the devastation. I wonder if the snows of that winter were giving one final, refreshing drink to Great Salt Lake as their way of saying their last goodbyes.

Up to 60 percent of our body is made up of water that contains the same amount of salt in relation to water as the ocean. We taste that salt in our tears. There are still similarities between fish and humans—the webbed skin between our thumb and fingers, our smooth belly fat. I became entranced with the idea that we are really land dolphins—curious, playful, social. But unlike our sea cousins, we have forgotten our original home, despite the fact that we carry its blueprint within our cells.

There is a Welsh word called hiraeth, pronounced "*here-ayeth*," that describes a longing for something that has been left behind or has been taken from you. The Welsh poet Leslie Norris, who lived in Utah Valley for over twenty years but grew up in Merthyr Tydfil, wrote a poem called "A Sea in the Desert" that described a sea that "came fawning to my door" in Orem as he slept. When I first moved to Cedar City's high desert, I dreamed of Sandbridge, a four-mile stretch of beach in Virginia north of the Outer Banks where my family spent summers. My body craved tumbling in the breakers and the salt spray or walking at sunset to see the water get darker and darker, rhythmic waves lapping the sand. I missed the ocean in an almost animalistic way. At dusk, I'd watch the sun fall below the horizon west of the Escalante Desert and wait for "nautical twilight," when fading rays scatter a deep oceanic blue throughout the sky, and first stars appear.

Within the concept of *hiraeth* or longing rests grief, from the Latin gravis, loosely related to the English "grave." When I drove to the farthest southern edge of Great Salt Lake's predecessor, to the start of its vanishing point from over ten thousand years ago, I wished I had thought to carry one of my ammonites with me—the one on my necklace, or the polished refined piece propped in its stand on my dresser. Most appropriate would have been the one still curled in its limestone deathbed. Should I have buried it somewhere along Beryl Highway? The Paiute Indian Tribe of Southern Utah was finally federally recognized in 1980. Every year in June they hold a Restoration Gathering Powwow on their portion of reinstated federal acreage, celebrating the bringing together of what was lost. Coal Creek runs to the west, across the road from the tribal headquarters, between them and the land their ancestors used to explore for centuries.

Each Sunday I drink water from a small cup as a sacrament—a word derived from the Latin for Sacred Oath, with roots connected to the Greek word for "mystery." Each week I give a Sacred Oath to remember a symbolic Living Water as a form of renewal. I sing hymns with a congregation of descendants from some of the Welsh and Scottish families who first settled near the Iron mines, who consider themselves the original founders. Within the blood of my fellow congregants runs the River Taff or Loch Lomond; within mine, the Atlantic and the Shenandoah River. Like many of our northern counterparts, we are not indigenous but interlopers, living under the misguided legacy of our predecessors who didn't understand at what cost would the desert "blossom as a rose." The pioneer descendants who have ranched much of the high desert now sell acres to developers; rows of Great Salt Lake townhomes pave their way over a depleting aquifer. We don't know what will happen up north. I do know that at the southern rim of the Great Basin, we live in the ghost town of an inland sea. Our ancestral memory of abundant water won't change the fact that we are drinking dry what little was left behind—even as inside us all lies an ocean.

Feather Tracts Seen

Sarah May

Your naked bed turned towards the sun
cracks form on the surface and run deep
our exposed bellies tied together
fractured webs etching maps on our skin
praying for water
for shelter amongst the sagebrush and dry grass
praying for rest

Your desert is a forgotten place
where we come together to remember
praying for the sacred
facing the west as the sun disappears
our cracks all we are left with

You have been deemed unlovable by many
but your beauty and holiness never diminish
you continue to shapeshift
death as transformation
the greatest gift you have given to me

We exist in the same world
on parallel paths
our softness oppressed
by doctrines of patriarchy
of those who fear our power
who exploit out of fear

born of a desire to thwart mortality
they fear dying
we understand death is pain
alchemized into power

My body has experienced
many deaths
perpetually changing and mutating
my feminine form
the ultimate embodiment of love
even when I reject her
she protects and forgives me
my arcs and bends
the ultimate vessel for forgiveness
a promise of a new life
a new world

Your body and mine are one
Intertwined with love and courage
to let the darkest parts of ourselves
be held and seen
adored for the things
we thought made us unlovable

Waif

Holly Simonsen

Four men disassemble
the modular visitor center
into three pieces

The frontage road
in January's haze
is no place for visitors—

I pump my gloved and fisted hands,
                the hearts beat,
             six crows are reluctant to scatter

My boots won't grip the ice
that shags Blackrock—
            what they've found,
                they've emaciated

Finally, a variegated feather
flutters down

        Ferruginous Hawk
        Cooper's Hawk
        Red-tailed Hawk
        Prairie Falcon

Our home is only sometimes an island;
take a tooth to the body of your own

Float

Claire Wahmanholm

When I moved to Salt Lake City in 2012, I knew exactly four things about it.

I knew about the Mormon church. I knew the city was in the desert. I knew that Jean Baudrillard, whose *America* I read without really understanding it, called the city a "symmetrical, luminous, overpowering abstraction," and Great Salt Lake's waters "hyperreal from sheer density of salt."

All of this made the city seem more extreme than any other place I had lived. The desert of it, maybe, or the religiosity, the fact that a single body of water held such power over the region. I came from Minnesota, where lakes are famously abundant, so this had a certain allure—the allure of scarcity, of the ends of the earth.

I imagined Great Salt Lake as a dead lake. I pictured an enormous stretch of blank water, ringed by nothing. A surface that was simultaneously there and not. A mirage.

When we first arrived in Salt Lake City, I was surprised by how close the lake was to the city itself. "Oh!" I remember saying to my husband as we came down the mountain pass on I-80 for the first time, "the lake is *right there*." And whenever we had out-of-town visitors, we would take them to the steps of the Utah State Capitol and point to Great Salt Lake shimmering to my right. "See how close it is?" I would say.

I had a casual, benign interest in the lake. It was assumed that, at some point over the next handful of years of graduate study, we would visit it. Of course we would. It was the Western

Hemisphere's largest saltwater lake, it was the namesake of our new home, it was—I would quickly learn—a globally important ecosystem, and it was right there.

For three years, we lived so near to Great Salt Lake that when the wind gusted in the spring and fall, we woke up to a salty layer of dust on the windowsills.

But we never went.

I tell myself, now, that we were simply too busy: I had academic and artistic obligations. I had family and social obligations. We quickly established routines, and everyday life rushed to fill the spaces between those footings. We went to concerts; went to the grocery store; went to brunch; went to the ER; went to the vet; went bowling; went for runs; went for walks; went to Halloween parties; went to readings and receptions; went to Park City, Deer Valley, and Alta; went to Craters of the Moon, Arches, Canyonlands, Moab; went to Vancouver, Toronto, Seattle, New York City, Los Angeles, London, Denver. *There it is*, we'd say, cruising over it on our way in or out of the Salt Lake City International airport, the sun glancing off its flat face and into our eyes.

And then somehow three years had passed, and we were moving back to Minnesota. We were in the van and heading East on I-80, back the way we came, the lake winking in our rearview.

■ ■ ■

Now, I scroll through the Google reviews of Great Salt Lake to see what I missed.

No one expects the internet to be a place of nuanced engagement, but I am still taken aback by the tone of some of the reviews.

> *not real suer [sic] what all the hype is about was not impressed* (2 stars)

> *The water doesn't even like this lake. Lake is a strong word for this smelly pond. Time to let this go* (2 stars)
>
> *Went in summer. smelled like a morgue. so many flies that they form layers upon the lake. It's water with a lot [of] salt in it. Not revolutionary* (1 star)
>
> *Worthless lake. Nothing cool about a way salty lake* (1 star)

I am mortified by the cavalier dismissal of a 13,000-year-old keystone ecosystem, sure, but I am also mortified because this attitude feels too close to what might have been going through my head during the years we lived in Salt Lake City. *It's a big lake. Whatever. I hear there are lots of flies.*

▪ ▪ ▪

While most of us probably associate the word inertia with the realm of physics, in its original Latin it simply indicated a "want of art or skill" (from inert, from in-art/artless).

As an artist, I am suitably chastened by this etymology.

I don't know what we had been waiting for, or what would have jolted us out of our assumption that *the lake would always be there, so why rush?* And even if we had gone (I tell myself now, trying to justify our inertia), I suspect it would only have been to check the lake off our bucket list, to say we'd done it. And a bad reason is worse than having no reason at all. Except that I often do things just to say I've done them. I love bucket lists. I have been dutifully chipping away at my own for years. I have run three half-marathons; I have published three books; I have gotten two tattoos; I have gotten an undercut; I have dyed my hair several outlandish colors; I have taken psychedelic mushrooms; I have eaten at a three-star Michelin restaurant; I have donated almost a gallon of blood.

Many of the things on my list have taken longer to accomplish than a trip to Great Salt Lake. And so I worry we didn't go see the lake not because we were too busy but because we just didn't think it was worth seeing.

The longer we lived there, the more the lake's allure receded. It became less of an idea and more of a real place, which required real time, gas, planning. It had lost its mythic proportions. It had moved from *hyperreal* to *real*. It was just a lake.

■ ■ ■

If someone had said *The lake will be gone in five years*, I wonder if we would have made the trip. But I wouldn't have believed it. The lake has existed since the Pleistocene; how could it disappear within five years?

But that is the number, according to a dire report published in early January 2023. Compiled by a group of scientists, educators, and environmental advocates, the report notes that excessive water use has resulted in the lake's all-time low levels (nineteen feet below average), and that without an additional influx of a million acre-feet per year—starting immediately—the lake will vanish.

When we arrived in Utah in 2012, Great Salt Lake was very much alive, its abundant brine shrimp and brine flies supporting millions of migratory birds. Water levels in the lake were at the highest they would be that decade, at fourteen million acre-feet. The levels are now half that. In some places, the lake is now a mile away from its previous shoreline.

In 2012, news coverage and public discussion of the lake rarely focused on the arsenic, lead, and mercury-laced winds that would buffet the Wasatch Front, decreasing the average person's life expectancy by about two years; it rarely highlighted how much the PM 2.5 levels would worsen in an area where poor air quality has already led to an increase in miscarriage and risk of stillbirth.

In 2012, I didn't hear anyone calling the desiccation of the lake a "potential environmental nuclear bomb" or an "ecological, economic disaster" or using phrases like "existential threat."

▪ ▪ ▪

The water levels keep dropping, and we still have not visited. As the lake's desiccation becomes more certainty than fear, I worry I would only visit now because I'm drawn to the seeping tang of disaster. I would only visit to see the hundreds of dead, rotting grebes and *feel like I was walking in a grave yard* (2 stars). To stand and look at the lake and think *Very sad to see the low water mark in all of recorded history...* (2 stars) or *So sad it's drying up, but I'm glad I was able to see it before it's gone forever* (5 stars)?

▪ ▪ ▪

I am at the spa down the street, checking in for my one-hour float session, checking off another experience from my bucket list. I am thinking about Great Salt Lake as the person behind the desk tells me I will float in ten inches of 98.6-degree water concentrated with 1,000 pounds of Epsom salts. Float tanks are about 30 percent salt, similar to the current levels of Great Salt Lake's north arm, which is now too salty to support algae, brine shrimp, or brine flies.

The attendant walks me back to my room, where I shower, work ear plugs into my ears, and ease myself into the tank.

I float instantly. It is incredible. It takes me several minutes to relax my body entirely. I keep catching myself trying to use my muscles to support my neck or my arms or my head. *Let go*, I have to say over and over again. *Trust the water.* I am afraid that the saltwater will get in my eyes, but it stops right at my temples.

At first it is tricky to know what to do with my arms and hands. The tank is wide enough for me to float with my arms outstretched, but that doesn't feel natural. My elbows want to come down, come in, toward my ribs. I notice that palms up feels more effortless than palms down. Finally, I figure out that the most natural position is palms up, elbows down, in a gesture that I visually associate with supplication or surrender. This feels alien to me. It's not what I would have expected. When our bodies are at their most natural, their most free, is this the position they take? Surrender rather than control? *Does* the water know best?

▪ ▪ ▪

If you Google *places to see before they disappear*, you are flooded with articles: "15 Breathtaking Places to Visit Before They Disappear"; "Bucket List Places To Visit Before They Disappear"; "27 Attractions People Need To See ASAP (Because They Won't Exist In 2030)"; "50 Places That Will Be Affected By Global Warming"; "9 Tourist Attractions That Could Vanish Due To Climate Change."

Great Salt Lake isn't on any of those lists. It is not Instagrammable the way the Great Barrier Reef, Venice, the Seychelles, or the Galápagos are.

In the same way that charismatic, photogenic animals (tigers, pandas, polar bears) fare better in conservation efforts than, say, invertebrates—even though invertebrates make up 79 percent of species on Earth compared to mammals' 3 percent, and even though they're arguably more essential to overall ecosystem health and resilience—I wonder whether Great Salt Lake will suffer from not being "pretty" enough to save. From not being *useful* enough to us. From not giving us enough *bang for our buck*.

▪▪▪

it's a smelly place, like a dead seashell. Once you drive by, you can smell from a distance. Also, it's a large body of water without good use for drinking or irrigation. I hope one day we will have a good use for it besides tourism (4 stars)

This is literally once in a lifetime thing because I'll never go in that water again. The lake is absolutely disgusting. There are thousands of bugs in the water and the smell is similar to manure or worse. We only went in the water to float (one time only, checked it off the list and never going back in unless someone pays me a minimum of $500 lol). The lake is pretty from the shore but that's about it. The Great Salt Lake is way overrated (2 stars)

▪▪▪

"Perhaps the biggest deficit we have in facing this crisis is trust," write the authors of the January 2023 report. "Conservation measures have been taken throughout the watershed, but many water users and providers do not yet trust each other to shepherd conserved water to the lake. We desperately need transparency and shared sacrifice to reinforce trust and solidarity."

And though a survey conducted in September 2022 indicated that 80 percent of Utahns are concerned about the lake, I am worried that this won't translate into action, that not enough people are willing to put faith in data, models, first-person reports, the exhortations of scientists and activists. I am worried that people are not willing to put enough faith in each other.

And yet, sometimes respite comes. In the six months since

that report was published, an above-record snowpack has bought some time—possibly an additional two years. Furthermore, in early May the Weber Basin Water Conservancy District authorized the diversion of 650 million gallons of water per day into Great Salt Lake. And the Bear River was high enough this year to generate runoff into the lake. But more importantly, water conservation measures are actually being implemented.

Experts stress, though, that another two years on the clock is not an excuse to sink into inertia. We should be grateful for the extra time, but it alone will not be enough. Things are still precarious. The north arm of the lake has not received the influx of fresh water that the south arm has, and unless it does, the pelican population on Gunnison Island, which used to number around twenty thousand and which numbered precisely zero in June 2023, will not recover. This gift of two years could actually work *against* long-term conservancy efforts, since people may assume the problem is solved, that they can relax, that it's not such a big deal after all. People could succumb to "Great Salt Lake Fatigue." It could all still fall apart.

■ ■ ■

What does it mean to live an artful existence? Does it imply movement as opposed to stasis? A coming together? A coordination? Like birds taking to the sky? Turning as one in a murmuration?

I worry that floating—metaphorically at least—is the wrong stance. In the float tank, it is as if all weight has been removed from my shoulders. In the float tank, I am inert, passive, working toward nothing.

Maybe floating, like retreat, can be a recalibration before action—a summoning of resolve, a moment of hover between the long ascent and the plunge.

Maybe I will leave the tank having felt the world—and my

weight in it—differently. Rather than dragging myself over its surface, maybe I will feel like stepping more lightly, with more flexibility, with more faith.

■ ■ ■

I turn the lights off in the tank. As my eyes adjust to the darker-than-night darkness, a jagged red-blue shape—fish-shaped, bird-shaped, shaped like a lake—soars from the lower right to upper left of my field of vision. I imagine I am floating in the lake. I imagine the stink. I imagine not the clean plastic tub beneath me, but mud. The floaters teem in my vision like flies. I imagine birds by the thousands. Sometimes my arms or legs graze up against the edge of the tank and I am startled into remembering how small the tank really is. I imagine the claustrophobic feeling of it getting smaller and smaller.

I open my eyes as wide as they will go. I tell myself to have faith, to open my heart to the possibility that the affected parties—the lawmakers, the lobbyists, the industries, the farmers, the citizens—will continue to do the right thing. I try to make myself see it. I try to make myself see it as if I am *right there*, rather than 1,250 miles away. I try to picture the walls of the tank expanding away from me, the freshwater flooding in. I tell myself I will see the real lake someday.

Praise the Baby Pelicans

Willy Palomo

salt-white feathers tarred
like filthy and immaculate
prophets   we must all
be notorious ready to die
for your gospel of crack
and eggshell   each of
your feathers is a quill
a page of the book of life
black with our gasoline
nobody reads books
anymore for fear of what
is written about them
heirs of air and cloud
blood brothers of breath
and wind your bones
are snow that never melts
only glistens   you are
disgusting and pure
guilt-ridden and innocent
it pains me to see the twisted
hay of your feathers the weak
air melting beneath your
wings until you land like
a ripped grocery bag
eggs broken milk claiming
a continent on the tile

ravens will dive foxes sniff
they will join you in your
sticky grave devoured
by their hunger rest now
young one   this pain
is for the living

Brine Flies and the Dark Instead

Joel Long

This is how water moves, remaking what it does and does not touch.

—Elizabeth Rush

Around the entire shoreline of Great Salt Lake, some two-hundred-plus miles, lies a banner of brine flies, six feet wide, a perpetual stirring. I walk through the insects with my dogs to get to water, and these flies, in congress, pour a rounded wave at the widening circumference of every footstep forward. The flies do not fall backwards to my shins, seem uninterested in skin at all, uninterested in biting me, stinging me. A thousand wings buzz, join the millions of wings that surround the lake. Some see this chain mail of brine flies as a barrier to the water. I walk through; the brine flies part, let me find saltwater, let me wade into sinuous waves. As I leave them, brine flies fill every footprint I've made with shimmer and hum.

In normal years, thirty-seven million flies teem in just one linear mile of shore; midseason, billions clothe the circumference of the lake, from Black Rock to Rozel Point, pulsing with life. In the mile I walk on shore, each fly of the millions bears two wings. Each wing shapes multiple facets, translucent, stained-glass windows, fastened with leaden veins in the well-proportioned lancets of the High Gothic vogue. Beneath the window quivers one plump abdomen, a chitinous thorax where wings attach, where wings begin their blur and flight that takes this one fly and the thousands near me, out of range of my footstep.

From the thorax sprout six legs, each hinged twice and barbed to grip the microbialite mats or to propel the flies in twitches along mud near lake water.

Above their wings, the head turns with two tiny, complicated eyes and antennae probing from either side of the forehead. Every fly has a mouth that opens to the world, to its water and its algae, to water and its salt. Inside the head lives a brain the size of a poppy seed with the complex blueprint drawn in electric nerve for its movement, flight, fear, want. How much space does a creature need to make the desire to return to the world in another fly, another life, however brief its return? Their entire world yields often just three-days-brief, sometimes five, little more, but every day, a quick flash, flying.

My dogs chase gulls ahead of me. The gulls chase brine flies. A hundred California gulls, with tiger lily grins, fly or scurry along the shore with their mouths wide open, inhaling hundreds of flies at once, vacuuming down pail on pail of black rice with wings. The gulls are hungry. They need protein, thrive on this buzzing in their gullets, buckshot sensation of salty flavor and contentment. My dogs follow suit. My golden retriever Stanley opens his mouth to retrieve flies by the mouthful. Stella snaps her old girl shepherd's jaw along the shore and inhales a fold of flies, snorting, sneezing, rising back on her haunches, plunging her front legs in stinky black mud. Clouds of flies erupting with each lunge.

■ ■ ■

I first saw microbialites when I climbed down an embankment from the scenic view turnout on I-80. I was trying to get to the lake. I trudged through a swamp, rabbit brush, cattails, phragmites, holding my camera above my head, walked the railroad track past a corroded pistol dismantled—I thought, *mob killing, gun disposal.* I ended on the west side of Black Rock, carrying swampy wetlands in my heavy, soaked jeans. Closer to water, strange striations and domes of whitish rocks rose from the sand. In furrows between striations, bright saltwater stretched and bulged from the lake filled with organic matter, dark as reddish coffee grounds, fragrant. These white striations, microbialites, are living rocks formed from sediment excreted from the smallest microbes. When the lake is healthy, the microbes are healthy; microbialites are healthy. That March day, microbialites *were* very healthy. But they were alive in a different way. A fur of living brine flies draped their surface, thriving where microbialites thrive, the still waters in the channels between, perfect for feeding, perfect for making more flies.

This is not a normal year. I return to Bridger Bay on Antelope Island to photograph the place my daughters Hannah and Sarah floated when they were young, in 1994, salt water so buoyant that the girls in their brilliant dresses lifted like corks above, their vision skimming sky that lived in water. I walk where the girls floated. I walk through no water at all, walk on sand, mud crust, salt crust. Egg Island and Fremont Island stand for my pole star, steady hills from decades-old photos; now, I could walk to every island I see.

I walk nearly a mile before I reach wet mud and finally shallow water. I expect windrows of pupal casings. I'm hoping for flies. No flies shimmer on *this* shoreline. No birds chase flies. A column of water rests between the shore and an exposed berm of microbialites. The berm forms a shallow pond, attenuated along the island, that the biologists tested: 30 percent plus salinity, nearly double the salinity that can sustain fly larvae, eggs, and pupae. There are no flies and the microbialites, where flies fulfil their cycle, dry above the water in the late autumn heat. The silence of gulls and phalaropes here is a warning, a threat.

The life cycle of the brine fly is as quick as the wash cycle in my washing machine, from adult fly to egg to larvae and pupae to adult fly. Adult flies mostly live just three to five days, but they are three days of gorging on abundant food around microbialites, finding a mate and laying eggs before dying. Hotter weather speeds time up for the flies, and cold slows time down, their life span stretched, slowed, slurred. Many brine flies end obscurely in the throat of one of the hundred gulls prancing over the surface of rocks and water, or they end in the snap mouths of the many other birds, grebes, golden eyes, phalaropes, who depend on these flies for sustenance.

If I hadn't been enamored with strands of water reflecting gold near Black Rock, barren hills of the Oquirrhs that day, I might have noticed eggs in the water. I might have scooped up water and dark sediment to find rice-colored larvae, a quarter inch long, larvae grazing the water in my palm for cyanobacteria or bits of algae, not normally provisions I bring myself. The larvae live the longest chapter of the brine fly life. They feast beneath grooves of water, fattening themselves to extend days when they can actually fly, and the plumper the larvae, the longer they will fly above water. Eat well, darlings.

I lifted one microbialite shard—it felt like a long crust of bread, breaking—and found its bottom littered with dark, segmented pupae, brine fly cocoons where that crazy magic metamorphosis occurs in a week or so. The audience never sees this brave trickery: plump white larvae, inside the chiseled pupae, crafted by the larvae, or in metamorphosis to full grown flies with all their machined parts. Within days, inside the pupae, larvae grow legs; they grow wings, all those cells in the larvae with their genetic design for the full body of the fly, head, thorax, abdomen, which in days after the fly hatches, will be capable of making eggs and sperm to fertilize the eggs in the ovum, the return, you see, this cycle of change.

When the flies emerge from the shell of the pupae, they have formed a bubble of air that surrounds the newly-formed body, a supply that floats them to the surface of the lake. The adult flies in their few days can return underwater by forming a new bubble of air. I call it the magic bubble, diving bell, old gentleman, scuba suit. In the bubble, the flies crawl down the microbialite terrace underwater and feed on algae and diatoms, enough oxygen in their gear for a fifteen second dive. When they surface, the bubble, this safety suit, pops, leaving the flies perfectly dry and groomed, ready for their closeup along with the thirty-seven million on this mile of shore.

In healthy years, discarded pupal casings line the shores of Great Salt Lake: the pulsing waters of the lake sculpt the casings into windrows that curl and curve like hair in Botticelli's Venus or his attending angels. Late evening, when the sun slants over the Oquirrhs, over the west hills of the Island, sun hits the windrows, the amber and obsidian casings, and lights them up, each fragment a miniature lantern that once held larvae turning to fly. Step back, and the windrow turns to a shimmering arabesque, copper polished by sunlight and departure. These curves lead the curious heart to slow waves of the lake, green, blue, and lightning.

Westminster College biologist Bonnie Baxter, who studies microbialites, said that she saw gulls floating in Bridger Bay. Emaciated and hungry, these gulls waited, not for millions of flies that would feed them endlessly, but for one fly to emerge from their silver bubble. One lucky gull would eat this grain of rice. Bridger Bay and White Rock Bay on Antelope Island are places I used to see windrows, where I walked through that ribbon of sequins, flies smoking from my feet.

It is not just gulls missing flies. Nearly the entire US population of eared grebes, nearly 4.7 million, come to this water to feed on brine shrimp and adult brine flies. These kajagoogoo, new wave grebes with their red, beyond-the-power-of-Visine eyes, will miss more than half their nourishment; the other primary food and fresh water for these birds, the brine shrimp, fare not much better than these flies. Shrimp bodies flash bright red in the water, a warning flare that the saltiness of the water threatens them and could destroy them. Diving birds, goldeneyes with sleek black heads come to the lake by the thousands just to eat ivory larvae of brine flies. Microbialites die, and water furrows evaporate. Larvae have no place to feed, no place to attach when they form pupae. Goldeneyes will eat no larvae, nothing but seeds to feed them.

When I get to the water, I'm surprised; brine flies skim the shoreline! I have never been so happy to see flies. I kneel down to view them, my knees soaking in briny mud. The flies flit about like a negative of shooting stars in fast motion. I see flashes of wings, motes of legs that scatter too fast, but the flies are alive. The carpet of brine flies is 95 percent depleted, but they are here. I'm stunned, however, by the absence of birds, by that quiet. I see not a single shorebird, avocet, stilts, no water birds, eared grebes, shovellers. Perhaps it is this late hour of day, but the birds that eat these flies and their progeny are absent. An uncanny silence of air hovers above the shore.

Years ago, I took students to a room in the middle of my old school, a room without windows. In my pocket, I hid the feathered shoulder of a pheasant, brilliant dead thing, a gift from my hunter colleague down the hall. After I closed the door, I asked the students to be silent then turned out the light—utter darkness. I clicked on a flashlight, held it above the pheasant wing in my hand and asked them to imagine the beauty of the Thing in the dark room: bird shoulder, puffed rufous feathers, hundreds arranged in rhythms, gilded with black parentheses, feathers elongating toward lines in my own white wrist, catching light. I asked them to perceive this wing, see it blooming from nothing—Being emerging from the dark, sound from silence, the sudden light, the strangeness, our own breath.

I retrace the exercise backwards, brine flies receding into the dark room, the gulls, the grebes, the goldeneyes and phalaropes, following the flies into dark, into that silence as the lake recedes, as the lake gets saltier and diminishes. I do not know what is left when I turn on the lights and see the faces of these young students, a pile of wings in my hand.

But in the dark, I forget freshwater springs. I forget watersheds, Lee's creek and its delta, water mixing with waters of the lake, a cocktail of salt and freshwater mixed *just right*. Springs near Black Rock where Garfield Beach used to be, hold water that seeps past dried microbialites in white mounds, seeps toward living microbialites near the receding waters, far from Black Rock, water filling the channels. At these liminal spaces where freshwater meets the elevated brine of the lake, refuge habitats persist. Salt finds balance with freshwater. Here, thanks to osmoregulation, brine flies will balance their interior salt with the salt around them. This acrobatic act is not too much in the refuge. It is not too much to keep brine flies living. The flies will find acceptable salt levels for algae, diatoms, and other food they need to live, even to thrive. These freshwater inlets build little arks in the flood of drought and salt. The arks will carry a flurry of brine flies to another time—let it be soon—when we find wisdom to allow the water to return to the lake and swell its shores again the flies will return to the shores. They will surround Great Salt Lake with the sizzle of their living. Ten million birds will find them.

The Monster Shrinks

Natalie Padilla Young

Sounds around his home begin, build again:
some cameras, scientists, some curious
locals—this collection
of water is worth more
than their parents claimed (*stinky,*

bug-infested, cesspool of brine).
The monster overhears concerns,
shrugs a few new kinds
of prayer. He never needed
critical-level speeches, felt how tight,

his home cinching
closer, quicker. Not surprised
but nervous his big body
might survive
the inevitable reveal. Not so suddenly

without water, well,
that wouldn't work. Then something else
starts.

The monster feels more room
to float, feels his home grow
inch by inch, gather higher
over his head. He studies the shoreline

days to weeks, weeks to

a new conclusion:
The water *is* still receding.
And so is he.

Crystals, salt crust, the distance
to the bottom—everything
bigger. Ducks, seagulls
bigger between his teeth, harder to chew
through. Lonely and alone for so long

it feels nice. Each month a little less
mass to worry, lug about,
cause ripples. The monster
calculates:
a few short years and then drift

away. No more
reflection. Smaller than the smallest
sea monkey, how easy to disregard
the facts
of disappearance.

Everyone Wants To be a Brine Shrimp

Nicole Walker

In 1847, as the wagons emerged from Emigration Canyon into what is now called Salt Lake City, a band of silver blue water streaked across the western horizon. The pioneers must have been enchanted by the promise of a lake, a refuge from the arid trek they'd made from Missouri. Soon enough, immigrants realized that the lake was too salty to be of agricultural use, but still this valley held to its perceived promise. Rivers ran from the mountains to provide fresh water to grow the homeland they desired. Although Shoshone, Goshute, and Paiute peoples had practiced irrigation for years, the settlers began in earnest to divert that fresh water to their crops and homes and, eventually, businesses and mining operations.

That diversion has worked so well that these days, Salt Lake City boasts one of the fastest growing population centers. To visit Salt Lake—the capital of the second most arid state in the country—is to be surprised by how green the landscape is, how Edenic in its emulation of Illinois grasses, Missouri hawthorns. Linden and maple trees line the wide city streets. Lawns Lego into perfect squares in front of bungalows and duplexes, mini-mansions, and ranch houses. Golf courses undulate across wide patches of town. Farmers grow beets and corn and alfalfa for horses and cows. The settlers took the mountain water destined for that western-edge, blue-gray lake and converted it instead to the geometries of green that color the valley.

Great Salt Lake holds the remains of Lake Bonneville, that ancient lake, once vast and as full of as many species, maybe even more, than your own gut biome. Earlier climate changes, like the end of the ice age 14,000 years ago, forced Bonneville to retreat into its shallow, western edge. The water evaporated. The salt stayed down. No longer teeming with myriad sea creatures, now Great Salt Lake teems only with brine shrimp, the only creature that can survive the salinity of a sea that collapsed on itself, doubling down on its minerals, then doubling again.

Although the pioneers didn't find the lake useful to their purposes, the lake is not useless. It supports millions of migratory birds. An algae unique to this lake prefers the heavy salinity of Great Salt Lake and feeds the billions of brine shrimp that feed those migratory birds. In addition to feeding the birds, the brine shrimp are harvested to feed aquariums around the world.

But descendants of those pioneers mostly ignore the lake like one avoids the garbage dump. Just as a landfill does, the lake sends gases into the atmosphere and liquids to the water table, while everything else will linger until some of that lingering becomes useful again and a brilliant start-up figures out how to mine the landfill for its gems. But unlike a landfill, the dump trucks have stopped depositing their wares. Snowmelt once funneled its watery goods west and down. Snowmelt feeds alfalfa farms to feed cattle now. It waters lawns. It fuels industrial turbines. It washes cars and dishes. It flushes waste. It spins laundry. It fills water bottles. It quenches everyone's thirsts but the lake's. In October 2022, the water level in Great Salt Lake reached a historic low. A rail causeway divides the lake in half, causing the north side of the lake to become saltier as freshwater is prevented from reaching the northern end. The salinity is now too high even for the life that has adapted there. And, the water, a great, protective blanket, holds down the toxins that have been dumped there, trapping what has been buried by mining operations—arsenic, antimony, copper, zirconium, mercury, selenium, and other heavy metals. As the water evaporates, those toxic metals will be exposed to wind which will carry them up to the Wasatch Mountains and beyond to Wyoming. The only thing that doesn't evaporate and get blown eastward are the brine shrimp. Tiny enough to fly, they prefer their sticky, hostile habitat. But even lovers of hostile environments call uncle when they can't breathe.

▪ ▪ ▪

When I was five years old and had just learned to read, my mom and dad sat on the couch on either side of me and read a book about how bodies became pregnant. Although it was a children's book, the writing was clinical and the pictures stiff and uncomfortable. This was just before *Where Did I Come From?* came out—the more comic, cuter images of clouds and fat babies version of oh-my-god-I-didn't-even-ask sex-ed explainer. The formal and thin characters of my book must have displayed some of their body parts in this unwarranted and unwanted lesson but the image I remember best was the pencil dot in the middle of the page that represented the egg. The narrator explained that the egg was *this* small—barely visible—and that sperm, even smaller than that pencil dot, could only be seen through a microscope.

The smallness of babies struck me as miraculous. I loved small things then and now: miniature teacups, miniature pigs made of marzipan, and miniature bears the size of miniature toy poodles. The idea that humans grew from an egg the size of a pinprick fertilized by a swimming thing several times smaller than that egg amazed me. Throughout my childhood, I studied *A Child Is Born* with its romantic language and each stage of the fetus depicted as if someone were in the womb with a camera. The photos have been manipulated to magnify and light the tiniest fetuses to make them look more babylike, but I was always drawn to how alien the babies looked. An embryo at six weeks of growth is still smaller than an adult brine shrimp. It also might look a bit like a brine shrimp, with its tail a bit like a tadpole.

This six-week embryo swims in a uterus that forms an ecosphere to itself. Everything the fetus needs is provided by the mother. Some say that the book *A Child Is Born* elides the gestater's existence since the camera pays no attention to her identity or the work her body does to protect and to grow this shrimp. A study in the journal *Science* investigating endurance exercise events found that pregnancy equates to running a marathon every day for 365 days. No one watches films or TV shows about pregnancy as an extreme sport, but if you ask a pregnant woman how she's feeling, she will exhale deeply at you and bow her head so you can slip the gold medal over her head, though she must be careful not to knock the baby, once it's born, in the head with the medallion while she nurses.

▪ ▪ ▪

I didn't mean to fall in love with brine shrimp. In 2017, for my birthday, my friend Angie gave me an ecosphere—an egg-shaped glass enclosure in which three brine shrimp swam among oxygenating plants in a carefully balanced, magical kind of system. The brine shrimp were meant to live six months. Over a year later, most still swam between the tiny, oxygenating branch that produced the algae that fed the shrimps.

That year, I took the ecosphere on a book tour through California. As I explained in *The After-Normal*, an abecedarian about how climate change affects albatrosses, frogs, igloos, grasses, opossums, possums, and whistles, I passed the brine shrimp around the audience to show how their habitat is a synecdoche for our planet. This carefully balanced glass egg is as perfect as the earth. The brine shrimp are perfectly fine as long as nothing upsets the balance. I held up the sphere and said, "These are magical creatures in a magical chemical system. All food is provided. All waste is recycled. All chemicals equally distributed just like a perfect atmosphere." Analogy made, I handed out blue and green marbles. "These are your tiny planets. Don't lose them." I strike metaphors too hard sometimes, but everyone took their marble and carefully slipped them into purse and pant pocket. A year later, I met someone at a writer's workshop who had been at my talk. He produced a marble from his pocket. "I always keep it with me."

I am enchanted by brine shrimp. They are known adapters, but I wonder, as the lake dries, becomes more saline, can they survive this extreme and extremely fast change? Can the brine shrimp adapt to life in a habitat of a wide range of salt concentration? Brine shrimp grow to be about a centimeter. They are the largest creatures in Great Salt Lake. Because of their ability to adapt to different levels of salinity, they live in both the north and south arms of the lake. Brine shrimp eat microscopic algae *Dunaliella veridis. Dunaliella* are soft and nutritious but adult shrimp can eat all kinds of cyanobacteria and diatoms, which grow well in the south arm of the lake but struggle to grow in the over-salty north.

The better-balanced south arm of the lake takes good care of its tiny creatures, providing sustenance as well as space to grow. What brine shrimp lack in individual size, they make up for in abundance. Over seventeen trillion brine shrimp live in Great Salt Lake. An eared grebe, just one of the millions of birds that feast on the shrimp, eats between 25,000 to 35,000 per day. As one of the primary migratory bird stopovers, Great Salt Lake provides the food necessary for birds to make it to their next stop north and then feed them thoroughly on their way back south again. It takes a lot of energy for migratory birds to fly up and down continents. Seventeen trillion brine shrimp are just the right amount to sustain the metabolism of ten million visiting birds.

■ ■ ■

If you Google "What should pregnant women . . ." Google will autofill the rest of the question for you with the word "eat." Then Google will return to you 671,000,000 entries. Six hundred seventy-one million isn't as many webpages as there are brine shrimp in the sea, but the internet teems with delicious information to strain through the baleen that is your brain. Similac, a predominant brand of baby formula, occupies the first entry. If there is a perfectly designed-for-wellness drink for babies, why isn't there one for pregnant humans? Not only do we have to distill the advice, we have to shop for and concoct our own nutritional intake. In the Google list, Johns Hopkins Medicine is the fourth entry. Since there is no Similac for pregnant people, Johns Hopkins advises pregnant people to eat their food the hard way. With cooking and with teeth.

Once you start manufacturing humans, the internet/world/Johns Hopkins becomes invested in your diet. The list of foods to eat is short. The list of foods to avoid long: food trucks, carnivals, fast food, delis, raw sushi, and fresh cheeses like feta, queso fresco, blue-veined cheeses and Camembert, and smoked seafood. When I was pregnant with my first child, I felt hemmed in, hampered, envesselized. I did not want to be a walking environment. I felt like an aquarium—belly on display, John Hopkins shaking the right kind and right amount of flakes of fish food (cooked not raw) into my tank, taking my pH balance daily (blood work, ultrasound, weigh ins) to make sure I wasn't fucking anything up.

Embryos are not as sturdy as brine shrimp who feed on algae and live with bacteria. Bacteria from foods like deli meat and raw cheeses potentially threatens the fetus's native environment. Nine months of no queso fresco, no hot dogs, no sushi, no Caesar salad, no pâté turn the pregnant person's body into a laboratory. We're running experiments in here. Try not to contaminate with your regular person, regular turkey slices, regular raw-fish eating ways. It's a fragile, delicate environment—you don't want to upend the balance.

■ ■ ■

Brine shrimps are sensitive to their environments but not particularly fragile. Adept at adapting to extreme situations, they come prepared with strategies to extend their survival. Brine shrimp are gender tamperers. Sometimes, environments prompt changes in their sex, sometimes other environmental changes require them to adapt. Brine shrimp have no say in the salinity levels in the lake but they do have the capacity to employ their plasticity in order to adapt to radically altered environments.

When conditions in Great Salt Lake become especially hostile, dormant brine shrimp embryos lay protected inside cysts until conditions improve. The science journal *Frontiers in Physiology* published an article, "The Brine Shrimp Artemia: Adapted to Critical Life Conditions," that reads:

Under extremely critical environmental conditions, for example when seasonal lakes dry-out, Artemia takes refuge by producing a highly resistant encysted gastrula embryo (cyst) capable of severe dehydration enabling an escape from population extinction. Cysts can be viewed as gene banks that store a genetic memory of historical population conditions. Their occurrence is due to the evolved ability of females to "perceive" forthcoming unstable environmental conditions expressed by their ability to switch reproductive mode.

In addition to turtling up into cysts and waiting for the water to return, female brine shrimp can reproduce asexually by parthenogenesis or regular-sexually with males who are slightly smaller than they are but still cute. Parthenogenesis requires no oversight by the internet nor Johns Hopkins.

I want to take stock, or even purchase stock, in these potentialities. I want to hoard my gene bank for when environmental conditions become more hospitable. I want to live beyond severe dehydration, beyond evaporation, beyond wind-blowing my chemical brethren asunder. I want to have the kind of patience for my species as brine shrimp have for theirs.

As Great Salt Lake changes shape, the brine shrimp are acting up—they're drying out, ready for the next world. They're tantalizing their male partners then faking them out, flipping their naughty bits into head gear. Is Great Salt Lake dying? Possibly. But the brine shrimp are prepared, just in case.

In what reads a bit like a eulogy, Terry Tempest Williams wrote in the March 25, 2023, issue of *New York Times* about the lake: "The malignant colors, shapes and smells eerily mirrored the imaging of my mother's late-stage cancer. I knelt to caress the water body of Great Salt Lake, my henna-painted hands now tattooed in intricate designs by the feathered bodies of dead brine shrimp." Later, she uses "she" pronouns to refer to the lake. Twitter users excoriated Tempest Williams for equating a body of water to a woman. They made fun of her for giving human status to a lake. Maybe it was the mother idea that bothered them. Women take up enough space, I imagine they felt.

I too have trouble with the gendering of lakes and nature but not for the same reason. If you name it "she," it will suffer at the hands of "he." Maybe if we called things Father Lake, Father Nature, we'd be cowed into carefulness. No father likes it when you chip the paint on the walls of the house, let alone coat the floor of a waterbody with detritus like mercury. Being a mother means your body takes the brunt of its children's nutritional needs, their fetal desires, their in utero demands. If the earth had been a father, not a mother, maybe we wouldn't have depleted her like a fetus depletes the calcium of her host's bones.

▪ ▪ ▪

The brine shrimp situation is dire in many saline lakes, not just Great Salt Lake, but researchers watch in real time salt crystals stack where water molecules once piled. As agriculture, residential use, mining, and damming increase, less fresh water reaches the lakes. As the lakes become more saline, the brine shrimp stocks shrink. The northern arm of the lake has been oversaturated with salt for a while now, but now even Gilbert Bay, on the other side of the causeway, has reached 27 percent salinity; no brine shrimp have been found in the bay. Researchers at Utah State University compare Great Salt Lake to Lake Urmia in Iran. Both have similar depth, size, and geographical setting. "Lake Urmia has already lost most of its ecological and cultural function—but Great Salt Lake has not yet crossed that precipice." You can hear the ellipses burbling out from the "yet."

Already, birds suffer the lack of food. Utah Public Radio reported that 95 percent of all eared grebes stop at Great Salt Lake. Eared grebes, once they stop to rest, don't fly again for nine to ten months. They live much of their lives on Great Salt Lake, feasting on brine shrimp. There is no other place for them to stop in the western United States. If 95 percent of the eared grebes rely on the brine shrimp of Great Salt Lake, then 95 percent of eared grebes will die.

■ ■ ■

In the human body, cysts are small egg follicles that don't grow to ovulation. You learn a lot about cysts when you're trying, and failing, to get pregnant. The dream is to stimulate an egg follicle into ripe and receptive material—like Jell-O awaiting bananas. Or, in Utah, sometimes carrots are installed inside the Jell-O. Heck, sometimes even hot dogs, although that may be too on the nose in this metaphor. Imagine a cyst, hard-shelled like a fully developed chicken egg. No way in. No way out.

Fifteen months after the party Angie threw, one of the brine shrimp did die. Then things inside the ecosphere got a little strange. The water turned murky. The two remaining shrimp stopped moving. Light reflected against the glass instead of through it. I missed my tiny orange friend. I was worried about the other two. I moderated the temperature as best I could. I tried not to shake the egg. I didn't take the shrimp on any more road trips. A year or so after that, another shrimp died. Then the next. I shouldn't have been so sad—they lived seven times longer in that bubble of a planet than they were supposed to. But I thought they were amazing little guys so I grieved and looked to find another ecosphere but the only ones I could find were made of plastic instead of glass.

▪ ▪ ▪

Great Salt Lake grows and shrinks. In 1983, snow stacked itself deep in the Wasatch Mountains. Skiers skied until May. Then, the temperature spiked and all that snow seemed to melt at once. Streams that meandered through Liberty, Fairmont, Murray parks turned into raging rivers. The road that severed the town east from west turned waterway. Sandbags lined the street, Utahns lined the sandbags, watching the snowmelt slide westward toward the lake. Governor Bangerter enlisted industry to solve the problem flooding. Great pumps siphoned floodwaters from the lake and blew them into the salt flats just west of the lake. Or they would have if they'd turned them on. Evaporation and aquifer suck restored the lake to more reasonable boundaries. The pumps still await their destiny.

By 2003, twenty years after the Great Flood, astronauts studied Great Salt Lake from space. The halophilic bacteria in the north, saltier side of the cause reflected red, the shallow pools wave turquoise, umber, russet lengths into space. The outlines of the lake, though still visible from the Space Station, constrict. Since 1986, when the lake stretched to Bangerter's pumps at 4,212 feet, the lake has been in retreat. In the fall of 2002, the lake hit a twenty-year low, measuring 4,198 feet. Twenty years later, the lake is at its lowest level ever recorded, 4,188 feet. Those who measure the water level have become a different kind of astronaut—you can see them suited up in hazmat gear as they walk across toxic waste once buried by water to reach the edge of the lake to measure what it has lost.

■ ■ ■

Brine shrimp should be easy to grow. If something can survive in salinity three to five times greater than the ocean, if "hardiness" is the adjective always modifying the shrimp, if these shrimp can adapt to live in waters whose salinity spans 14 percent to 27 percent, then shouldn't you just be able to drop those brine shrimp eggs in a bucket full of salt and water and watch them hatch. Called Sea Monkeys in another marketing life, people used to order them by mail. Harold Von Brunhot visited a pet shop and thought that brine shrimp, on display awaiting their fate as fish food, could be a great way to teach kids about nature. He named them Sea Monkeys because brine shrimp tails whip behind them in the form of a question mark, similar to monkeys, hence the name. That night, eating leftovers with my visiting in-laws, I carefully spooned a teaspoon of cysts into distilled water. I dumped in some salt, turned on a pump for aeration, and set some glow lights above to warm the make-shift tank. Erik and I didn't sleep that night. The lights were bright. The pump was loud.

Erik elbowed me. "It sounds like someone is peeing." I told him the eggs needed air. It should only take twenty-four hours but when I looked the next day, nothing happened. I remembered, fertility is hard. I added some more salt.

I gave up on the brine shrimp eggs and dragged Max to PetSmart, its own kind of adaptation. We were going to get some already hatched shrimp. And some premixed salt water made by the same experts who make fish tanks for display and possibly helped organize Lake Bonneville when she receded to her Great Salt Lake stature. The Internet warned me. Hatching brine shrimp is not as easy as it looks. Even harder, possibly, than hatching chickens or squirrels or babies These puppies need all of your attention. Also a light that never goes out and a water heater. I asked the man at the PetSmart if he had any brine shrimp.

"Just ones in the refrigerator."

"They're already dead, right?"

"Yeah. They're dead." I looked in the fridge and they looked like the shrimp from my ecosphere. The ones that had died. I missed them. I would have revived them if I could have.

But I couldn't so instead I asked the guy for some salt water from his big red garbage bin of salt water. He filled up my mostly clean milk jug.

"Can you recommend a heater? The brine shrimp need it to be 72 degrees to hatch."

"How much water do you need to heat?"

I held up the milk jug he had just filled. "A gallon."

He handed me a tiny heater and I handed the cashier $17.99. I was now into this for something like $40 and several twenty-four-hour periods of disappointment. It was fine. I had been disappointed with the fertility of the universe before.

■ ■ ■

The winter of 2023 provided some relief for Great Salt Lake. With snowfall over 800 inches in the Wasatch Mountains, the lake rose three feet this spring but the lake level sits at 4,191.9 feet elevation. A better number would be 4,200 feet which would allow some give and take. The snowmelt of 2023 will help but it would take years of that amount of run-off to fill the lake.

As it stands, the north side of the lake is dead except for the few bacteria that turn the water pink. The legislature contributed a whopping $232,000 to mitigate the release of toxic dust. The brine shrimp are stuck in small pools.

Perhaps it's time to turn Governor Bangerter's pumps around! Attach those pumps to every hose bib and irrigation pump in Salt Lake and send the water to its original destiny. How much can humans do to fix the problems they've made? The poet Audre Lorde said about the patriarchy that "the master's tools will never dismantle the master's house." Human demands and innovations filled a lake with toxins then turned the convection oven onto high, evaporating the protective blanket. The brine shrimp have a cyst plan. What do we have besides rusting pipes?

■ ■ ■

Have all natural processes gone haywire? And if so, should we intervene, even when the results may be purely delightful? To get pregnant should have been a natural process, but after two years, it was time to call in industrial favors, rig pump to follicle, and see what science could produce. Spontaneous generation, spontaneous combustion, spontaneous sex—these things can happen inside the home but if you want to ensure success, sometimes you have to turn the systems inside out. Thanks to human innovation, the systems are on display as if through a window. Look closely at the anatomy. Put the shrimp under the microscope. Let's see what we can do here. Intrauterine insemination isn't a magical procedure. It takes the pure science of conception and adds one ounce centrifuge, some stirrups, and the muscle it takes to plunge a syringe.

The process wasn't the one I wanted or expected but the result was still enchanting: Next week, I'm driving from Flagstaff to Salt Lake with my kids, Max and Zoe. We're going out to the bird refuge, which is flooded, but the drought comes back quick in the West. For now, the grebes find food. Perhaps I can scoop a few brine shrimp into a jar to see if I can rebuild that once-perfect sphere.

Alchemy

Holly Simonsen

All earth is marked by water
                                        and I am no different
there is compound between (NaCl)   us
and element (Mg)
ignition
conflagration
and only one of us can douse the other

                                        The distillate is not gold
                                        or lead
                                        or an apple, ripe in the orchard

■ ■ ■

    Fossils still have beaks
    and feet and other cartilage, sometimes

Despite the dissolution of soft spots,
the crown of my head deepens around an ancient shore
The lake is a puddle
and I am evaporate

                        Someone else will burn a tree tonight

SALT

Alex Caldiero

*

SALT
the title alone
makes this a poem

*

body
never
found
is
eco-
logically
correct

*

the shelf life
of a sigh
in early summer air

*

a snake
across
my path
would mean
something

*

so much depends on nothing

*

stones sleep
with eyes
open

*

cant wait
to speak
with no punctuations

*

One day a
lie began
to believe itself

The rest is history

*

A glass
of water

You thirst

You drink

*

I
plagiarize
my own life

*

I write my pain
and words have no feeling
I write my pain
and words have no feeling

*

as you finger
your hand
as you handle
the pen
as you pen
your name
as you name
your poison
as you poison
your mind
as you mind
your thought
as you thought
you would

*

poem
breath

poem
breathe

poem
breathes
poem

A way way away

Charles Waugh

She wakes in the night, wind rushing over the skylights. Gusts like whipcracks, like they will tear the roof from the house, slice through the guttural howl.

She rises. Slips through the darkened bungalow. Triangles of white light the floor from the streetlamp outside.

Down the stairs, in the basement, at the furnace, she checks the filters. Gray, red, brown, but still some chalky white. Still some use in them. All year the blower pulls air from all over the house, through the filter, and pushes it back all over the house, cleaner. She'll need new ones soon, but they can wait.

She checks the bedroom. The children, ages five and seven, sleep. Little snores mean they are congested again, breathing through their mouths. Without waking them she gently rolls them to their sides and the sound of their breathing smooths into a susurring rise and fall.

She goes back to bed and lies awake. The glacial wind still grinds. She lists the things that must be done, the things she herself must do, the things she once did, the things she should have done, the things she will yet do, on endless variable repeat. The rasping wind turns to spatters of rain that sound first like fistfuls of gravel on the roof, the siding, the windows, and then grows to a steady crushing static to which she is finally found by sleep.

In the morning, she dresses the children, feeds them, washes their faces, oversees the brushing of teeth, hugs them, kisses them, and at the door arranges their outer layers, rain pants and jackets, rubber boots, filter masks, goggles, hoods cinched tight. They look like bug-eyed aliens now, sound like Darth Vader pulling air through his helmet.

The children dash from the house into the waiting yellow bus. It roars ahead half a block, stops, waits, three more children similarly enshelled dash from their homes and into the bus, the door flicking open and shut as if it has swallowed them. It roars ahead again, stops, waits, eats another dashing child. Roars ahead. The bus ride takes nearly two hours, but this has become the way it must be done.

She wears her own goggles, her own mask, her own protective outer layers. Outside, she assesses the results of the previous night's storm, sees it on every house on the street. The bungalow has been plastered with a layer of gray-brown mud. Already a professional crew with some kind of loud whirring steam cleaning machine has nearly finished the neighbor's home across the way.

She hoses the mud from the roof, the siding, the windows. She scoops fixer from one of the sixty-pound sacks stacked in the garage and shakes it out, a scoop at a time all around the house where the gray-brown mud now lies dark and soaking into the earth near the foundation.

She wonders whether the fixer fixes anything, whether the house is now as toxic as she feels. How much arsenic might be in the mud? How much is too much? How many times does it take before it soaks its way inside?

Later she showers to scrub at her skin as if she had not been wearing the hazmat suit. She knows the suit is impermeable, but it is difficult to reconcile logic with fear or fear with logic, whichever way it goes. Now that her husband is gone, if she succumbs, who will care for the children? A wave of nausea surges up through her, delivers her breakfast to the shower floor before she can even think of the toilet.

She knows the solution is simple. She must move away. This

is no way to live, here on the shores of a once great lake, now just another source of the toxic metal spew whose wind spun dust splatters her home every time it rains. But where will she go? Her home is here. No one will buy it. She does not have money to move away, to support herself without work to find another job, another house, another school, another life. She herself has become fixed, as bonded to the surface of this toxic, desiccating earth as the arsenic around the foundation. With her foot she sweeps the mess of undigested cereal to the drain, presses it through the little holes, lets the hot water rinse it away.

There must be a way, she thinks. But if it exists, she cannot see it.

Outside the wind picks up again, blows a low and rustling fugue over the pipe that vents steam from the shower.

A way, she thinks. A way way away.

Black Rock Vespers

Joel Long

They will never find us though the highway
Is near. They might see us amid a thousand
Gulls blending the glare of light on lake,
This late image we might think we see first
Through a pinhole in a shoe box so we won't
Go blind. And there we'd be scattered in spray
Against the back of the box, a particle
Amid the image projected, not so different
From particles gulls make or the range
Of mountains, Stansburys, and the island,
All turned blue now, shaped like water, built
By water that leaves ghosts in steps
That quiver late, the old shores fossils
Remember in gleam, but now, it is ours.
We are lost to everyone who wants to find us.
We come here to be lost and shaken by light
The color of tiger lilies next to the blue iris,
Waves on waves, sheen that opens the door.
We practice for departure, perfecting our part.

"A Noise Like Thunder": Great Basin Experiments in Scale and Time

Sarah Fox

I moved to Logan in the summer of 2004 to work on a master's degree in history at Utah State University, where I'd been granted an editorial fellowship at the Western Historical Quarterly. I was interested in Western stories of place, and the fraught entanglements of communities, environments, and federal power which have played out here since the advent of settler colonialism, but I had not yet settled on a topic for my research.

I found it in a jumble of half-unpacked boxes in my new apartment on a stifling August afternoon. Flipping through Terry Tempest Williams' Refuge: An Unnatural History of Family and Place, a book I hadn't read for several years, I noticed the map of Great Salt Lake and located my new home in Cache Valley on the top left. I re-read the dedication ("For Diane Dixon Tempest, who understood landscape as refuge") and the Mary Oliver poem "Wild Geese" that followed. While trying to make sense of my place and my work in the world after I graduated from The Evergreen State College, I'd copied out "Wild Geese" and adopted it as a sort of mantra for myself. Speaking directly to the reader, Oliver's poem invited us to share stories of our despair, reminding us that no matter our confusion, loss, loneliness, or heartbreak, we were in fact grounded in places, in deserts and rain and prairies and rivers, part of an ongoing world with a place in the "the family of things." Re-encountering the poem here, alongside a map of my new environs, felt like an invitation.

I sat down amid the boxes, reabsorbed in Tempest Williams' gifts as a storyteller of place. Chapters named for the birds who called the Bear River Migratory Refuge home throughout the year were subtitled with the steadily rising levels of Great Salt Lake from 1982–1983, plotting the reader's sense of place, time, and environmental change against a landscape (and vulnerability) shared by the human and nonhuman.

As the daylight drained from Cache Valley, I finished the epilogue, "Clan of One-Breasted Women" and sat quietly, reeling. When I'd read it years earlier, I had failed to absorb the revelation of the epilogue, the "unnatural history" in this story of place: the cancer stories the book documented were potentially linked to Cold War nuclear weapons testing upwind in Nevada, which had blanketed the region in radioactive fallout throughout Tempest Williams' childhood.

I'd heard references to "Utah downwinders" since moving to the area, but I had not yet realized what Utah was "downwind" of. As a Washingtonian, I associated "downwinders" with the farming and Indigenous communities exposed to radiation during WWII and the Cold War plutonium production at the Hanford site. I'd wondered how on earth Utah could be downwind of Hanford. The next day, I went to campus and checked out books on the nightmarish history of nuclear weapons testing in Nevada.

■ ■ ■

In November, Tempest Williams visited campus to read from her new book, The Open Space of Democracy. In the book-signing line, I introduced myself, tried awkwardly to explain to her what her work had meant to me, and shared that I was thinking of writing a master's thesis on the Utah downwinders. She encouraged me with warmth and care, then grabbed a flier from the table and wrote down a phone number for Salt Lake City journalist and downwinder activist Mary Dickson and told me to get in touch.

I stared at Mary's name and number for weeks, nervous about asking someone to dredge up their trauma for my research, uncertain of what good my inquiry into the topic might do anyone. I knew it would be difficult, if not impossible, to verify the connection between particular nuclear tests and particular diseases in the downwind areas, at least with my skills as a historian, but I was determined to learn more about what had happened here. Finally, I gathered my courage and called. Mary was gracious and warm on the phone, and willing to be interviewed.

She invited me to her home in Salt Lake, and told me about her childhood, how common cancer was for people in her family and neighborhood. She recounted how she survived thyroid cancer while co-editing a Utah newspaper as a twenty-something journalist in the 1980s, but never connected her illness to the radiation from the tests, even though she was writing about the southern Utah Downwinders for her work. Mary told me that when she met fellow journalist Carole Gallagher to learn more about the Gallagher's book project American Ground Zero: The Secret Nuclear War, Gallagher told her "you know, you got it from the testing." When Mary disagreed, pointing out she'd grown up in Salt Lake, Gallagher showed her researcher Richard Miller's map of areas of the United States crossed by two or more clouds from atmospheric nuclear tests in the 1950s, which shows so much fallout across the intermountain West it is almost impossible to make out the borders between the states: Northern Utah and Southern Utah are indistinguishable. After our interview, Mary insisted on feeding me dinner. As I drove home, I watched the silhouette of the Wasatch Range roll by, thinking about how the peaks had cradled the fallout clouds drifting in from Nevada, and how the rain that fell in the mountains and ran down the canyon rivers and into the irrigation systems brought the radioisotopes directly into Mary's childhood milk, produce, and the places her family lived, played, and worked.

I spent the next two years travelling around the Great Basin region listening to the stories of other Downwinder activists, walking cemeteries to pay my respects to their loved ones, and poring through archives and microfilm reels and legal records. I learned more than I ever wanted to know about the Atomic Energy Commission's wanton disregard for human health and environmental integrity during the period of atmospheric nuclear testing in Nevada, and I was haunted by stories of birth defects and cancer clusters in the downwind region.

▪ ▪ ▪

As a born and raised Pacific Northwesterner, my Utah sojourn in the early 2000s was defined by a tangle of topophilia and topophobia. I was entranced by the canyons, rivers, and peaks of the Wasatch and Uintas, dazzled by redrock country, comforted by the wetlands of Cache Valley, and seduced by the expansiveness of the Great Basin sky, but I also laid awake at night in the grip of a new kind of dread.

Initially, I ascribed this dread to a problem of cultural geography: I had moved too far from the incoming and outgoing tides of the Salish Sea and Pacific Ocean, which had defined "west" for me since I was small. I shied away from Great Salt Lake and the landscape of salt flats which surrounded it, telling myself it was because I was unnerved by saltwater that was not governed by tides. If pressed, though, I couldn't explain my antipathy: it took me a year to bring myself to the lake's edges. What I found there is still with me, decades later, and is inextricable from other learning I was doing at the time.

Six months after moving to Utah, I sent a song called "Landlocked Blues" to a friend back home, and she shared it with someone she knew; her friend wrote back to me directly to say he liked the song, and promised to visit the Salish Sea for me and toss in a rock. We started to write letters, and soon we were taking turns driving the eight hundred odd miles on weekends to visit each other. In the fall of 2005, during one of Ryan's visits to Logan, I handed him my copy of Refuge, suggesting he might find it interesting to read while I was working on campus that day. When I returned to the apartment a few hours later, Ryan announced we were going on a pilgrimage: he wanted to visit two of the sites she'd described in the book, the Bear River Migratory Bird Refuge, and Nancy Holt's Sun Tunnels in the Great Basin Desert north of Great Salt Lake.

■ ■ ■

It was a short drive from Logan to the refuge entrance outside of Brigham City, and there was still ample daylight to read the site's pamphlet as we made our way along the twelve-mile loop through the part of the refuge described as "Unit 2." The pamphlet explained that the marshland area at the Bear River delta had once spanned some forty-five thousand acres, providing a massive oasis for migratory birds. I thought about the teeming plant and animal life of the river deltas in the Pacific Northwest I'd grown up alongside, and reasoned the Bear River delta must have been a place of tremendous significance for local Indigenous peoples, but the pamphlet made no reference to the Shoshone, Paiute, Bannock, or Ute peoples. It did provide the impression of "Explorer John C. Frémont," who in 1843 described how the sheer number of birds "made a noise like thunder."

The next paragraph explained how, predictably, "as settlers moved into the area, ambitious projects were undertaken to divert great quantities of river water for use by upstream settlements and farms" and the marsh habitat began to shrink. By

1920 only a few thousand acres remained, and outbreaks of Avian botulism during this period killed birds by the "hundreds of thousands." In response to these changes, and alarm from the public and game conservation organizations, the river delta was designated a National Wildlife Refuge in 1928. Fifty-five years later, Great Salt Lake began to rise.

The pamphlet described the damage to marsh vegetation and bird habitats wrought by the incursion of salt laden floodwater during this period. We read about the optimistic "plan of action" instituted after the floodwaters receded to restore the marshland habitat. "To date," the pamphlet affirmed, "close to one million cubic yards of earth has been moved to restore and enhance the Refuge. Forty-seven primary water control structures have been restored along with forty-seven miles of dikes."

Late-day birdsong was all around us, and the sun glinted off the waters amid the grasses and reeds. I felt a flush of gratitude for the care which had been employed to preserve and restore the refuge after the flooding, marred by a ripple of irritation about the casual way the pamphlet glossed over the earlier near-destruction of the marshland by early settler engineering.

▪ ▪ ▪

Darkness seeped in around us as we left the refuge. We passed signs for Promontory Point, the historic meeting place of the transcontinental railroads. I remembered visiting the site with my family on a cross-country road trip: the replica nineteenth century locomotives, nosed together so intimately on the track; the interpretive placards about victorious tycoons and sturdy workers, and Chinese laborers made to work the most dangerous jobs. The landscape around the site had struck me then mostly for how monochromatic it seemed. Driving past the signs in the fading light, I thought about how exponentially that feat of transcontinental infrastructure had increased resource extraction, Indigenous dispossession, settler colonialism, and ecological change.

We left the pavement as night settled thickly upon the landscape, headed west on dirt roads around the northern edge of Great Salt Lake in search of Holt's Sun Tunnels. This was before smart phone maps or affordable GPS navigation devices, and soon we were profoundly disoriented. Jackrabbits sprang out in front of the car with regularity, and while we could see lights occasionally in the distance, we never seemed to arrive at their source. We laughed grimly, remembering that we were passing south and west of the property of military industrial contractor Thiokol: the lights began to feel conspiratorial, like markers for stories I wasn't supposed to know.

I learned later that Thiokol acquired the land north of Great Salt Lake in 1956 to build large solid-fuel rocket motors for Minuteman missiles, part of an intercontinental ballistic missile program started in 1955. Like many Cold War era defense contractors, Thiokol hadn't gone dark with the purported end of the Cold War. While I was busy falling in love and trying to write a master's thesis in history, Thiokol was producing equipment for the so-called War on Terror. For years, they'd been burning toxic waste in the open air of their property, sickening so many local cattle that they were compelled to pay an eight-million-dollar settlement in 2001. A few years later, Thiokol became known as known as Orbital ATK, a subsidiary of aerospace/defense company Northrup Grumman. Today, it produces items like "illuminating flares," "small warheads" and "infrared countermeasures."

One cluster of lights remained steady, and we hoped it was a town. We discussed plans to proceed directly to a diner for coffee and pancakes and reorientation. When we bumped out of the darkness and onto street lit pavement, we found the shimmering town was only a gas station in Snowville with no hot coffee or pancakes to be had. We fueled up, stared at the map, and headed back off the pavement and into the darkness.

We passed back into the confusing tangle of unmarked roads until, at long last, we spotted a small cluster of vehicles and campers. It looked like a trailhead parking lot, and we pulled up and threw down our sleeping pads and bags with relief. Eager to see the tunnels we had wandered so far in search of, we set out across the playa with our headlamps, puzzled when the tunnels did not materialize in front of us. Despite my confusion and weariness, I was fascinated by the form of the earth materializing in my headlight beam, a landscape we had driven through for hours without really apprehending in any embodied way. The cracked surface, so clearly shaped by water, was unlike anything I was familiar with in the Pacific Northwest: desiccated and sparkling, fossilized and ancient.

We returned to our sleeping bags and fell asleep under the stars. I noticed the glow of sunrise on my eyelids at the same time that I heard the yelling and rolled over to discover a naked man with a rifle was running toward us, screaming that we were trespassing. We evacuated our campsite with urgency, noticing as we did that in the light of day, it bore a much stronger resemblance to a meth lab than an art installation trailhead parking lot. He ran after us as we drove off, hoisting the rifle overhead as our tires spun playa dust into the morning light. Watching his naked figure recede in the rearview, I was reminded that there are many different ways of being in a place.

■ ■ ■

When we finally found the Sun Tunnels later that morning, I wondered uncharitably if it had been worth all the trouble to get here. Aside from the careful angles at which they were set to each other, the tunnels were indistinguishable from large concrete culverts I'd seen waiting to be installed in salmon streams back home in the Northwest. We stood inside them, stared through them, and took in the play of light and shadow they created in the open landscape. Holes in the tunnels admit light in the shape of four constellations: Capricorn and Columba, Perseus and Draco.

Holt built the installation in 1976, intending, she said, "to bring the vast space of the desert back to human scale." In this, she succeeded, certainly. After our disorienting misadventure through the dark landscape, we now had a reference point of some solidity, a decidedly human-scale landmark from which to contemplate ageless practices of mapping stories onto the stars.

Standing with the tunnels behind us, we oriented ourselves to the southwest. We were only a short distance from the Nevada border, perhaps three hundred miles northeast of the test site, where from 1951 to 1962 approximately one-hundred nuclear weapons had been dropped out of airplanes, shot out of cannons, detonated atop towers and attached to weather balloons. The force of the explosions sucked up the materials of the desert floor, materials I imagined were not so different from the dried lakebed beneath my feet. As those now-irradiated materials ascended in the iconic mushroom cloud shape, thousands of feet above the desert floor, prevailing winds carried them east, most of the time. The trajectory of these fallout clouds could never be certain, but, fully cognizant of the potential of human health harms from radiation exposure, the Atomic Energy Commission dictated tests only take place when the wind was blowing east, away from densely populated California, and over the Great Basin and Great Salt Lake, and across the more sparsely populated Indigenous, rural, and agricultural communities of the Intermountain West and Southwest.

The Wasatch mountains behind us to the east had funneled the fallout materials into the watersheds and neighborhoods where Mary Dickson and so many others lived. I hadn't spoken yet to the Western Shoshone downwinders who lived immediately downwind of the NTS, or the Navajo and Puebloan downwinders who lived further south, amid the interconnected, also-radiological disaster of the Cold War uranium industry, but I was beginning to glimpse the scale of the disaster unleashed in this part of the world in the name of national security, imperial might, capitalist growth, and scientific knowledge production, writ large. In the face of this kind of history, the silent vigil of Holt's Sun Tunnels felt more poignant: a refusal to disavow this landscape as so many others have.

■ ■ ■

We made our way east, around the northern periphery of Great Salt Lake. We clattered along the unpaved Central Pacific Railroad grade for hours, dodging potholes, and occasionally passing small, sunbaked cemeteries, the only remnants of small railroad towns like Matlin and Kelton. Hours into our trek across the basin, we spotted a large, white animal moving across the salt flats to the south of the car. It was a dog, miles from any source of fresh water or food we could see. We got out and spoke quietly to it, tried to tempt it with food and water, and waited for a time to see if it would come closer. It contemplated us from fifteen or twenty yards, and then turned and strode slowly to the south, toward the lake. We watched it go, wondering aloud if someone had dumped it out here, or if it did in fact, live nearby.

Within ten miles of pavement, we blew a tire. As Ryan set about changing it, I shaded my eyes from the midday sun and walked across the playa, thinking about ghost dogs and ghost towns and ghost toxins. The sunlight glinted off the salt flats, and I could not distinguish between water and land: my sense of Great Salt Lake and my sense of historical time both bent in the firmament. We drove back to Logan on the spare tire.

Six months later I finished my master's thesis. Four years later Ryan and I got married. Five years later we had a son, and four years after that, my research on ordinary peoples' experiences of radiation harm in the region was published as my first book, *Downwind.*

Today, communities along the Wasatch Front are threatened by a new toxic dust problem blowing in from the west, tied to a new fluctuation in Great Salt Lake that once again threatens the millions of migratory birds who rely on its ecosystem. The rivers and streams which descend from the Wasatch and sustain the lake's levels have been diverted for irrigation and other human uses. By January of 2023, the lake had lost over 70 percent of its water and 60 percent of its surface area. As the lakebed dries, dust bearing heavy metals like arsenic, lithium, magnesium, mercury, and lead will be swept up by the wind and swirled into the air people breathe along the Wasatch Front, a problem which will only worsen as the lake continues to shrink. Brigham Young University ecologist Benjamin Abbott has suggested the disappearance of the lake could lead to "thousands of excess deaths annually from the increase in air pollution and the collapse of the largest wetland oasis in the intermountain west[.]"

Residents of the Wasatch Front are not the first to confront the public health implications of a drying salt lake. Since the early 1960s, the saline Aral Sea in Central Asia has been steadily disappearing, drained by irrigation diversions undertaken largely for cotton cultivation. As the lakebed of the Aral Sea has been exposed, it has created what researchers describe as "a desert which acts as an active particle emission area. Particles can be dust, salt, or pollutants like heavy metals and pesticides." While a plethora of variabilities make it difficult to prove a direct causal connection between the Aral Sea's disappearance and a regional spike in "infant and maternal mortality, and debilitating respiratory and intestinal ailments," numerous studies have indicated such problems are likely linked to inhalation of particles from the lakebed floor. "[C]ardiovascular issues, cancer, and DNA changes in the body that may lead to disabilities" have also been identified when saline lakes disappear.

The disappearance of Great Salt Lake is the product of less than two centuries-worth of settlement along the Wasatch Front, a tiny blip in the deep history of Indigenous land tenure in the region, which dates back more than ten thousand years. State leaders have engaged in a flurry of legislative measures to halt Great Salt Lake's disappearance, setting aside forty million dollars for the Great Salt Lake Trust to purchase water rights that might help raise the lake's level. The trust's advisory board includes members representing "adjacent landowners, agriculture, bird conservationists, aquaculture, mineral extraction, water districts, and wastewater facilities[,]" but other local stakeholders are conspicuously absent. Primary among these are Indigenous peoples. Darren Parry, a former chair of the Northwestern Band of the Shoshone Nation writes "[w]e have never been given a seat at the table, yet we manage the resource for thousands of years…, subsequently affirming that, to assume scientific knowledge is superior to Indigenous wisdom, that kind of thought process can be harmful." The absence of the region's Tribes from decision-making about Great Salt Lake's future is as glaring as their absence in the Bear Lake Refuge pamphlet I pored over so many years ago: both omissions are in keeping with a dominant settler society attitude that falsely assumes Indigenous people—and their ways of knowing this place—are a relic of the past. Grappling with the result of the settler experiment on the edges of Great Salt Lake will require all the wisdom that can be brought to bear. In the post-WWII orgy of nuclear weapons production here, Indigenous communities and white settler communities were both consigned to be collateral damage in the pursuit of national security and global nuclear hegemony. Today, both are once again vulnerable to another environmental justice crisis: the toxic dust of the disappearing Great Salt Lake.

Our places of refuge are also the places that teach us about loss, entanglement, and love. They show us the gaps in our own knowledge about place, power, and the past, and the places where we must make kinship and common cause if we are to head off worse disasters. My time living in the Great Basin taught me volumes about the power of grief and love to fuel social movements, and the capacity of ordinary people to make sense of what is happening around them, and in their own bodies. These, in the end, are the scales with which we are most equipped to make sense of the world, to choose a future where the sound like thunder is not bombs, but thousands of birds, reminding us of our place "in the family of things."

Driving Across the Salt Flats While Listening to Homer's Odyssey

Justin Evans

A full Utah moon—
yellow, fattened,
rises behind me
in the last moments of day,
before dusk is erased.

Slowly, it sheds its onion skin
becomes a worn silver dollar
as it slides parallel, hovers
over this ancient basin,
silver light reflecting salt,
salt reflecting back.

Beneath the black, sagebrush
rooted in the alkaline flats
sways like sea anemone
waiting for the tides.

Millennia have passed since water
graced this small pocket of earth,
but at night a person can become lost
within the depths of this wine-dark sea,
only headlights and the constant mirror
of the moon to show the way.

That Which Passes Through

Andy Hoffmann

The curves of stone protruding from the lake's surface make for stopovers, points of pause for migrating birds and homesick poets, the story of exiled wanderers, nomadic song infused with the spirit of abandoned horses. In the landscape: rusted bloom wilts at island's edge; railroad causeway divides the lake, one side pink, both sides frail; vanished languages in wind and drift of playa; debris of the Bear River Massacre coagulated in salt. Scents and visions flicker: of nomads like Neal Cassady who, born in downtown winter 1926 Salt Lake City, set out as a blaze along the sides of dry drainages across America, anointed subversive hero in novels and poems; of Thomas Wolfe, during his 1938 car tour, passing by Great Salt Lake and making notes, fascinated by the orchards ("the irriguous ripe of the sudden green"), and repelled by Salt Lake City emanating "the old feeling of Mormon coldness, desolation—the cruel, the fanatic, the warped and the dead."

Indeed, while unaware of Mormon tussle with charity and greed, Wolfe was not wrong to introduce death, for his was but a few months away. And perhaps he intuited something of ancient hunters, how they were evangelized and disappeared in the storm of soulless doctrines and manifestoes. Perhaps he sensed something of the future when fruit farmers would trade fertile ground for vast stretches of pavement. What he couldn't have guessed is the survival of ancient gatherers, those still spotted in shadows and haunting the lip of mirages in woven black shawls, how they become shapeless in the heat of tainted sand, leaving in their path rock pits filled with twigs and roots that, when steeped, make good medicine to dispel sorrow and despair. When following the trails of gatherers along the lake's edge, it's not unusual to meet thin vapors smelling of cigar.

The water we call the lake is in constant flux, has disappeared in the past and will disappear again. We might say the water, like Thomas Wolfe, like you, like me, like elk and birds, is passing through. Facing east from the crust at the edge of water, it's easy enough to locate traces cut into the hillside of Lake Bonneville, formed 30,000 years ago and spanning twenty thousand square miles at its peak, a body of which Great Salt Lake is a remnant. Above the top bench run hills and ridges. The hike up Dry Creek is one of many trails to get there, passing a gated community to gain the trailhead. The gated community with gatekeepers aplenty, is a museum to the sedentary, the sovereign, and the separate. A story older and more harsh than the ancient Mesopotamian walls of Uruk. Southeast of the gate the trail appears between clumps of oak and leads up a sunlit drainage, a good place to sit with clusters of white sage. From there it doesn't take long to make the ridge where one can imagine the reclusive poet Cold Mountain overlooking the city, writing as he did on rock, "Where the dust blows through these heights, / There once shone a silent sea."

Great Salt Lake is a mercurial plateau within a multiplicity of interconnected layers. The lakebed is a condition, a conditioning, a breathing constellation of scale. Buddhists might see the lake as a sutra, a cryptic scripture bending the corners of being and becoming and the karma that cuts between. Like a diamond, the lake, a shamanic flower of dust.

Dark enigma, this lake, these mountains, the effervescent moon of ch'i. Vast, the world of sight. South—the city, the suburbs. West—the lake, the mine. North—cold wind, the hummingbird, the fire lookout on Desolation Peak. East—the condor, the hurricane, the wheat. Shifting topographies, all.

Tracing currents of bone and feathers, three white pelicans cross through clouds as a fading song, off for the day to feed far from nests on the lake's Gunnison Island. Fox and coyote navigate what is now a land bridge to the island formed by the receding water to feed on pelican eggs. Which is to say, white pelicans, momentarily speeding on thermal updraft, having passed through and stayed a while, are now on their way to the other shore.

The freeway connecting Denver and San Francisco runs beside the lake's southern edge. In 1975, after falling to a historic low in 1963, the lake was on the rise and white pelicans were safe from coyotes just as Anne Waldman, author of the chant poem "Fast Speaking Woman" from a book of the same title, made her way from Colorado through the ribcage of these lands to City Lights Books, across from Vesuvio Café, North Beach, California. While nearly fifty years have passed since publication of City Lights Pocket Series No. 33, the poem lingers in mycelium covered by soil shaded by shrub.

As a blooming poet and dakini, Waldman disrupted binaries, gave birth to the liminality of tundra, "seeds of future poetic fire" that continue to root within those who snake words from volcanoes and charnel grounds. "I'm the angel woman," she sings,

I'm the white-devil woman
I'm the green-skin woman
I'm the green-goddess woman
I'm the woman with arms
I'm the woman with wings
I'm the woman with sprouts
I'm the woman with leaves
I'm the branched woman
I'm the masked woman
I'm the deep-trance woman

Etcetera. And so she rolls line after line in arterial transfixion. A shapeshifter "attracted to shamanic energies of all kinds," Waldman's movement from cosmic angel/goddess/devil to arms and wings and branches of earth evokes the magic of shadow falling across the ridge and onto the lake, a phantom upon the water and distant islands. So it is "woman" in constant transformation that mirrors a nomadic landscape where twilight clouds carrying lakebed dust burst over the plains, burying warehouses and freeways in the rhythm of geologic time.

Waldman's summoning of trance in the unifying of heaven and earth is but one outcome of the chant, and one of many acknowledgements of her debt to Oaxacan healer María Sabina, whose 1956 recording of sacred song-poems Waldman came upon and was inspired by. When cleansing the spirits of the diseased in ceremony, Sabina was known to transmit messages of "little saints" through the veil of Christian icons. Sabina's language is not her own, but instead comes through her by way of the medicine, the sacred mushrooms, Psilocybe caerulescens, that grew in fields near her village, those gendered and "torn up out of the ground" for ceremony. Waldman honored Sabina's path as healer and speaks to consuming mushrooms and peyote herself to gain a closer relationship to enchanted language. Even so, just as the lake bed is stained with arsenic, so too is the transfer of Sabina's magic language from Mazatec to Spanish to English corrupted with colonial ambition and appropriation. Waldman, "passionately in love with the magics of the phenomenal world," understands the terrors of transmission and the suffering it caused Sabina, just as she realizes that such poetries contain the power to liberate consciousness, thus her responsibility to share: "I learn by books," Waldman fast speaks, "I learn by singing / I recite the chant of one hundred syllables / I write down my messages to the world / The wind carries them invisibly, / staccato impulses to the world. . ."

As those working with poetries born of wind, Sabina and Waldman might ask us to follow the trail to cliff edge, from ridge to river to lake, drawn by lunar utterances into the fertility of cracks. It is there, surrendering to valleys of rift, we rise into the aberrant truth of ourselves, the truth of deforestation and the anxiety of trees, the truth of subaquatic spirits and evaporation, the truth of identities as fragile as the pathologies from which they are born. Poetry is the shadow realm of the wild, irrevocably unsettled in its beautiful and grim behaviors.

And as poetry is an energetic field to be discovered and experienced but never owned, so too is the lake a terrain of transformation that is as much the sage fields of the Great Basin as it is salt water and brine, as much mountains and clouds and snowfields as it is birdhouse and wetlands, as much the storms breaking over valleys of the Sierra Mazateca as it is tributaries of the Wasatch and Uintas. Everything in flux and impermanent and entangled. Including the poetry and poets who passed through.

Many have passed through. Thousands. Millions even, and millions more. Some stayed a while, others passed like cloud and storm. Some stopped to meditate at the lake. Many did not. Anselm Hollo passed through and stayed a moment. Allen Ginsberg. Joy Harjo. Pablo Neruda. Bruce Weigl. Amiri Baraka passed through. Gary Snyder. Emerson, Rimbaud, Whitman, Lorenzo Thomas, Jayne Cortez. Alice Notley passed through—"I've got your keys so you can go home now and translate your poetry / into language of angels in bark clothes or darkest maroon at dusk." Diane Di Prima passed through. Jack Kerouac. Robert Smithson and Nancy Holt passed through, leaving tracks. Gertrude Stein: "I liked going over the Salt Lake region the best, it was like going over the bottom of the ocean without any water in it. . ."

Yielding to ridge and ravine, vortex and parabola, I head to Black Rock by the lake, drop over a low shelf and walk a path through salt to the water, sinking. To circumnavigate the lake will take the rest of my life, perhaps longer. Here, at dusk, I am a dark dance of freeways and formulisms, embrace science as a means to name and measure, just as I roll with Keats' tenuous threads of uncertainty and chance. It's easy to be seduced, laid upon, impregnated by that which unfolds in the heat of language, a continuum of consciousness that compels me to seek what I can touch and smell, like greasewood adapted to alkaline flats, or the crusted boulders holding the shape of the *Spiral Jetty.* Tongue upon branch and leaf, the message from bush is to be expected: you must change your life. For now, I meditate on ashen blue shimmer and expanse, a view of Antelope and Stansbury islands through industrial haze.

Yes, and what then?

Bear witness to traffic sprawl, rivers dammed and diverted, lake level dropping in swoons. Move close to the disappearance of birds that leave with and without warning. Prepare to say adieu, adieu to poets and poetry that arrive in each one of us, depart when we do, as we must. Jack Kerouac, poet and storyteller, inspired by Wolfe's heraldic self-study and Cassady's blistering burnout, after two months solo in the Cascades as a fire lookout and ready to leave his cabin on the peak, writes in Book One of Desolation Angels:

> *Fairwell, Desolation, thou hast seen me well—May angels of the unborn and angels of the dead hover over thee like a cloud and sprinkle offerings of the golden eternal flowers—That which passes through everything has passed through me and always through my pencil and there is nothing to say—*

Kerouac passed through as humans do in human ways. In his case, an abundance of grudge and alcohol led to a lonely death. The fall of a famous writer looping in resentment is predictable. It's when thinking that mountains and lakes also appear to falter that I must remind myself that not all things speak with a human tongue. Meeting Kerouac at the crossroads and bidding him farewell, now cradled by the long reach of water, I hold space for separation and loss as my pulse spirals toward a beckoning stillness. In this slender drift, freeway noise disappears. I am so very dry and tired, the sky darkens, I breathe sand, salt, muck, the planet's rotting fish.. And birds rising from the marsh? Ten birds, thirty, five hundred? Coyotes, foxes, snakes to follow? In expanse of twilight, eyes half open, gatherers of roots and herbs arrive and blow smoke upon my head, scratch faint hieroglyphs in the bark of the tree growing from my chest. Exquisite clouds, this migratory flood of wings. Arms spread wide in a cosmology of verbs, white pelicans enter my mouth and nest in my throat, just as brine flies hatch in the shallows of my heart. For a moment, and only for a moment, the lake swells in a ghostly chorus that empties into the breath of all things, seeping into rock and sand and sky. Haunted as I am, as the lake must be, hummingbird hovers in the echo of water before flitting toward the reflection of a sun setting in the body of an earth that dreams in voices that fill our lungs and flow through the veins of plants.

Report from Antelope Island

Joel Long

After Carolyn Forché

The island docent told me last year's owls were dead,
the babies killed by coyotes or racoons late spring.

The owls came back anyway. The owlet survived,
screeching from a June poplar, looking at me coyly

from beneath a wing, fuzzy with newness,
but her eyes were amber in which the beginning

of the world was stilled, the color after the fire
cooled, yoke yellow, pupil, black center of things.

The springs dried up in the high hills, so men
in helicopters haul water to the peaks for wild sheep

to drink; they won't come down where we are,
won't come down to pools of dust where bison bathe.

It is an island you can walk to, a dry thing, fox
dead by the roadside, the gums framing teeth in ash.

One boat rest on ground in the marina, twenty docks empty.
I step into the cracked earth, once, twice, sink in mud

warm on my shin, the stink of it, the salt, brine shrimp,
decay. It is an island you can walk to, lake holding breath.

If I can look directly at the sun and not go blind, the island
suffers. Beauty mute, a lake sliver punctures the bubble sun.

A pronghorn runs through moth mullein to get away
from me. Don't fear me, I say. It fears me. I know why.

Still-Life with Birds

Rob Carney

Everyone paying attention knows the West is in serious trouble. Australia too. A whole planetary roll call of places: wildfires, record heat waves, fill-in-the-blank drought—*mega*, *decades-long*, *state-of-emergency*, *extreme*; any of those adjectives will do. And the heat? A hundred million mussels baked right there and reeking in the tide pools.

And inland isn't any better. No, each river, each body of water, is setting new records for lowness every year. I'm not an ornithologist, but I still know how to ask: If moored boats are practically dry-docked in their slips, then what does that mean for all the migratory birds depending on the wetlands? Picture it like this: You're trying to drive cross-country—say, from Phoenix to Billings to Seattle to Alaska—then back home, only you can't, not really, because these geese have bulldozed every rest stop, and some egrets have blown up all the gas stations, and even the monarch butterflies are getting in on the action, raining down poison on the off-ramp restaurants then setting the next-to-last grocery store on fire. So anyway, trouble.

Last summer up at the reservoir, there was a heron on the dock; its shape, all its movements: calligraphy. Two pelicans, a seagull, even cranes, or at least I think so; they were too far away from the boat to be sure, just a dozen white blurs along the shoreline.

My son Quentin said, "I guess I missed the cranes; I wish I'd seen them."

"Next time," I said. "There'll be other days."

I hope that's true.

The Great Sassy, Salty Lake

Eli McCann

Over the years, friends who didn't grow up in the Salt Lake Valley like I did have asked me about Great Salt Lake—about recreation, about my memories playing along its shoreline. "Yeah," I've tried to explain. "The thing is, most people don't make it out to the lake all that often."

"Oh? Is it far away? Hard to reach? Restricted in some way?"

"No," I clarify. "It's none of those things. We just, I don't know, we don't really visit it."

"*Never*?" they ask, surprised the way one might be to discover a Parisian hadn't bothered yet to lay eyes on the Eiffel Tower.

Suddenly a memory flashes through my mind. "There was this one time. . ." I'll begin to say. My voice will trail off. The image becomes wavy.

By age fourteen, I had never set foot on an island. So, when my Boy Scout leaders announced we'd be camping on one, I felt like I had just won an exotic tropical vacation to a place with swaying palm trees and ukulele music.

We were told it was called "Antelope Island."

Sure, it didn't sound like "Aruba" or "Oahu" or any other word that conjures to the mind white sand beaches in front of never-ending blue waters the temperature of a comfortable bath illuminated by a setting sun silhouetting breaching mammals with mystical powers. But it was allegedly an island, and our imaginations allowed us to see whatever we wanted.

Yes, this was an actual, real island. One that belonged to us and our neighboring Great Salt Lake. Even better, this was an island accessible to two large vans packed with hormonal adolescents that smelled worse than the lake itself. Not by boat, but by car, somehow. Did this technically mean it wasn't really an island? We didn't ask that. No reason to risk spoiling the allure. We packed a trailer full of cheap mountain bikes, many borrowed from families around the neighborhood who had extra and crammed ourselves and our hand-me-down camping gear into a couple of rickety vehicles pointed northward. I'm sure I had seen the lake before this, but I couldn't recall a time doing so up close. An hour or so after leaving home we departed the freeways of our budding civilization and made the quick journey across a causeway and toward the large brown mound of land dotted with bison and midges.

We ventured through the island's dirt roads slowly, staring out at the vast lake, brimming up to the edges of the shoreline, reaping the ongoing benefits of a good snow run-off from mountains we could see on the other side of the water. We arrived at Bridger Bay just in time to set up a small camp on the rugged beach and undercook dinner. The salty winds began to blow toward us as the setting sun across the bay assisted the chaotic sands in blinding us, prompting our dutiful scouting troop to retreat under the protection of our cheap nylon homes. It wasn't more than an hour before my best friend Sam and I found ourselves holding the ceiling of the tent off our faces—our arms extended upward in a push-up position, fighting the wind that had easily collapsed our shelter in a way I still find humbling. After the battle with the elements raged for an hour or two, we slinked through the tent and searched for a zipper in an attempt to peek out to investigate and locate our best neighbors for refuge. Instead of sturdy standing dwellings, we found, stretched across the beach, a dozen flattened bags half suffocating our fellow troopmates whose arms, it was clear, were similarly being used as last-ditch emergency tent poles.

I don't think any of us slept that night, an inconvenience normally weathered alright by fourteen-year-olds. Our adult chaperones wore the experience on their faces and in their shoulders, physical manifestations lost on us and drowned away through our excited chatter about our island adventure we couldn't wait to share as a war story, surely to be exaggerated over the years.

That afternoon we mounted our mountain bikes with tires inflated to varying degrees by the one leaking pump someone had been half wise enough to pack. We fought the winds, the midges, the sand. We meandered across narrow rocky trails, occasionally treacherous enough to turn the ride into a hike, our bikes packed onto our backs and leaving black grease stains that would never wash away from our shirts. One of our troop leaders, Wayne, a childless man who no doubt wondered what sins he had committed to deserve any of this, carried bikes by the twos for those of us who eventually grew too fatigued and dehydrated to manage on our own, this, thanks to a combination of poor planning and the absence of grit.

I think our camping trip was supposed to last two nights, a fact our surprised parents surely tried to confirm late that evening when we boys were dumped onto our front porches by exhausted neighborhood dads who no doubt allowed the smells of our unshowered bodies to answer whatever questions anyone had about why they had pulled the cord on the whole thing.

For years we'd tell anyone who would listen about the time we survived the lake—that Great Salt Lake just down the street that we don't seem to visit as often as a Parisian might a tower.

"Oh, it couldn't be that bad," my friend Daniel told me fifteen or so years after that camping trip when I regaled him with my miserable tale. He had just suggested we go to the lake for a swim. We had recently signed up for a distance triathlon. It was a spur of the moment sort of thing—done out of peer pressure. Neither of us had ever done a race like this before and neither of us had ever really done much lake swimming. Our race would require us to swim in an icy reservoir and the internet cautioned us that traipsing through a large body of water in a thick wetsuit couldn't be accurately simulated in a temperature-controlled pool with lines painted on a clean illuminated floor. No, we'd have to find some body of water nearby for a number of training swims. Daniel had suggested we give the giant lake not ten miles from town a try.

I told him this seemed like a bad idea to me, and I recounted my scouting story again in case he missed it the first time. The wind. The salt. The midges.

"I'm not suggesting we go camping on the island," Daniel told me. "Let's just head out there and try an open water swim."

I ran out of excuses around the same time I started to wonder if I had exaggerated the harshness of the elements in my mind. Besides, even if I hadn't exaggerated those things, it was possible that adolescent experience on the lake was an anomaly, more uncommon than breaching whales and white sand beaches.

We heaved our newly purchased wetsuits, fresh out of the plastic bags in which they had arrived, into the back of Daniel's vehicle. And then we set sail down I-80 toward Saltair, the once-abandoned concert venue near the southern shoreline—a ghost, a reminder of a time when proximity to the lake and the recreational opportunities it possessed wasn't wasted on the residents of our community, a time when a pilgrimage to the lake was a cherished rite of passage. We figured if Saltair was a good enough place for our teenage grandmothers to dip their toes in the lake, it must be good enough for two novice swimmers looking for a place to take a dip. Minutes later we parked in an empty lot down the road from the concert venue, just next to a small campground. It was early spring and a cold rainstorm from that morning had doused the shoreline and cooled the air to but a whisper above foggy breath. We pulled on our tight wetsuits and set off on a barefooted journey to the water's edge where we anticipated a slapdash plunge and athletic swim.

The terrain between our car and the lake had moon-like qualities, disabling our depth perception and ability to decipher how far we'd need to walk. We stepped over sharp rocks and carcasses we couldn't identify. We swatted away a critical mass of midges that had taken an interest in us. Finally, our feet touched water, cold, but that's what the wetsuits were for. Displaying a level of optimism that is funny to me now, we immediately pulled on our goggles and took a few cautious steps anticipating a steep drop of the lake floor and water depth that might be swimmable. Our footsteps grew less cautious and slow as we proceeded, minute after minute, to trudge through the icy water that never seemed to extend above our ankles.

Our swim turned into a hike the same way my Antelope Island bike ride had done until, after twenty or so more minutes, the water finally reached our knees and we decided it was time to try to swim it.

As we placed our faces in the water, our noses were filled with what we ignorantly assumed must have been sulfur. The intense salty taste reached the backs of our throats after forcibly clearing our sinuses and we pulled our heads out of the lake and expelled the water the way a geyser might shoot out steam.

"I had no idea it would be this salty," I yelled.

"Did you think the lake got its name by being sassy?" Daniel responded.

We'd have to try a new technique for our swim, one which kept our heads out of the water entirely. And so we swam, if it could be called that, our hands scooping mud from the lakebed, our faces pointed up toward the sky in an attempt to escape any splashing. The vastness of the lake and the emptiness of the surrounding terrain made it impossible for us to confirm whether we were actually going anywhere. After ten or so minutes of undisciplined thrashing, we forfeited to the lake and stood up to begin our long journey back to our car. We trudged again through the water, which leveled up just above our knees, and then receded to our shins, and then to our ankles. By the time we reached the comparatively dry land, our feet were numb enough to no longer feel the pokes of the vast shoreline's rocks. When we arrived at our car, we realized we had failed to bring an airtight bag for our wetsuits—we'd have to make our drive back home with the dripping swimwear soaking the interior of the vehicle with the potent waters of Great Salt Lake.

Just before we climbed in to drive home, I took one more glance across the lake, stretching far beyond where I could see. Off in the distance the brown mound of island where I had camped as a boy poked up around the green and blue waters. The winds rushing over the lake seemed to whistle. Great Salt Lake—this unrelenting, mysterious ancient sea—had now conquered me twice. I should have disliked the lake. I should have vowed to never return. The rays of a nearly setting sun made the water glisten and shone on a handful of gulls like a spotlight.

"What are you thinking?" Daniel asked me, noticing I had gotten lost somewhere in thoughts of boyhood adventures and a piece of Earth I seemed to be seeing for the first time.

"I don't think I ever want to try to swim in it again," I said. "Or camp on the island. Maybe this lake is just never going to be my playground."

I shook my head and goosebumps ran up my forearms in a wave.

"But there's no denying this place is breathtaking."

Two Ex-Mormons Swim inGreat Salt Lake

Kylan Rice

You told me I would float by virtue
of having a body. I wouldn't have to think about it
while not breathing. Instead I'd focus on the sound
of compounds in my blood, for once feel lighter
than that thunder, herding toward a precipice
then swerving last minute away. The plan
was to arrive
just as the difference disappeared
between the surface & the sky. To lie
suspended in a dome of pink, only knowing up
from down should birds in murmuration pulse & then
recoil overhead: the coming
-apart, or shivering when touched,
that I have always feared. I couldn't touch

the bottom when I tried. I didn't know ahead of time
that this was something I would want to do: resist
my own resistlessness. We brought gallon jugs
to wash each other after, in the dark, or else risk stiffening
with salt, but you stayed longer, somewhere
out there, while I bathed alone & waited on the shore.
The dirt road back was full
of rabbits crowding out of view. The slow knock
of a hawk

against your headlights, gash of gold
& red. You think nothing is out there,
then the levels recede. A jetty
turns up shiftless with crystals, their sharpness sharper
in the dark, not knowing when you leave the ground
will cut your feet, your wound
cleaned instantly & glittering.

"It was as though, for a time, I didn't exist": Great Salt Lake & *Carnival of Souls*

Michael McLane

Herk Harvey made just one feature film in his long career—1962's *Carnival of Souls.* The project was born when Harvey, on his way home to Kansas from Los Angeles, pulled off the highway to wander the ruins of the Saltair resort. By then, Saltair was land-locked, looming over the dried bed of Great Salt Lake while the waters had receded far into the distance amid a long drought. He sensed a place as haunted by its past as by its uncertain future. What grew from that short encounter was a story of a woman named Mary Henry who is likewise haunted, caught in limbo between past trauma and a community either indifferent to her plight or eager to exploit it. So much of Mary is liminal—caught between cities, jobs, navigating both the labyrinth of leering men in her new home and the gothic ruins of Saltair, which call irresistibly to her despite the ghouls lurking beneath its boardwalks. In many interpretations, Mary is caught in the final seconds between life and death, time and consciousness expanding and contracting in ways that leave her impossibly disoriented. The last we see of Mary's life is her footprints angling out from the resort toward the shallows of Great Salt Lake. Suddenly, she is gone—dilute, evaporative, a precipitate spun out of solution.

■ ■ ■

I wanted to write a straightforward essay on Great Salt Lake, to parallel it with an underappreciated film. To tell a story in a nice, neat arc—not unlike each day I shared space with her, the sun catching the glint of water in the morning and setting the shallow western horizon between the Oquirrhs and Antelope Island ablaze every evening.

But life on the periphery of Great Salt Lake is episodic. I think this is true for many who live nearby. The mountains tower over us; the cityscape envelops us in a sea of concrete and façade. Great Salt Lake dwarfs the city, but lays low, a long shadow. Everywhere, waters are diverted, rerouted, put in culverts, both literal and figurative. Daylighting them takes effort or sensory intrusion—a thousand birds alighting a once, a lake effect snowstorm, the smell of die-off, the specular reflection of mountains in salt mirrors as you speed from one state to another at 120 mph. We stare or listen or breathe a little more slowly. What feels intrusion is a momentary integration, a memory, synesthetic and nameless.

▪ ▪ ▪

In the film's opening moments, Mary inexplicably walks away from what should have been a watery grave in a Kansas river. The world shifts around, or perhaps within, her and she finds herself increasingly alienated from her community, precipitating a sudden move to Salt Lake City to take a job as a church organist. She experiences ghostly hallucinations and dissociative events in which the world carries on around her though others are incapable of hearing or seeing her and she incapable of hearing them. These events are cued for the audience by a wavering or rippling in the shot as if mirage or stifling heat.

After a terrifying dissociative event in a department store, Mary tells a psychologist who ostensibly has come to her aid, "It was as though, as though for a time I didn't exist. As though I had no place in the world. No part of the life around me."

▪ ▪ ▪

I remember when I first encountered Mary Henry, her arrival in the Salt Lake Valley, the silhouette of Saltair looming outside her car window. Home was immediately recognizable, yet new and unsettling. I had been to Great Salt Lake many times, had camped there, knew the sight and sounds in daylight and darkness. And yet, the ruins of Saltair (long gone by my birth) coupled with her increasing affinity for, and fear of, place felt oddly familiar. I was smitten with the film's unrepentant disregard for conventional storytelling, with its awkward/sinister embrace of my home geography, and with Mary. She is defiant, not only of death, but of the insularity she finds in Kansas or in Salt Lake City and of those who would manipulate her. She is the human embodiment of the water she gravitates towards—oozing otherness, preoccupied with the desolate and the undone, with a sense of time or perception beyond those around her, with the mythic and the ambiguous that they overlook. She is not particularly lovable or even likeable. She is not inherently a protagonist. She simply is.

▪ ▪ ▪

Great Salt Lake has had many lives, many more than most lakes. You can trace them in the mountainsides that surround Salt Lake City, the inverse of the tick marks for a growing child. The fingerprints of the departed sea are visible far south and north of Great Salt Lake's waters. Great Salt Lake is a being gathering itself in—a projection of a kind of provincialism perhaps, one convenient to our current needs and desires. She is a complex being that reminds us at times of death and always of the sublime—time and scale outside our grasp. A being that is simpler to forget or to ignore, a process made easier by contraction. This betrays the outsized reach of this inland remnant, the life so impossibly legion dependent on its salt and snow, its evaporative shadow and safe harbor islands. But a shallow pool is far easier to ignore than the lapping sea, even in the desert. This is especially true in arid lands, where mirages gather—reflections, fever dreams of high desert depths, irrepressible growth and green.

▪ ▪ ▪

I'd spent nearly every day of my life at the bottom of that inland sea, what Gertrude Stein called "the land salt lake land where there is no sea," shaping a life by its remnant and the mountains that contained it.

After her near drowning, Mary Henry flees west, where she is immediately captivated, unnerved, overwhelmed by Great Salt Lake and its ruined pleasure palace, where generations of Mormons set aside their millenarian concerns and were light on their feet on the dance floor above and even lighter in the waters below.

But you can still drown in only inches of water. We know this from experience, a kind of aspiration peculiar to particular places, particular shallows. Keep your mouth closed, especially in saltwater.

▪ ▪ ▪

Religion casts a pall over Mary's existence. She is a talented organist, a skill sought out by a church in Salt Lake City, whose priest initially welcomes her with open arms. However, it becomes readily apparent that Mary has little connection with the church or to any overt spirituality. During a conversation with her boardinghouse neighbor, Mary states "to me, a church is just a place of business."

It is unclear whether Harvey had any knowledge of Mormonism or Utah, though it seems fair to assume that it was minimal. Mormonism makes practically no appearance in the film—the church featured is clearly of another branch of Christianity, Mary's landlady offers her coffee, and Mary is boarding in a co-ed house during a time such quarters would be rare. But it is Harvey's treatment of the city itself—a kind of bastion of virtue bordered by wilds and dangerous outside forces—and the insularity of its culture and residents that rings true for many who call it home. Mary is a transplant, an outsider, strange to those around her. There is a coldness to those with whom she interacts, an efficient hospitality mixed with caution.

Mary, in her awkward state of limbo and in her almost incomprehensible draw to the lake, represents not only unwanted outside influence but an embodiment of disconnection with the wilds and the waters at the city's doorstep. Moreover, there are few places in the world where the phrase "a church is just a place of business" resounds more fully than in the epicenter of Mormondom's real estate and industrial empire.

Mid-way through the film, the priest who presides over the church where Mary is the new organist offers to accompany her to Great Salt Lake, though he refuses to cross fences blocking entry to the resort grounds. Though he offers legal arguments for not trespassing, he is clearly unnerved by her drive, her connection to loss.

He pleads with her, "What attraction could there be for you out there?"

Mary responds, "I don't know. Maybe I want to satisfy myself that the place is nothing more than it appears to be."

■ ■ ■

Great Salt Lake has always been more than it appears to be, though it took me many years to learn this. It is inhospitable in so many ways—temperature extremes in summer and winter, blinding sands and winds, overpowering smells, the sheer volume of time and space and silence, offset occasionally by cacophonous and uncountable movements of birds above or flies at ground level. The scales of life and death are always at odds here.

It is also easy to forget Saltair—a resort designed to celebrate the simple act of swimming. Despite the dance halls and roller coasters, the big bands, and the light displays, it was the water, the strange, "dead" sea that lured another of God's chosen people to wholesome entertainment at the edge of a great desert. People jumped from the piers and boated nearby. The pylons on which the resort rested were mostly covered by water. Taking the waters. Baptism. Immersion. Remission of sins.

By the time Herk Harvey saw the hulking Moorish exoskeleton from the interstate, the resort had caught fire twice, a 1931 fire resulting in a total loss. In fits and starts, attempts were made to rebuild and resuscitate, each marred by Depression or war, or shifting interests. By the 1940s, the water was receding and it was at its nadir in the early 1960s. As the lake literally disappeared from view of those in nearby communities, so too did their use for its amenities. Great Salt Lake shimmers faintly in the distance, a haunted, liminal space that mirrors the threshold that Mary inhabits following her plunge into the water in the film's opening scenes.

Fortunately, Harvey could not forget the building or the lake. He convinced officials in Utah to allow him to use the site for filming for a mere $50. The lights and noise created by film crews working on the long-abandoned site so unsettled nearby residents that the police were called on multiple occasions. While Saltair's ruins are the heart of this Gothic tale, Mary's trouble rises not from the building itself, but from the shallow waters beneath it. Her tormentor, known only as "The Man," and his acolytes (which include a decaying doppelganger of Mary at one point) are born of the water, primordial, instinctual, relentless.

■ ■ ■

One night, while driving I-15 near the Salt Lake/Davis county line, I saw and smelled what seemed a distant memory—thick fog gathering around the overpasses and the accompanying smell of sulfur, plumes of steam rising from storm drains and culverts. I left the interstate and drove slowly back down Beck Street.

My father worked as a Yard Master at the now defunct Union Pacific Top End Yard for many years. He took me to work with him occasionally, and I can remember the view from his tower—an amalgam of railyard, industry, scattered residential, and a receding patchwork of wetlands fed by a complex of geothermal springs beneath it. For millennia, the area had been critical to the larger Great Salt Lake ecosystem, and had been home to large populations, both human and non-human, particularly in the winter when the springs kept the ground warm and the game near. After Mormon settlement, the area, and the springs in particular, became a recreational, medical, and spiritual focal point for the city. Bathhouses and resorts abounded. Baptisms, dances, curative sessions, and boating events filled the weekends. A dedicated train line ran between the Lagoon amusement park to the north to both resorts in the Beck Street area and then out to both Saltair and Garfield Beach on Great Salt Lake.

But industry, Depression, war, and the looming promise of mountain recreation all took their toll. The resorts floundered while industry boomed, particularly as the proximity of railroads and oil refineries made the area a hub for the burgeoning military-industrial complex during World War II. Culverts robbed the areas of wetlands, Superfund sites replaced bathhouses. But the springs still gurgled away here and there, steam pouring from drains, and culverts, seeping from the hillsides, the water still slowly making its way to Great Salt Lake.

As I drove Beck Street that night, the shadows of industry and the ruins of recreation were wrapped in the fog of the springs. The ghosts of the landscape, of waters disappeared or hidden, wafted from the ground, obscuring the final traces of a part of the city that had once been loved. If they could not be saved, they should at least be remembered. They were potent symbols—the lost appendages of a larger body atrophying not far away.

▪ ▪ ▪

Much like Mary, *Carnival of Souls* seemingly didn't belong in this world. The film received a dismal reception upon its initial release. Critics and audiences alike were confused by the film's play with genre, its lack of sympathetic characters, male leads, love interests. It was an outsider even in the horror genre, lacking the gore and sexuality of grindhouse, splatter, and other exploitative cinema.

Were it not for Harvey retaining television rights to the film, it would have receded into obscurity. Eventually, the film made its way back to midnight screenings in theatres and its cult following blossomed, counting the likes of David Lynch and George Romero amongst its fans. Twenty-seven years after his death, Herk Harvey's sole feature film retains it macabre singularity as well as a treatment of issues of male dominance and the exploitation of women that is well ahead of its time.

Most films get one life, if they are lucky. *Carnival of Souls* has had at least two or perhaps, more appropriately, it has had a life that, like Mary Henry's, refutes linear time as well as the seemingly certain deaths imposed by taste and profit.

In light of increasing visitation to Great Salt Lake, renewed and concerted efforts by multi-agency groups and rapidly increasing numbers of residents, and an increasingly nuanced understanding of the issues facing the larger ecosystem of Great Salt Lake, the film has potential for continued life as not only documentation of ruins of the recreational heyday of the area, but also a poignant metaphor in the character of Mary, whose experiences mirror and amplify the trajectory of Great Salt Lake amid the growth of Salt Lake City and its increased participation in the American military-industrial complex. As the push for personhood for Great Salt Lake intensifies, Mary offers a cautionary tale, one of acknowledging trauma and granting agency before it is too late.

■ ■ ■

In 2016, I collaborated with Jaimi Butler, a biologist and former associate director of Great Salt Lake Institute (GSLI) at Westminster College, to lead a conference session for the annual National Endowment for the Humanities Conference. The session took place on Antelope Island in Great Salt Lake.

Butler's love of Great Salt Lake is layered and complex. She beams when she talks of its pelicans, its brine shrimp, and its hidden places that she and others work to keep safe from those predatory or careless. She has experienced the grit of the lake and its environs, both literal and figurative, in ways few others have—in her work as a biologist and her prior job on brine shrimping boats—and her efforts highlight the importance of stories and shared experience in conservation and placemaking.

We were on the beach and she asked everyone to pick up a bit of sand and look at it closely.

"This is oolitic sand," she explains. "It is named for its egg-like shape and it's only found a few places in the world. Much of it starts as brine shrimp shit." This was simplistic, but she had their attention now. She explained the long and delicate process by which a tiny fecal pellet becomes a kind of inverted pearl, building up layer after rounded layer of dissolved minerals long after it has left its host's body.

Later, she and I ate lunch away from the others, talking about the receding waters around us, an issue to which GSLI and others were already raising the alarm.

"You know," she says, "as the water recedes and the lakebed dries, those sands will be blown all over the valley."

"So, it's a literal shitstorm," I ask.

"Indeed. But there's far worse in that sand than shit. You and I both know that."

▪▪▪

Mary Henry again, ostensibly to the psychiatrist: "I don't belong in the world, that's what it is. Something separates me from other people. Everywhere. They're everywhere. They're not going to let me go. Everywhere I turn. There's something blocking my escape. It's trying to prevent me from living."

This is just before her discovery that 'they' are, indeed, everywhere, disregarding her cries for help and foiling her attempts at self-preservation.

▪▪▪

What rises from the receding waters of Great Salt Lake now? Tragedies mostly. Some are born of what we have taken, diverted water shifting the salinity of fragile ecosystems or exposing microbialites whose growth is measured in centuries. Others are a result of what we have given, arsenic and other heavy metals deposited by industry on the edges of Great Salt Lake. They lie in wait as the water recedes, rising like ghouls with the wind to haunt the small town turned metropolis, "trying to prevent [us] from living."

▪▪▪

However, these lands are also generative. Mirages and doppelgangers. Scale and time curves in on themselves. Robert Smithson understood this. Nancy Holt understood this. Alfred Lambourne had a sense of it. Herk Harvey got a small taste of it as he strayed from the highway late one evening to wander the edge of a lake in retreat: "The hair stood up on the back of my neck...the stark white of the salt beach and the dark quiet of the deserted buildings created the weirdest location I had ever seen." Wallace Stegner worked at Saltair as a young boy, though his fond memories were complicated by both adulthood and the trajectory of the resort itself: "If I had been a thinking or prescient creature, I might have felt the shadowy quiet under the pavilion as a threat or omen...something there was that didn't love pleasure domes, that wanted them down."

What Harvey and Stegner both sensed in those moments was a place with its own agency, a life outside the needs of human drives and developments. It reads as something sinister in both cases, though that speaks more to our own need to believe we can control the natural world and are not at its mercy. What Stegner saw as "the shadowy quiet," Harvey reimagined as "The Man" and his ghouls, risen from the ruins of forgotten dreams to torment a woman who occupies space on the fringes of a society both manipulative and indifferent.

▪ ▪ ▪

In an early scene, the priest admonishes Mary for her introverted personality, telling her, "but my dear, you cannot live in isolation from the human race, you know." His confidence in her ability to stir her own soul and those around her does not last. After she has a dissociative event in the church, he fires her, accusing her of blasphemy. His parting words are emblematic of her interactions with nearly every male in the film, a pattern of admonishment/reassurance/abandonment: "I feel sorry for you, your lack of soul. . . but that does not mean I am abandoning you." He promptly walks away, not to be seen again until long after he can be of any help.

Equally poignant are her interactions with John Linden, the man across the hall from her, and whose social and sexual advances are endlessly ignored and discouraged by Mary, leading to a similar pattern seen with priest. His frustration is recurring, leading him to ask "What, you don't like a man to hold you close?" It is a question he posits throughout the film, one to which Mary responds in different ways, finally landing with the affirmation that "I am not afraid of men."

■ ■ ■

There is a ghost town now far from the edge of the lake. The railroad once ran there, offering a short, brutish life for a community in the middle of nowhere, at the bottom of the sea, so desiccated now that the scattered wood of buildings has curled and contorted, contracted and petrified. A short walk from the foundations is a graveyard. Every body buried there is that of a child's, none older than five or six. I try to imagine leaving them behind. The last to leave town looking back. The tiny symmetry of life in this place, our shallows marks saved and undone by salt and heat.

Great Salt Lake is not afraid of men.

■ ■ ■

The insularity and hypocrisy that drives Mary mad is one side of home. It is part of living in a bowl. A high-pressure system and relentless thirst. It makes forgetting easy. Just as the little points of resistance to that insularity at times made it easier to forget where we were.

I tried to leave it behind. But salt cures. On the hands or in the heart. They called it flyover country. One day soon that may be true. If the water continues its retreat. If the sea floor rises to claim the city. And even then it will be our own familiars, almost invisible to the naked eye, rising from the sand.

▪ ▪ ▪

Great Salt Lake has been, and continues to be, subject to extractive and exploitative gazes. "The Man" in this case is similarly both singular and legion, both metonymic in the form of an ineffectual, indifferent, and insidious Legislature and embodied in the precipitation ponds, electrolytic facilities, mines, radioactive waste, and developments that surround her, reduce her bit by bit.

It is easier to exploit a place forgotten. "Life Elevated" is alpine, is peak views and pristine streams, or lake effect storms and perfect powder. It is not life in the valleys, in the wetlands or the desert flats. The realities of life in a delicate and difficult system are laid bare at Great Salt Lake. It is love on her own terms. For many, Great Salt Lake is other on a grand, geologic, and sometimes menacing scale. Otherness is pejorative and so it is othered. This betrays the inextricable ways in which she makes life near her both possible and pleasant, but it is convenient for those who measure import solely in financial terms, in tons and acre-feet per year, in magnesium, salt, and shrimp.

▪ ▪ ▪

It is within such shifting frameworks of interaction with the non-human world that this fractured narrative of cultural and geographical horror, as well as feminist defiance, is offered a third life, though perhaps one with a more positive ending than that of Mary Henry. Henry's character offers an unsettling parallel for Great Salt Lake while the film's dialogue is emblematic of attitudes and treatments of Great Salt Lake that were already well established by the time of its release and were so embedded by the onset of the twenty-first century that they threaten to facilitate the death of Great Salt Lake in a few short years.

And yet there is hope. But that hope exists not so much in the film's bleak ending, but by the rereading and reinterpretation of several generations of viewers, in the place its story now occupies. There is further life for the film and for the lake in that process. I can't help but think that Harvey would recognize, as I do, the embodiment of Great Salt Lake in Mary's gaunt figure and somnambulist retreat from a world that is constantly endangering her. Her cries for help feel out of place, unfamiliar. Something is lost in translation or shifting priorities. Though it is one possibility, Mary's ending need not be that of Great Salt Lake's. Rather, the multitude of voices through which Great Salt Lake now speaks, from plummeting bird populations and withering wetlands to toxic sandstorms and unpredictable snowpacks, are being heard, and not only by specialists trained to listen for them, but by students and artists and wide swaths of the general public who are waking up to the notion that the real dangers lay in any boundary, real or rhetorical, that separates her from the rest of us. For us to belong in this small sliver of the world, Great Salt Lake must be allowed to belong in it.

Water to Survive, Not Thrive*

*(*Local Government Information Poster seen around Salt Lake City)*

Rachel White

Shriveled vinca vines, stiff
& sun browned lawns slope
toward inland sea—in place
of sagebrush, rabbitbrush,
bitterbrush that used to feed overwintering deer—

brittle brown stems
barely alive in sweltering heat, I'm still watering
in vain, I don't like to neglect
and kill, yet I am

struck by the fact this water lives
at Great Salt Lake, belongs
to nesting birds who migrate
across hemispheres,
monarch butterflies too,
what will they do

when every pond,
lake and spring is gone,
allocated by cities unsuited to
their place?
All numbers down

except for people, and temperatures,
each year hotter than the last—
seasonal records shatter,
an infinite hall of mirrors witness to earth's scupper
as aridity expands

day by day becoming
year by year, at first
slowly, season after season,
then catastrophically,
all at once.

Cantos for Great Salt Lake

Brooke Williams

1. "Canto: [ˈkan,tō] NOUN / A major division of a long poem."

2. Dragonflies perched on each feathered head of eight tallest twigs—evenly spaced.

3. No water. Invisible water. The weight of it once held down the ground which has now shattered into a thousand cracks.

4. At first, we went to Great Salt Lake—her Islands, the marshes at her edges, Great Salt Lake, herself—for the birds.

5. *The Great Salt Lake: Present and Past*, was published in 1900. Its author, James E. Talmage, is my great-grandfather on my mother's side.

6. *The Great Salt Lake: Present and Past.* What about her future?

7. How can the dragonfly remain motionless while the feathered seed head moves so wildly beneath her?

8. *Meadowhawk, Sympetrum*:small red dragonflies seen over most of North America. Perching with wings

drooped forward.

9. I would not say their wings are "drooped." They're strategically positioned, draped forward and down. What are they hiding?

10. Those feathered seed heads: "You're looking at phragmites. They are very prominent along the shoreline near the entrance booth and across from the marina. They're beautiful, and terrible." Trish Ackley, Park Naturalist, Antelope Island State Park.

11. Today, from the car on the causeway, we've seen three live birds: two black-necked stilts, one American avocet. An eared grebe lies dead on the dry, cracked mud. Leaving the car to get closer to the old edge of the lake, we're blocked by webs sealing the space between sage, rabbitbrush, and phragmites.

12. Old edge, as the lake has not been near here for years.

13. January 2023. We join poet Nan Seymour during her winter vigil, camped on Antelope Island. She stays at Great Salt Lake during the months the Utah Legislature is in session. There are laws that could be passed that would help Great Salt Lake. This vigil's power is not only to raise awareness, but to change the dark story unfolding at Great Salt Lake.

14. To Nan, Great Salt Lake is a person.

15. I grew up on Salt Lake City's north bench, watching the sun set on Great Salt Lake. She formed foundation and backdrop to our lives, measured time and weather, and

in a way was our moat against the world. Now she's disappearing. The warming climate, up four degrees in a century, is only partially responsible. While some of her water is diverted to supply the Wasatch Front's growing population, most of it goes to farmers growing feed for cattle in other states. Threatened are ten million migratory birds dependent on Great Salt Lake's now-collapsing ecosystem, billions of dollars lost in the mineral, agricultural, and tourism industries, and the health of a million valley residents, as they breathe in the arsenic-laced dust churned up from exposed lakebed blown across their lives.

16. I have not always used feminine pronouns when referring to Great Salt Lake.

17. Brigham Young once referred to Great Salt Lake using feminine pronouns. He was my great-great-grandfather, on my father's side.

18. To celebrate the Fourth of July in 1851, Brigham Young led a contingent to Great Salt Lake. During his speech he gave a toast to Great Salt Lake which was recorded by the *Deseret News*. "As she has hitherto been oblivious to the birthday of freedom and independence; may she this day be awakened to her sense of duty, and seek by her briny sympathies to preserve the Union, till she shall become a component part thereof, even if she has to pickle it."

19. "May she this day be awakened to her sense of duty," he said. What were her duties?

20. Nan Seymour: "What would Great Salt Lake look like if

we succeed? If Great Salt Lake legally becomes a person?"

21. Great Salt Lake is fighting for her life. We're in the midst of a great learning.

22. Comfort the disturbed.

23. We begin by imagining. "What if the Earth loved us back?" Robin Wall Kimmerer.

24. Perfect orbed webs, the spiders who created them bull's-eyed in their centers.

25. Spider silk is highly flexible, extremely stretchable, surpasses steel in strength, and most importantly, can be formed into a mesh that would stop a bullet.

26. *Neoscona oaxacensis*. Predator. Antelope Island's most common spider. An orb-weaver, these spiders build their perfect round webs between any two structures, usually sagebrush. The females perch in the center of the web while the males haunt the edges.

27. Brine flies, *Ephydra cineria* and the larger *Ephydra hians* hatch by the billions, forming vibrating grey clouds. They have no time to eat, only five days to live and mate before dying. Five days assuming they aren't ambushed by the meadowhawk. Or frenzied, they don't fly into the orb-weaver's web. Or surrounded by clouds of them, we don't breathe them in, trap them with our nose hairs, wipe them dead off our teeth.

28. The route of the invisible breeze-body mapped by the moving feathered seed heads.

29. This hot day, one of 34 over 100 degrees.

30. While Terry had been going to Great Salt Lake to watch birds for a decade, my first time was with her, on an early date.

31. That cold day, hovering just above freezing, light intermittent snow, almost fifty years ago.

32. For Terry, Great Salt Lake is a person, always "she" and never "the," a subject to be interacted with, not an object to be manipulated and used. After two months writing and three levels of editing Terry's story, "I Am Haunted by What I Have Seen at Great Salt Lake," *The New York Times*' "Style" team, added "the" to "Great Salt Lake" each time it was mentioned and replaced "she" with "it" in the last moments before print deadline. "Take my name off," she told her editor. "This is no longer my story." Her editor responded, "Give me three minutes." All the "thes" were removed. Every "it" was replaced by "she." Great Salt Lake's personhood, restored.

33. By using feminine pronouns while referring to Great Salt Lake, Brigham Young was not personifying her. Rather, he included Great Salt Lake under the heading of feminine with his wives and daughters and all women which he considered resources, objects. Brigham Young was clear that a woman was to bear and raise the children, be subservient to her husband and honor the Priesthood which he held and she didn't (and still doesn't). Brigham did support women moving beyond their roles as wives and mothers to more professional work, but only when necessary to compete with the growing economic and political influence of non-Mor-

mons. Women. The feminine as resource. Object to be owned, used, and manipulated.

34. Great Salt Lake is granted personhood. Officially. Legally. Success. Imagine it.

35. Talmage rarely refers to Great Salt Lake's natural wonders, or beauty, or nature, and then only when quoting others. He writes, "I trust rather the scientific observer, whose love for the beautiful, while no whit less than that professed and held by his brothers, poet and painter, is kept within the bounds of truthful decorum."

36. Beauty but only that which is "kept within the bounds of truthful decorum."

37. "May she be awakened to her sense of duty."

38. Great Salt Lake as object.

39. Wild, evolutionary beauty: Truth greater than the sum of all truths. Truthful decorum has no bounds.

40. Nan: "When we sing to Great Salt Lake, she sings back to us."

41. Great Salt Lake, as subject.

42. Garfield Beach and Saltair. At their height, 160,000 annual visitors.

43. Saltair. Built by the Mormon Church, it first opened in 1893. It was more popular than Garfield Beach, which served alcohol. Saltair shut down shortly after the "Gi-

ant Racer," the world's largest roller coaster ride, collapsed in one of the windstorms for which Great Salt Lake is famous. It stayed shuttered until 1962, when Herk Harvey rented it for fifty bucks to film *Carnival of Souls.*

44. On screen. In a huge vacant haunted building, a burlap mat flies down long and steep metal surface. I knew that slide and that mat and was horrified. *I am five or six. We've taken the train across the salt flats to Saltair for the day. This is a very big deal. My father coaxes me and I sit down on the burlap mat and tuck my feet into the pocket sewn into the end of it. The attendant pushes me off before I am ready and down I move at a speed I am way too young for.* In the movie, the haunted burlap mat slides down empty.

45. Great Salt Lake's water is a "valuable source of useful products...Indeed these briny waters have already begun to yield their chemic riches." *Great Salt Lake: Present and Past* embodies the Mormon position that "man" has the divinely inspired position at the center of God's creation with dominion over the earth and all living things. *However, all are stewards—not owners—over this earth and its bounty and will be accountable before God for what they do with His creations.*

46. Dominion is control. Dominion—and stewardship—are only applicable with objects to be manipulated and used, not subjects we interact with.

47. Great Salt Lake deserves legal personhood. Success: The lake at the center, no longer in the periphery. Reverence as baseline.

48. What do we take from Great Salt Lake? Every year, 2.8 million tons—lithium, potash, sodium chloride, potassium sulfate, magnesium chloride, magnesium metal, chlorine gas. Mined *every year.* Chemic riches.

49. Salt. Mined, now, two million tons every year.

50. Salt. Harvested for hundreds of years by Native people. Northern Shoshone. Diné. Paiute. Cheyenne. Crow. Nez Perce. Their migrational salt paths from every direction, the spokes of a giant wheel, Great Salt Lake its hub.

51. This from Darren Parry, Northwestern Shoshone, raised north of Great Salt Lake, near the Bear River: "The one thing that people don't understand is, I was raised by a grandmother who spoke about water, land, plants, animals, as kinfolk. [She] told me that I needed to treat that relationship just like I would a person, and so we honor the land. We honor the water."

52. For Native people, resources are subjects to interact with. For white colonizers resources are objects to be manipulated, bought, sold, used. White colonizer armies treated other as objects to be. . .

53. Objects are massacred. The Bear River Massacre occurred on January 29, 1863. Four hundred North Western Shoshone people were killed by US Calvary in the worst slaughter of Native Americans in US history, although few remember it. "They flanked the Indians," says Darren Parry, and the river "became their last resort." Some jumped into the river but were shot, and others were swept away in the current and drowned.

54. If constructed by the Utah Division of Water Resources, the Bear River Development Project will begin a few miles south of the Bear River Massacre site. At a cost of $2.9 million, a ninety-mile pipeline connecting up to four new dams, destroying irreplaceable wetlands, will divert nearly half of the Bear River's annual flow into Great Salt Lake.

55. The Utah Division of Water Resources is a taker. Who are the other takers? Say them out loud.
    Compass Minerals.
    Great Salt Lake Brine Shrimp Cooperative.

    Kennecott Utah Copper Corporation *Rio Tinto.*
    Mineral Resources International.
    Morton Salt Company.
    US Magnesium. Formerly MagCorp.
    Cargill.

56. Great Salt Lake deserves legal personhood. Success: No more mining. No more using or manipulating her.

57. Water. We take water that once flowed into Great Salt Lake. Most of it to grow alfalfa. Most of it to feed distant cows.

58. Grant Great Salt Lake personhood. Success: Grow food, not feed. No more alfalfa exports.

59. In 1952, a causeway was built off Antelope Island's southern tip, connecting it to the mainland for the first time. A new causeway was built from the northern tip in 1969. In 1983, rising lake water flooded the island, isolating it until 1993, when the lake receded and the

causeway was repaired. Now over a million people visit the island each year.

60. Draw a line between the dragonflies and the draped webs. Do not cross it.

61. This causeway. Along it, a black pipe, five feet in diameter, lays on the ground, a ditch being dug to its side. To take water from Great Salt Lake? Impossible. To put water into Great Salt Lake? Since white settlement, any water flowing toward the lake from the east or north has been considered wasted.

62. What have we given?

63. "Effluent: [ˈeflōōənt] NOUN / Liquid waste or wastewater discharged into a river or sea." Or lake. Or Great Salt Lake.

64. The giant black pipe, the final effluent pipeline. The project revegetating and restoring surfaces (including wetlands). *Higher water quality: more attractive effluent; elimination of nutrient load*; "Keeping water flowing to Great Salt Lake is a priority."

65. Confusing. But what water? Object or subject? Still an object. Send waste into deeper water west of Antelope Island, instead of the shallower Farmington Bay where it causes toxic algal blooms.

66. Wastewater into Great Salt Lake contains: Industrial wastes, pesticides, cyanotoxins, metals—antimony, copper, mercury, lead, zirconium and arsenic. Chemic riches?

67. Grant Great Salt Lake personhood. Success: No more effluent.

68. On our first date, that overcast day, Antelope Island cast in black and white, Terry and I marveled at a large perfect cottonwood tree, dead in the distance, a dark contrast to the light grey bleakness. I took a photo, which I framed and gave to her as a gift. For the next few years that cottonwood marked the transition we'd made from our everyday complicated inundated world, to the world of wild birds and broad water. Then, one day it lay on its side, windfall.

69. Now, new apartments, like unopened boxes that just arrived. Strip malls, Maverick, Subway, Burger King oozing toward Great Salt Lake.

70. The state of Utah is officially doing everything it can to convince us that it is doing everything it can to put water back in the lake, while doing very little. No evolution, no shift from object to subject. Only use. Only manipulation.

71. Those with the power know the truth, which they hide if it erodes their power.

72. The truth: Great Salt Lake's ecosystem is for LULUs: Locally Unwanted Land Uses."Places to hide a bombing range; a huge Superfund site called US Magnesium; a new state prison, a bigger Airport; Kennecott copper's giant stack and toxic tailings pond; sewage-treatment plants, mineral-evaporation lagoons, dumps. And the latest: Inland ports with giant warehouses, intense truck traffic.

73. Great Salt Lake should have personhood. Success: "Lulu: [lü-lü] NOUN / One that is remarkable or wonderful."

74. First, we learned the birds: their size and silhouette, their coloring. Then long legged or not, then blue or green or cinnamon teal. Then yellowlegs or willet. We began to see them. We watched them.

75. We played flight games with our hands: *Whose flies like this?* Hand, fingers spread, vibrating: flycatcher. Fingers extended, hand twisting erratically: turkey vulture. Hovering/vibrating: kestrel. Fingers undulating: great blue heron. Fingers clenching in pulses: stilts. Fingers making strong rhythmic waves: ravens. Fingers, methodically stretching: white pelicans.

76. Nan folds white paper into origami white pelicans with a child at a street fair. The child's parents watch.

   "Why pelicans?" they ask.
   "We're making ten thousand to hang in the Capitol," she says. "To publicize their disappearance from Gunnison Island in Great Salt Lake."
   "What happened?"
   "Great Salt is so low that the island is no longer an island and their nests and young are no longer protected from predators."
   "But Great Salt Lake is fine now, right, after last winter's record snowfall?"
   "We'll need eleven more winters like that."

77. Comfort the disturbed. Disturb the comfortable.

78. Then we studied bird eyes, looking into them back a million years.

79. Eared grebes have red eyes, which may help them see better underwater.

80. The dragonflies: predator/prey. My friend Ron has a photo of a young loggerheaded shrike impaling a common green darner on a thorn.

81. Brine shrimp. *Artemia* (sp), prey. Talmage, *Great Salt Lake*, 1900. "The larvae of the tipula may be taken anywhere near shore during the warm months; and the pupa cases of both species are often washed ashore in great numbers, where they undergo decomposition with disagree able emanations. Of the lake animals, the *Artemia fertilis* (or *Artemia gracilis*) commonly known as the brine shrimp; exists in greatest numbers."

82. Great Salt Lake's ecosystem attracts ten million migratory birds—250 species, annually. For many, brine shrimp are the prime food source fueling their migrations. Add them up, say them out loud.

    One million northern pintails.
    1.4 million eared grebes.
    250,000 American avocets.
    65,000 black-necked stilts.
    250,000 red-necked phalaropes.
    Blacked-billed plovers.
    Snowy plovers, world's largest assemblage of.
    Red-winged blackbirds.
    Short-billed dowitchers.
    32,000 long-billed dowitchers.

Long-billed curlews.
60,000 ruddy ducks.
Tundra swans. 75 percent of all those in the United States.
Trumpeter swans.
Marbled godwits.

Now, say their names out loud again.

83. Brine shrimp mining. Each year twenty-one companies suck brine shrimp cysts from Great Salt Lake, valued from $10 million to $60 million. The unhatched cysts are fed to tropical fish. Hatched, they are eaten by fish and crustaceans being raised for human consumption.

84. "During a cruise upon the lake in September 1892," writes Talmage, in his Great Salt Lake book, "our party found the crustaceans; swarming in the open water. When near the middle of the lake, with a small tow-net we gathered a quart of the shrimps in the course of a few minutes. Thereupon we resolved upon an experiment the subsequent recital of which has shocked the gastronomic sensibilities of many friends. Reasoning that the bodies of the artemiae are composed largely of chitin, we concluded that the question of their palatability was at least worthy of investigation… By a simple rinsing with fresh water, the excess of lake brine was removed, after which the shrimps were cooked with no accompaniments save a little butter; and a suggestion of pepper. They were actually delicious."

85. Beyond birds, to the coyote traversing winter ice. White ermine becoming brown weasel, adapting in early spring. One bobcat. Occasional deer.

Smaller. The spiders. The butterflies, bees, wasps, the dragonflies and brine flies. Mosquitos. Gnats. Brine shrimp. Millions of unseen, foundational microorganisms.

86. Eared grebes eat brine shrimp which eat algae, which flourishes when Great Salt Lake is 12 percent salt. With Great Salt Lake now at 17 percent salt, the algae suffers. The brine shrimp and the eared grebes go hungry when the algae suffers.

87. When no one is there to hear it, does a tree falling in a forest make a sound? "No one" according to author Erik Jampa Andersson, refers specifically to humans. Thousands of other species would surely perceive a tree falling. Sound does not require humans to exist.

88. "The human-centered story is killing us." Andersson.

89. With time, would Brigham Young's vision of women have transformed from resource and support—from "rib" to "those who carry the magic of creation"? And would his vision of the feminine changed from subservient to divine, the adaptation on which our survival may depend?

90. Evolution is adaptation.

91. Nan: "Great Salt Lake will be restored by ordinary people willing to show extraordinary love."

92. Last winter, walking the edge of Antelope Island, we count dead birds. 496 rotting eared grebes float in the shallows. Did they die together, hungry and weak and

killed by a sudden storm? Counting dead grebes becomes part of Nan's vigil.

93. Personhood: Earlier this year, Brazil's Laje River was granted legal personhood, guaranteeing its natural flow and protecting the forest it runs through. The Whanganui River in New Zealand and Spain's Mar Menor lagoon received personhood status in 2017 and 2022 respectively. Terry writing in *The New York Times*: "The Rights of Nature is now a global movement granting personhood to rivers, mountains and forests. In Ecuador, they have granted constitutional rights to Pachamama, Earth Mother. In the United States, Lake Erie was granted personhood in 2019, allowing citizens to sue on behalf of the lake. Although this right was invalidated by a federal judge, this is the new frontier of granting legal status to a living world."

94. Those advocating for personhood for these water bodies believe that they are living with an existence that doesn't depend on humans. It is not a simple resource for humans; it becomes an entity that has a right to live, to evolve naturally, to have its natural cycles.

95. Give Great Salt Lake personhood: She is a subject to interact with; not an object to manipulate and use.

96. America has given personhood to corporations. What?

97. Great Salt Lake deserves legal personhood. She is hurting. We should help her as we would any hurting person. Stop the cause. Support healing. Maintain contact. Support. Love unconditionally.

98. Great Salt Lake is in between what she was and what she will be. What will she be? Imagine it.

99. Great Salt Lake is adapting, evolving.

100. Success: Great Salt Lake rises. She loves us back.

Antelope Island's 'Last Great Buffalo Hunt'

Scott Morris

In the eighteenth and nineteenth centuries, Euro-Americans spread from maritime farms, towns, cities, and states along the Atlantic and Pacific coasts, toward the center of the continent, in a relentless process of settler colonialism. In addition to being a story about demographic, economic, and historic phenomena, this was an ecological transition catalyzed by settlers replacing indigenous species. They intentionally imported familiar plants and unintentionally transported seeds lodged in the dung or fur of livestock; they trapped, baited, and shot 'vermin' and carefully tended the bloodlines of sheep, goats, cattle, and horses. A keystone transition of this larger social and ecological transformation was the replacement of bison with cattle across the continent's grassland and montane ecosystems. Though bison were better adapted to the environment, settlers preferred cattle for their docility and manageability.

The 1926 "Last Great Buffalo Hunt" on Antelope Island reveals how ecological changes, capitalism, and commodification intersected in the American West. That November, hunters shot most of the island's 350 bison—descendants of the millions that once roamed North America just a few generations earlier. Wealthy sportsmen from across the country eagerly joined this heavily-promoted event. A private company owned both the island and the herd, and after attempting various unsuccessful profit-making ventures during the four decades since bringing bison to the island in 1893, the owners conceived the hunt as one final desperate attempt to make the herd profitable. News of the hunt spread widely, drawing both interest and condemnation from across the nation. The bison of 1920s Antelope Island and their ancestors had survived the continent-wide ecocide that took the homelands of perhaps thirty million bison and turned them into irrigated fields, hay meadows, ranches, grazing lands, and other agricultural arrangements. They had survived the dislocations, importations, and reintroductions of the 1880s and 1890s, and in 1926 they faced another existential challenge—surviving market conditions and cultural memories that encouraged and enabled hunters and sportsmen to travel from thousands of miles away to shoot a bison and bring home its robe and head.

▪ ▪ ▪

In the late eighteenth century, as French, Spanish, and Anglo-American colonial projects began to push towards the core of the North American continent, bison were the linchpin of grassland ecosystems. These herds stretched from the Appalachian Mountains in the East, to the Great Basin in the West, and from nearly the Valley of Mexico in the South all the way North to Great Slave Lake. Products from the bison contributed to indigenous economies, societies, and cosmologies. Contemporary scholars and activists like Ervin Carlson (Blackfeet Nation), Leroy Little Bear (Blood Tribe of the Blackfoot Confederacy), Rosalie Little Thunder (Sicangu Lakota), and Fred DuBray (Cheyenne River Sioux) have deepened our understanding of this contribution. In short, humans and bison were co-creators of a shared ecosystem.

Great Salt Lake sits near the edge of bison's historic western distribution. According to historians Dan Flores and Andrew C. Isenberg, North America's pre-contact bison population likely fluctuated around thirty million, oscillating with changes in climate and resource availability. Bison skeletons were found by nineteenth century settlers in Echo Canyon, Utah Valley, and other drainages of the Wasatch Plateau. An archaeological site near Great Salt Lake's Willard Bay has also been shown to contain bison bone dating to the times of the Frémont peoples (400 to 1300 CE), and Frémont-era petroglyphs depicting bison have been found as far south as today's Kane County.

Early Euro-American explorers also ran into living bison. Escalante recorded seeing bison tracks in September of 1776 near the current Utah-Colorado border, and two beasts were killed by the expedition members near the Green River in Utah. American fur trappers reported seeing bison in the valley of Great Salt Lake, and Peter Skene Ogden left an account of seeing them in the Cache Valley in 1828. Five years later, Captain Joseph Walker's westbound detachment of the Bonneville Expedition ran into their last bison on the northwest side of Great Salt Lake.

The memories of contemporaneous native leaders are perhaps the best source. The Ute chief Wanship, who Mormon chroniclers described as wearing a long buffalo robe over his shoulders, "gathered around his waist in folds like a Scotsman," reported in 1841 that he "remembered a time when buffalo passed from the mainland to Antelope Island without swimming." Wanship was reported to be living on the island when the Frémont expedition explored the lake in 1845. The Ute leader Wakara also recollected that when he was a boy (he was born about 1808), deer were abundant and "buffalo more plentiful than Mormon cattle."

In any case, bison were not frequenting the Wasatch Front by the time the Mormons arrived in 1847, but they had been within the living memory of Native people living there. The island was on the edge of their habitat, the kind of place grazers would visit during verdant years but avoided when climate shifted drier and warmer.

After at least a half century without bison, they were to return, thanks to Buffalo Jones, a hunter-turned-conservationist, and an Ogden newspaperman and politician named William Glassmann. Buffalo Jones and Glassman partnered up in the late 1880s to establish a ranch near the south shore of Great Salt Lake. They brought thirty-five bison in on a retrofitted cattle railroad car, seven bulls and twenty-eight cows.

But the experience of these thirty-five, and that of their descendants, was to be much different from that of their free-roaming ancestors. Glassmann was not trying to return the animals to Utah out of some notion of ecological holism: He wanted to make money off them. He held an interest in the nearby Utah and Nevada Railroad, as well as real estate west of the Black Rock and Garfield Beach Resorts. He sold Jones on his vision of a combined zoo and game preserve on the south side of the lake. Animals could be sold to zoos, tickets would be sold to visitors wanting to see the rarities, and his real estate holdings would increase in value. Plans for Garfield City were drawn up, which would be centered on the Buffalo Park and an expanded waterfront and baths resort. Some lots in the town were sold to Eastern buyers, and some visitors did come to the Buffalo Park, but within two years the paper town had collapsed.

▪ ▪ ▪

On January 17, 1893, Glassmann sold twelve bison, three yearlings, and nine mature animals to John Dooly and John White, who, in the form of the Island Improvement Company, owned most of Antelope Island. Dooly bought the island from The Church of Jesus Christ of Latter-day Saints for one million dollars. They were reportedly motivated by a desire to turn the island into a large game reserve for all animals indigenous to the west, while also profiting off sheep and cattle ranching.

By 1896 the animals had begun to reproduce, with fifteen

total bison on the island. Dooly, White, and the ranch hands of the Island Improvement Company adopted a strategy of leaving the sometimes-dangerous animals alone, unless one became problematic, at which point it would be killed for profit. The meat went to mostly eastern customers looking for an exotic taste, the head would be skinned, stuffed, mounted, and sold, and the robes would be turned into high-end rugs and wall hangings.

More money was to be made by catering to mostly eastern upper-class sportsmen looking to travel to a rugged western locale and reenact the conquest of the continent through a private hunting trip. In December of 1896 the first commercial hunt came to Antelope Island in the form of an expedition to kill "The Mighty Sullivan of Satan's Gulch," an old bull with a reputation for destruction and misandry.

The bison took to their new home. The island's isolation certainly helped. For today's reader familiar with Antelope Island State Park, it's hard to imagine the Antelope Island of the 1890s—a remote, windswept island a few days' travel from Salt Lake City without the conveyance of the modern automobile causeway. By 1911, the one hundred bison on the island were already one of the largest herds in the United States. By the 1920s, the 300 members of the Antelope Island herd represented a sizable portion of the animals extant—all federal reservation herds put together numbered only 1,100 bison.

Land managers soon found other opportunities for making money from the Antelope Island bison. In 1922, the hunting and stampede scenes from The Covered Wagon were shot at the spot now called Camera Flats. Seven bison were killed in the process of the shoot. The silent film was the highest-grossing movie of 1923, and was reportedly President Warren G. Harding's favorite, with a special screening at the White House. The director of the film, James Cruze, responded to the criticism over the slain bison by saying "Don't grow sentimental over the seven.

The folks out there would like to get rid of the whole herd and they would, but for the sentimental hubbub that is always raised when they talk of rounding out the buffalo." The animals were sentimental reminders of the America of the past—but rather than blocking grazing cattle from productive habitat, perhaps that nostalgia could be packaged and sold.

Bison ranching hadn't worked; the animals refused to abide by the fences ranch hands erected for their containment and attempts to develop a market for their meat never really took off. The harsh conditions out in the lake provided sanctuary from other grazers and predators, but it didn't make for an easy life. Rather than bison meat or bison robes—products that drove nineteenth century economies—the twentieth century product would be a packaged experience, a tourism product that could allow upper-class sportsmen to relive atavistic fantasies of the Wild West.

▪ ▪ ▪

In April of 1925, a year before the Last Great Buffalo Hunt, the Antelope Island herd was sold to A.H. Leonard. Leonard jumped into an escalating series of get-rich-quick-schemes that were designed to squeeze greater returns out of the Antelope Island Bison herd. His first plan was to sell the animals to zoos across the country, but they proved too wild to catch and too hard to transport off the island. His next plan was to convince the federal government to buy him out by establishing a National Park containing the island and its bison. To this plea he was met with "Congressional Apathy." So rather than sell the bison, Leonard planned to sell an experience—one last great buffalo hunt catering to rich hunters who would pay top dollar for the privilege while making room for more profitable and more easily managed cattle.

The leadup to the hunt saw a flood of activism, mostly from

Easterners who were horrified by the prospect of the wholesale slaughter of one of the last bison herds on the continent. A letter-writing PR campaign led by The New York World and joined by Eastern Governors, Mayors, and Philanthropic groups was rebuffed by Governor's Office stationery curtly informing the writer that "the buffalo herd are privately owned."

In Utah, the *Ogden Standard-Examiner* ran a long piece on August 22, 1926, about the plans being laid for the coming hunt, under the headline "Famous Utah Buffalo Herd Doomed; Will Shoot Over 300 this Autumn." Letters of protest flooded Governor Dern's office from Los Angeles, New York, Chicago, and other distant cities. More sympathetic letters arrived from closer, including a sportsman and eyesight specialist in Boise and the Idaho Fish and Game Protective Association, who cheered on the governor's measured attempt to find a solution. Utah constituencies were mixed; a protest came from Ogden and Salt Lake's Lone Pine Hunters Club to "place themselves on record as being emphatically opposed to the proposed slaughter of the bison herd on Antelope Island."

The governor's outgoing mail shows a desire to defuse the controversy. On May 14, before the nationwide ire had been raised by the media, he wrote to the Land Office to enquire which of Great Salt Lake's islands were still public domain that could be made into a state park. The next day he wrote to a senator with the idea of a private fund drive to buy the herd, which he felt was out-of-reach for the state to fund themselves. His replies to his critics remained patient and calm, filled them in on the facts they were misunderstanding, and constantly repeated that he had been assured by the owners that 60 to 75 bison would be preserved to re-propagate the herd.

One letter, from New York, made a nostalgic appeal to Dern as a Westerner, writing "no doubt your parents and grandparents were on the prairie when the buffalo roamed, wild, same as mine were." Another letter from New York was sent just after its author returned from a trip to Utah and uses the tourism potential of the bison as a justification for their preservation. Hunters wrote in to argue that the proposed bison hunt violated their notions of sportsmanship.

By the end of October, as the activism reached a fever pitch, Governor Dern was losing his patience with the eastern outrage. By October 29, in a reply to the Izaak Walton League, Dern defended the hunt, making the case for the priority of sheep and cattle, and calling the misrepresentations in the eastern press "an injustice to the state of Utah and its people."

▪ ▪ ▪

Regardless of the protestations from near and far, the hunt proceeded as planned.

"Buffalo Hunt on Antelope Island Opened Tuesday…Famous Sportsmen Are on the Ground," declared a page two headline in the Salt Lake Telegram on November 2. The bison herd's owner had received 130 applications from people hoping to participate in the hunt. Leonard had promised the Governor he would spare 60 to 75 bison, but after this surge in interest he revised that down to 40. The hunt was wrapping up by late November, but not before a group of 35 of Brigham City's Boy Scouts and a few adult leaders went to Antelope Island to gun down a bison for a Community Day Barbeque.

The results of the hunt are difficult to quantify. Some sources say that all but twenty-five cows and calves were killed, while others claim that only one hundred of four hundred animals were taken. In any case, it seems that Leonard stayed more or less true to his commitment to Governor Dern: to allow a few dozen to survive but otherwise clear "surplus animals" off the private property and make as much from the hunt as possible in the process.

■ ■ ■

After the hunt, the company soldiered on and consolidated control over the island. Max Harward, who lived and worked on the island from 1938 to 1950 as the son of the company's foreman, provides some insight. He reported that in 1911 there were over one hundred bison, and by the late1930s the herd numbered between thirty and forty, and stayed about that size in all the years his family lived there. Harward blamed inbreeding and overgrazing, with no mention of the 1926 hunt.

An appraisal in 1967 assessed the value of two thousand acres at the island's north end for a potential state park. The challenge wasn't simply determining land value, but calculating how this purchase would affect the livestock company's year-round transhumance operation. "Rarely nowadays is it possible to develop a ranching operation here in the West where the total livestock enterprise covering a year-long business is in one contiguous block of land," explain the Report's authors. The appraisal marked a turning point when Antelope Island's "highest and best use" began shifting from ranching to tourism and public recreation."

In 1969, the state of Utah completed its purchase of two thousand acres on the North end of the island for a State Park, and an automobile causeway from Syracuse was finished later that year, dramatically increasing access to the island. This northern causeway was an improvement over a causeway built in 1951 that connected Great Salt Lake's south shore to the ranch house on the southern half of the island. The southern causeway was intended to allow access to the island, but it also had the ancillary benefit of preventing raw sewage from Salt Lake and Davis Counties from flowing West towards Saltair and other beach resorts on the south shore. In 1981, the State bought the remaining 26,000 acres, ending commercial ranching on the island.

Six years after the state took control, the first bison round-up was carried out as an effort to control the population level. In the decades after the Last Great Buffalo Hunt the population had rebounded heartily, and without natural predators, the grazers were threatening to overwhelm the biotic balance on the closed system of the island. The state's biologists consider the carrying capacity of the Island to be about 550 bison, and 100 to200 calves are born into the herd each year, making predation in the form of state-sponsored-capitalism necessary.

Bison hunts still happen on the island, but just a few a year, with most of the excess animals auctioned off, usually to increase the genetic diversity of other herds. In 2021, 238 bison were put up for auction, netting the State more than $300,000. This is a success story for state-led ecological restoration that may provide a blueprint for other parts of the Great Salt Lake Basin and further afield.

Across North America, Native people are leading the way on bison reintroductions. Representatives from nineteen Tribes gathered in the Black Hills in early 1991 to discuss the reestablishment of bison populations on Native land. Early collaborations were consolidated in 2010 as the InterTribal Buffalo Council. The Council has grown to eighty-two Tribes and has helped introduce and manage more than twenty thousand bison on a million acres of tribally controlled land. From a low of 541 individuals in 1889, conservation efforts have grown the continent's population to about 31,000 bison in sixty-eight herds. Another half-million bison-cattle hybrids are raised on private ranches and feedlots.

■ ■ ■

Bison, especially those that visited or lived on Antelope Island, have been assigned a shifting value by the human societies they co-created the region alongside. Different groups assigned different values; native people place them at the center of a vibrant indigenous economy and cosmology, while the industrial capitalism of the late nineteenth century valued them exactly at the price of their hides' leather. To the 1890s entrepreneurs who reintroduced them to the island, they were worth the expected volume of zoo exhibit ticket sales or a federal buyout. In both the 1926 "Last Great Buffalo Hunt" and the late twentieth century establishment and popularization of Antelope Island State Park, we see the value of the bison shifting again, as recreation boosters and officials offered a packaged opportunity to relive an atavistic fantasy about cowboys and horsemen in the Wild West. In the twenty-first century, we see the value of the bison reclaimed by tribal governments as an opportunity to exercise sovereignty and provide for the spiritual and economic sustenance of their members, with support and collaboration from state and federal land management agencies.

Aridification exacerbated by climate change and persistent low lake levels threaten the Antelope Island bison herd. In their pre-contact, free-roaming state, they visited the island on wet years but avoided it when the glaring Basin sun blasted the scant vegetation. If each decade moves the Basin in a hotter and drier direction, the bison herd will need to be evacuated and relocated, and the entire ecoregion will be ecologically and culturally poorer with the loss.

All the While

Alyssa Quinn

There's blood. Blood in the sky at the set of the sun and blood gushing from the ruptured blister on his palm. All of it is red and all of it stings.

He throws his shovel from him and pulls a bandana from the pocket of his trousers. Binds the bleeding hand. The cloth is dirty and thin and the blood blooms through it faster than you'd think. No sign of stopping.

The setting sun's red reflection glares up from the lake and he goes dizzy with the light. This place. He was a fool to come. Should've gone to the Klondike like the rest. But he thought he'd be clever, thought that while the droves raced north he'd strike it here, on this lonesome little island which he could keep all to himself.

Or almost all to himself. There are a dozen or so of them there now, their meager camps scattered along the island's west side and each sluice box empty as the next. He set up at a weak little creek with barely enough flow to move the ore through the riffles. He'd maybe be more concerned about it if there were any signs gold was present to begin with. A whole year since that good nugget was found and now, after weeks of digging, not so much as a dust. He's tired and antsy and hasn't bathed in days—the saltwater unnerves him, the way it upends gravity and sets his cuts to sear.

He peels the bloodied bandana from his hand. The bleeding's slowed but the blister's flap has peeled entirely away and the skin below is a raw meat pink. Shoveling with that hand'll be hell.

He lets out a small yell and kicks at the dirt.

Leaving the sluice in the creek, leaving his shovel where it lies, he takes off down the hill. He's done for the day. Heads for his limp little tent, rummages around inside, comes out with a fifth of whisky, half full. Then sits down on a rock, grips the bottle's cork with his teeth, yanks it out, takes a good swig.

At the edge of lake and sky, the sun descends to meet its double.

These past days he's been thinking of the thickness of the earth. So easy to forget how much depth there is to the land when all you see is surface. Even for a prospector such as himself, who spends his days picking away at the layers, surprisingly easy to forget there's more there than what he's revealed. So much more. Miles and miles. And it angers him. Feels as though the earth is keeping its secrets from him out of spite. If only it'd open itself up for him, reveal its ribbons.

He gets up and heads south along the shore. The light's failing fast now, the last lip of sun slipped past the horizon. He walks and drinks and dreams of wealth. The sun sets and the moon rises, pulling with it tides across the earth. Every step the prospector takes he is pulled back down by the planet's mass, the core grasping after him like a spurned and yearning lover. He walks and drinks and gravity exerts its forces on him. The moon lifts high and tight as a fist, casts its light on the lake where the beams dissolve to a sheen. Elsewhere a coyote calls and a pronghorn lips some sage and all the while below his feet the miles of rock lie cold and dark. A riot of ripples and seams, igneous protrusions and pressed sediment, anonymous fossils which will never see the light. And the gems, the precious metals, the pools of crude, this shadow self of human capital, the underworld of commerce. There all the while.

A cool sets in and the dusk turns to dark. The drunker he gets the more gravity toys with him; he stumbles, he staggers. Then drops to the ground, lies supine and stares up at the stars. He feels his body sinking heavy into the earth, feels himself bound to it, even as up above the Milky Way glosses the contours of eternity. There is a paradox in his body, a simultaneous upward and downward pull. Perhaps that's all a body ever is.

He sleeps. Dew collects on the grass around him, a crab spider crawls up his leg. From the holster on his hip, his gun digs into him. He tosses and turns. Dreams of a river run over with gold.

He blinks awake. It's early, the sky just beginning to lighten. He can hear birds though he cannot see them. There is a morning mist on everything like a shroud.

He pushes up to his elbows, groggy and sick from the whiskey. He closes his eyes and breathes slow to settle himself, then rises heavily to his feet. The lake is still, the island is still, the stars are invisible once more. A few swallows of whiskey remain in the bottle. He takes them, then heads back the way he came.

He comes upon his camp. His tent's slouchy silhouette against the dawn, the firepit blacked with coal. He sighs and runs a hand through his hair. Down shore a bit, he can see his neighbor at his fire, a pot set to boil. He's leery of this neighbor, who's always up before the sun, whose coffee and sourdough and fried eggs often wake him with their scents. The man works past sunset, bathes daily in the lake, then sits and smokes his pipe with the satisfaction of someone who's done it—struck gold. More than once he's thought to ask him if it's true, if he has indeed found anything. But he can't bear the thought of admitting aloud that he has not.

He'd like some breakfast himself but can't summon the energy to fix it. With nothing else to do, he wanders up towards his claim. Follows the furrow that is his creek. Comes over a little hillock and then stops. Up ahead in the middle of the creek is his sluice box, where he left it. Only it's not a sluice box any longer. It's smashed up. Smithereens. The shards lie there, the creek too weak even to wash them away. He stares for a full beat. Feels drunk still, feels tired and hungry and achy and damp. And now—and now—

He approaches the box. Crouches down. Every piece of it's broken. He can make out hatchet marks in the grain.

He rises to his feet. He knows who did this.

Back down the hill. His walk is a lumbering one, a forward-slanted staggering one. Back down back down. The man's sitting at his fire still, straining his coffee through a cloth. He hardly has time to look up and see his attacker barreling down the hill before he's there, barging into camp, throwing his whiskey bottle to the ground, where it smashes, then smacking the mug from his neighbor's hand and delivering a sloppy punch to his jaw. The coffee slops over the man's front, scalding him through his flannel shirt. He yells and jumps to his feet. *What in god's name?* he cries, but there's no answer forthcoming, just another punch, this time to the gut. He staggers back from the blow but manages to duck another and return it with an uppercut. His attacker stumbles backward, trips over the rocks ringing the firepit, then falls on top of the shattered whiskey bottle, whose shards dig into his back. He cries out. His neighbor's coming at him again but not before his hand's at his hip and he's drawn his revolver and aimed it upward. His neighbor freezes over him. Come on now, he says in a forced calm. *What's all this about, huh?* The man on the ground breathes heavy. You goddamn know what it's about. He cocks the revolver. *No sir, I'm afraid I do not. Maybe you'd be so obliging as to explain it to me.* The man on the ground laughs. *Jesus Christ you're smug. Even when you've got a goddamned gun at your chest. I knew it. I knew it all along.* His neighbor has a handsome, cleanshaven face. Too smooth for a man of their profession. The eyes too soft. He gets a new inkling about him now, a new suspicion. It fits. He always knew something was off about the man. *You can't even deal with a little competition. Got to go smash up my goddamn sluice box!* He brandishes the gun. *Sir, says the man above him, still in that careful calm. I swear I don't know what happened to your sluice box, but I can promise you I ain't been anywhere close to it.* The man on the ground laughs again.

It's then it happens. In the second before the man on the ground can squeeze the trigger, his neighbor has whipped his own gun out from its hiding spot at the back of his pants and, in one swift motion, raised it and fired. The shot socks straight between the eyes. The man on the ground goes instantly limp, gun falling from his hand, arms falling to the ground, head falling back on his neck, the thoughts falling fast through his brain. There's a gold light above him which might be the sun and a dark shape across it which might be a bird or a cloud or his own dying sight. And then even that is falling, falling forever as everything does, tumbling unending into gravity's arms.

來/Journey

Paisley Rekdal

Robert Smithson on AJ Russell's photo, "East and West Shaking Hands at Laying Of Last Rail"

This excessiveness of men
spilling, crowding
to mark their X of time

and money, I find
lamentable—their little moment
composed of paper

and light: alienated
spike, relic
in the hands of those willing

themselves be relics, too. Nothing
so linear as human
ego and desire, while the past

turns and returns, spirals
like these pelicans journeying
over the red

waters off Rozel, streams
of purple; yucca rimed
with pustules of dust.

Each one lifts, rises: finds

what only some part
of the cells remembers, nests

in the wreck
of what we've left, this bulk
of ruined train, its wheel wells turned

the rust
of flaking blood. Of course
they trekked the human

bodies from the crash
back out. We care
for our own. We care

nothing for our own,
making our lives material so as
to free us all better

to forget. Who remembers the names
behind those grasping
fingers in the photo?

Who recalls the dead
the UP ferried from its crash?
The metals they left not

as memorial to them, but because
it cost less
to leave the evidence

than drag it all back out.

Healing Generational Trauma for a Thriving Great Salt Lake

Darren Parry, as told to Brooke Larsen

In 1964, my family moved to Syracuse, right on the banks of Great Salt Lake. I was four years old then, and the causeway to get to Antelope Island was about a mile from my house. My grandmother would take me to Antelope Island, the Bear River Migratory Bird Refuge, and the marshes over in West Kaysville to collect duck eggs. Of course, we could go to the store and buy eggs, but my grandmother told me that it was important to learn about my culture through foraging. We harvested out of respect for our people. My grandmother told me about the importance of the lake; she said that there is healing in the water; she showed me how she used lakeside plants as food or medicine.

My relationship with Great Salt Lake and Antelope Island were always different from my non-Indigenous friends' relationships with these places. When I became a teenager, Great Salt Lake was the perfect slough spot for Sunday school. We'd ride our motorcycles out there, and hike around the island. My friends were apprehensive about Great Salt Lake though. They'd say "it smells" or, "there are too many bugs," and I think for a lot of Utahns that is the perception of the lake. If the lake is stinky and buggy, why would you want to go to it? Why would you care to save it?

I never thought about the lake like that though. For my people, the environment was a grocery store, it was a pharmacy, and it was home to our non-human kinfolk, as my grandmother always called the plants and animals. For me, Great Salt Lake is a sacred place. It is a place that our people have lived with forever: Our creation story began at Antelope Island. That was the center of our universe. Great Salt Lake, and the non-human kinfolk that inhabit it are our kin. Kinship has always meant one thing to me: relative. Think about how you treat your human relatives. You might have a mean cousin that you treat differently, but when I think about a relative or kin, it always fosters good feelings. My kin share my values; they have my best interests at heart. Growing up, I knew only one definition of kin. So when my grandma talked about our plants as kin, and the water as kin, and animals as kin, that told me that my relationship needed to be different than settler attitudes towards those beings.

Today, you turn on the news and you see how we don't treat non-human kinfolk like we treat a close human relative that we love. We treat them with indifference, we extract from them, we deplete them. We think about them as a commodity to be bought and sold, something we can make money from. I have never thought of a relative in those terms. I remember my grandmother picking choke cherries so carefully so as to not harm a single leaf on the cherry tree. She would carefully move a leaf out of the way and pick a strand of berries, and then leave a bunch, and then pick some more. Knowing that she treated those leaves just like she would treat her relatives taught me what kinship meant. If we treated our environment and non-human kinfolk the way we treat our human relatives, Great Salt Lake wouldn't need saving in the first place.

This kind of kinship reminds me a lot of the kind of work that we are doing to steward the land at the Bear River Massacre Site. The Northwestern Band of the Shoshone is one of the few Native American tribes in the US that doesn't have a reservation, but our identity is tied to the land. We learn who we are from the land. It has been so hugely important to us to steward the land where the Bear River Massacre happened. In 2002, when my dad was the tribal chairman, a foundation in New York bought twenty-five acres of the massacre site which they donated to the tribe. It was the first time in forever that our tribe had owned anything. When we got that land back, I remember the sense of pride that accompanied finally having stewardship over this land again, to have a place that we could call home. When I became the chairman, the next step was so clear to me: We had to raise enough money to get all of it back. Our tribe has some businesses, so we were able to put 2 million dollars towards purchasing the land.

My grandmother was always telling the story of our people, but she would tell me that the story of the land was equally important. The day after we purchased the land, I went to Utah State University and spoke with two professors in the department of natural resources. I told them I wanted to return the land to what it looked like in 1863 using my grandmother's plant diary. We went up to the site together, and, after looking at everything, they said it was absolutely possible. They said some of the native species might struggle because of climate change, but they had scientific models that could inform restoration efforts.

Since that initial meeting, we've been removing invasive plants and planting native plants. We've also been cleaning up watersheds. There's a major tributary that came out of the mountain and ran through the property that we call Beaver Creek. The pioneers changed it to Battle Creek and then they moved it into a ditch down the side of the road to use for irrigation. We now own senior rights on the Bear River, and we're using those water rights to restore Beaver Creek. We've laid the groundwork with farmers to get permission to create riparian buffer zones and reintroduce beavers into that ecosystem. We're collaborating with different groups, including Bio-West, and Sageland Collaborative. We're cleaning up the watershed to reintroduce Bonneville cutthroat trout with our partners Trout Unlimited and US Fish and Wildlife. We're planting 250,000 cottonwoods and willows. We've removed more than half a million Russian olives. The land is transforming right in front of our eyes.

■ ■ ■

Our stewardship of the Bear River Massacre site will have a long-lasting impact on Great Salt Lake. We're putting way more clean water into the system. We're putting our water rights back into Beaver Creek which will empty into the Bear River. The scientists at Utah State University have told us that one Russian olive plant drinks between fifty and seventy gallons of water per day. As we remove half a million Russian olives, we're saving a lot of water. Millions of gallons of water should make it downstream to the lake, but a farmer told me that that water won't make it to the lake because landowners downstream will use it. If we don't change how we govern water and use water, it may not matter what we do upstream. That's a huge focus for me now: I want to make sure that water we conserve upstream makes it to Great Salt Lake and isn't siphoned away. Even though we didn't start this project to save Great Salt Lake, our stewardship and restoration efforts should have a huge impact on the lake which highlights who we are as a people.

I see this restoration as a way to heal not only Great Salt Lake, but also our people from intergenerational trauma. My grandmother and other elders endured traumas from boarding schools, which continues to follow us. The only way you can really get past it is to talk about it—to use stories and culture to heal. As our stories are accepted by a wider audience, healing finally starts to take place. When our Native kids see that people are recognizing these imbalances that have been here since colonization and are ongoing, that brings healing. I think the same is true for the lake. You can't solve a problem until you acknowledge that there's a problem and are willing to take responsibility for it. Your relatives may have been part of the problem, so you have a responsibility in highlighting what happened, and then asking: What can we do to solve it together? We're finally recognizing that this trauma has happened to our non-human kinfolk. We're recognizing our role in that history. And by recognizing it, we can start seeing the error of our ways and make decisions that start repair.

Of course, the descendants of Mormon settlers have to acknowledge this history and take steps towards repair. That's the monkey in the room. I think everybody has to play a role. I live in an area in Cache Valley where most of my neighbors can say their great-great-grandparents settled in 1860, three years before the massacre, and that they've been there since. I look at them when they celebrate Pioneer Day on the 24th of July, and I hear what comes out of their mouths about how their families colonized the area. It is so hard for me to listen on those days. I just want to hear somebody say, "What our relatives did came at a huge cost to people that were already living here." I understand that history can't be changed, but it makes a huge difference to have some recognition and say, "I'm sorry for what my relatives have done." People will say, "Well, it was the Wild Wild West," But that doesn't mean there weren't people who knew better. So, can you apologize for your ancestors? Absolutely. I think it would go a long way towards healing generations of people have never heard an apology before.

The Church of Jesus Christ of Latter-Day Saints isn't what it was in 1847: Today, it is a multibillion-dollar deal run by attorneys. I don't know if they're capable of making statements of apology. I don't think they feel an obligation to apologize, even though they bear the biggest responsibility. Once, I sat in the Church's Presiding Bishop's office and talked about the Bear River Massacre. I could tell that he was getting angry with me; he eventually stopped me and said, "We didn't kill anybody."

I replied, "Well, on January 29, 1863, you may not have killed anybody. But you being in the Cache Valley, you coming to the Great Salt Lake area, that's what caused the massacre. Whether you fired a bullet or not, you're the cause." The Church could go a long, long way to heal a lot of traumas by apologizing. I think people want to see the Church apologize when they make mistakes, but I never hold my breath for that. Institutionally, they've made it a policy to not apologize, and that's sad to me because I grew up in their religion. I was taught by the Church that when I make a mistake, I repent, and I say, "I'm sorry." I follow this process because that is part of the doctrine, and the fact that the leaders can't do it themselves is a huge problem.

▪ ▪ ▪

I am a sixth generation Shoshone Mormon; I was born and raised in the Church; I served a mission to England; I've been immersed in the Church for a long, long time. It's complicated for sure, but I'll tell you why it's easy for me to stay when the histories, legacies, and present realities of the Church say I shouldn't. One of the reasons I can stay is because I've always believed in the ideal of Christ. When he came to the Earth, he came to the marginalized. He came for those people that have never had a voice. I've always tried to advocate for that too. I want to be an advocate within the Church for people who decide to stay and don't have as much of a voice. What Christ taught is such a simple concept and it tells me how to live in this world and be kind. That's one of the biggest reasons I stay. I'm hyper aware that the Church is run by people that I don't necessarily agree with most of the time, but I'm okay with that.

I can get more done the more I am immersed in the legislature if I'm not confrontational with the Church. Some will say I'm selling out. I just look at it as I want to get things done. If you want to get things done in this state, you must have a decent relationship with these people. Plus, my personality is such that I always want to find common ground. I have been able to navigate things better by having a relationship with my enemies; it allows me to get in doors that, frankly, a lot of my friends never enter. If I can get in that door, I feel like I have a shot. Brigham Young loved my third great-grandfather Chief Washakie because of his ability to get along and make it work, even though Washakie on many days was probably just cussing the process. There's something to be said for being able to sit down with your adversary and having a conversation—that's what it takes to navigate this world.

I have to be immersed in as many communities as possible because it is going to take all of us to solve Great Salt Lake's problems. I have been advocating for a Native American voice to be present in all of these governing institutions that the Governor and the legislature are putting together. Someone asked me, "What if they give you a seat at the table? What are you going to do? They're going to expect you to say something profound and have an answer that'll save it." But that's not the case. All I can do is share stories. Storytelling changes people's minds and it changes values because you're hearing it with your heart and not your mind. From there, you can actually make a change. That's what I have to offer. We need to infuse ethics of care with scientific knowledge. Is that an easy solution? No, it's not. However, it is easy to look at the ethics of care that have been infused in our worldviews all along.

I am always blown away when people want to know the Indigenous perspective. Growing up, my grandmother told me all the time that no one has ever wanted to hear our story. The only people that would ever listen to her were graduate students or professors doing work on her subject matter. The public didn't want to know; they were mean about it. She didn't have an avenue to tell our people's stories. The fact that I do have an audience tells me that our society is in a different place. Marginalized voices in our communities are finally starting to be heard.

As a storyteller, I've always felt a huge responsibility to deliver every time. Seeing how many groups are engaged in the fight brings me a lot of hope. The fact that they want to listen to a tired old Indian tell a story or two. . . that brings me hope. I always hope I'm able to do so much more.

Covered in Feathers

Sarah May

Dear Sarita,

Our stories are our bodies
Our bodies are our legacy

I see you
I see you in all of the moments
you sat at my shores
I cradle and hold within me
your words
your tears
your rituals
they are a part of my story
I love them dearly as I love you
you and I are the blood
of the same life force
existing
in the sacred space
between the earth and the sky
you know me and see me
as I know and feel you
you hold and listen
and create for me
and the lifeforms
that are fed by my shores

I want you to tell the world about me
to address the world as you address me
with the same reverence and adoration
I know you are afraid they will not see you
but trust that the right people will hear you
will find and hold you
they will hold us
they will hold our stories
there are those who need to hear your words
who need to feel they are not alone
I ask you because I know who you are
I know the power your creations hold
It is time to manifest the stars you embody

Knowing is to grieve
but grieving is to love
love is vulnerability
and bravery
love is facing all the parts of ourselves
light and shadow
seeing all of it and choosing love
over and over again
witnessing the complex layers
the ebb and flow
allowing ourselves to exist
with flow and reciprocity
sovereign entities
choosing to live in the deep intimacy
of being completely present

We hold the beginning together
our time endless
the forms that hold us
cycling continually

to that next place
souls parallel
to the songs of vulnerability and strength
voices hum together
letting go all we carry

Our stories are our bodies
Our bodies are our legacy

Stolen Time: Prisons, Profits, and Pollutability

Madi Sudweeks

I grew up in a picture-perfect suburb of Salt Lake City, Utah. Nestled into the southeast corner of the Salt Lake Valley, the city of Draper was reminiscent of many suburbs in the West. It was spacious, full of single-family houses with big backyards. It was also very white, wealthy, and extremely segregated. However, two things always seemed out of place in the image of a picture-perfect white suburban town. While driving north on I-15, the freeway curves around the Point of the Mountain. Here, you are welcomed into Draper by two massive developments. The first is the Geneva Rock quarry. The open-air mineral mine is enormous. Over my lifetime, it has quite literally relocated the point of the mountain as more and more of it is excavated away. The Point of the Mountain, which was created and has stood on geologic timescales, has been eaten away in the span of a few decades. This image acts as an omnipresent reminder of stolen time. On the other side of the freeway, another institution worked to steal time from bodies and left long-lasting scars; it just does so less visibly, behind barbed wire fences and ten-foot walls. This was the home of the Utah State Prison for over seventy years.

I grew up in Draper so the Utah State Prison was impossible to ignore. The prison did not fit the picture-perfect suburban lifestyle our community worked so hard to portray, especially in a town that prided itself on being "safe" and well-to-do (all the ensuing racial coding included). I cannot remember adults ever discussing or even acknowledging the reality of the prison's existence, despite growing up right next to it. The taboo only made it more intriguing for us as kids. I remember kids sharing scary stories about escaped prisoners who stole away children. I feel uneasy reflecting on these tall tales, especially as I have learned more about the prison-industrial complex. The stories we told underscore just how much the physical presence loomed in the shadows of our consciousness despite my community's attempts to ignore its existence.

History of the Move

In 2005, Governor Jon Huntsman and the Utah state legislature began an inquiry into moving the prison. By then, Draper was changing from a rural farm town to an up-and-coming suburb. This meant that the land, seen as "suitable" for a prison in 1937 because it was isolated farmland, had skyrocketed in value. In a system where land is the finite and foundational source upon which wealth can be extracted, the profit to be made from the sale of the land became the state and community's primary area of focus. I remember many discussions we had at home about moving the prison. My dad worked in construction and small-scale land development. So, like many, my dad's main concern about the prison's move was not based upon questions of the facility's safety but rather the value that property would have someday when the prison was moved. Likewise, residents at city council and other public meetings in Draper argued over the value of the land and said nothing of the value of the lives of the people living there.

The prison and the land it occupied, once seen as only suitable to house those deemed "unfit" for society, suddenly had a huge potential for development. This appealed to a state legislature made up of land developers and construction tycoons, and a community that was more than happy to get rid of the institution they had been working hard to ignore for years. The idea of moving the prison and making the land it occupied free for development became a primary driver in the push for relocation.

In 2014, the Utah State Legislature passed H.C.R. 8, Concurrent Resolution Regarding Moving the State Prison which declared that "the Utah State Prison facilities currently located in Draper should be relocated from that site to one or more other suitable locations in the state." This resolution also enacted S.B. 268 "Prison Relocation Commission," an appointed body of state legislators and leaders of the Utah Department of Corrections and the Commission on Criminal and Juvenile Justice, to work to "choose the site for the construction of new prison facilities."[1] In their 2015 final report, the Prison Relocation Commission unanimously recommended the new Utah State Correctional Facility site.[2] The state would build the new prison nine miles west of the Salt Lake City International Airport. This would relocate the prison from a residential area to a wetland area, ecologically sensitive and surrounded sources of industrial and "natural" pollutants.

Developing the Wetlands

Construction on the new Utah State Correctional Facility began in 2016. After six years and over one billion dollars, the 3,600-bed facility opened in July 2022[3]. People from across the political spectrum celebrated the development and improvements of the new prison facility. Republican Governor Spencer Cox lauded the development and opening of a "state-of-the-art corrections facility." After all the cards had fallen and the new prison opened, its one-billion-dollar price tag ended up

1 Stevenson et al., "Final Report of the Prison Relocation Commission: Improving Our Criminal Justice System by Building a Leading-Edge Correctional Facility."

2 Stevenson et al.

3 Miller, "Six Years and over $1B Later, the New Utah Prison Is Ready to Open."

being almost twice the initial cost estimate. This was primarily because of the soil conditions at the site.[4] The soil of the brackish wetland ecosystem near the south side of Great Salt Lake is soft and holds a lot of water. This was not a surprise to the state. The Prison Relocation Commission's reports detail the many geotechnical and environmental considerations for construction including the need for intensive and time-consuming soil mitigation, deep foundation systems, and the risk of liquefication.

To develop the 1.3 million square footprint of USCF in the remote area, state and Salt Lake City governments spent over $90 million to build seven miles of roads and thirteen miles of utility lines.[5] The challenge of developing on the shores of Great Salt Lake significantly increased the costs of construction. It also restructured the material conditions of the land. State officials claimed that although they knew the soil would be challenging to build on, it was even more corrosive than expected which required deeper foundations and increased costs. The state also attributed the overblown price tag to the impacts of the COVID-19 pandemic, a 5.9 earthquake that hit the area in 2020, and tariffs.[6]

The Prison Relocation Commission also clearly recognized that the proposed WSCF site was part of a wetland area and an ecologically sensitive habitat.[7] Conservationists and environmentalists flagged this because of the potentially devastating impacts of prison construction on the environment and the habitat of millions of migratory and local birds. Advocates from the Audubon Society and others protested the construction, particularly the risks of the large-scale pest mitigation projects like the draining of wetland areas and the mass-spraying

4 Miller

5 McKellar, "5 Things You Need to Know about the New Utah State Prison."

6 Woodruff, "Utah's New Prison Opens with Much Higher Price Tag than Expected."

7 Stevenson et al., "Final Report of the Prison Relocation Commission: Improving Our Criminal Justice System by Building a Leading-Edge Correctional Facility."

of pesticides that would be necessary to minimize the impacts of mosquitoes on incarcerated people, employees, and visitors. Although officials from the Salt Lake City Mosquito Abatement District and Utah Waterfowl Association warned about the obvious fact that mosquitos would be a major issue in a wetland area, the state of Utah did not heed these warnings. Advocates also pointed to how this project would further damage habitat, which was already in decline because of human intervention, and further endanger millions of migratory birds.

Wastelanding

The prison-industrial complex functions and maintains its existence by labeling people "bad" or "disposable" and erasing them from public society.[8] Many scholars and advocates of abolition have shown how prisons make people disposable. The state of Utah decided to move the prison from a highly visible and "desirable" area to one that is more easily ignored and deemed less "valuable." In this way, the incarcerated people at the prison become ever more erasable, even more disposable, via a process that author Traci Brynne Voyles has termed "wastelanding." It is a process that "render(s) an environment and the bodies that inhabit it pollutable."[9] By moving the prison to an area that was already deemed less desirable, the outskirts of the west side Salt Lake City near the wetlands of Great Salt Lake, the state enabled the further pollution of the site and, critically, the people who live there. Incarcerated people at USCF are exposed to a myriad of environmental justice issues, even beyond those commonly associated with incarceration.

On August 29, 2023, local media broke the news that mosquitoes at USCF had tested positive for West Nile virus. [10]

8 Pellow, "Toward a Critical Environmental Justice Studies."

9 Voyles, Wastelanding: Legacies of Uranium Mining in Navajo Country.

10 Harkins, "West Nile Virus Found at Utah State Prison Built on Prime Mosquito Habitat."

Carried by mosquitoes, the virus can cause lifelong disease in humans and other animals. Infected people can develop symptoms including headache, body aches, joint pains, vomiting, diarrhea, or rash.[11] A small percentage of people infected develop serious neurologic illness that leads to spinal cord and/or brain inflammation, which can be life-threatening. Although no cases of West Nile virus have been reported at the prison, the headlines point to a larger, underlying issue of the prison's location. Before the state moved over 2,400 people into the area, it had been the home of many non-human inhabitants, including mosquitoes. The ecologically sensitive wetlands near Great Salt Lake are prime mosquito habitats. The Prison Relocation Commission and state knew and accepted that incarcerated people at UCSF would be eaten alive by mosquitoes. They made the choice to not only place the prison in this location but also failed to protect the people who would be incarcerated there from the mosquitoes. For the first year that USCF was open, they failed to provide incarcerated people with resources or repellant to protect themselves from mosquitos.[12]

The failure to consider the wellbeing and lives of those who would be incarcerated at the facility reveals how systems of incarceration make people and environments disposable on all levels, even at the scale of a mosquito. The state even used conservation advocates as scapegoats for their own shameful inaction—blaming environmentalists' protests against widespread spraying of pesticides for the harm mosquitos inflicted on the incarcerated population. When groups like the Utah Physicians for a Healthy Environment raised concerns about the potential impacts of aerial pesticide spraying on nearby communities, the state used this genuine concern as justification for their inability to take any sort of action, and the incarcerated people at USCF bore the brunt,[13]

11 Harkins.

12 Harkins, "Inmates 'Getting Eaten Alive' by Insects at New Utah Prison. Officials Knew It Could Happen, Records Show."

13 Harkins, "Location of New State Prison Pits Safety of Inmates against the Future of Great Salt Lake Wildlife."

emphasizing how systems of power pit environmental issues against other social justice issues to discourage solidarity and maintain the status quo.

The Utah State Correctional Facility is located close to many polluted areas. The Prison Relocation Commission's final report reveals that the area "borders a former landfill (conditions unknown) and is associated with past military activities."[14] Although each of the sites studied as potential locations had their own environmental, cultural, and sociological factors, the I-80 site is described as the "most complex [to implement] relative to alternative locations."[15] The bureaucratic language obscures what goes unsaid here. The area is not a good site for development of what is in practicality, a massive residential facility.

Incarcerated people across the country face unique and heightened levels of environmental injustice and are subjected to disproportionate levels of environmental risks.[16] Activists and scholars, both inside and outside of prisons and jails, have shown how environmental injustice and the prison-industrial complex are interconnected forms of state-sanctioned violence.[17] Inside prisons, people are exposed to dangerous environmental conditions like heat waves, toxic materials, and disease. In the case of those incarcerated at the new Utah State Correctional Facility, it is important to understand how the environmental injustices that incarcerated people face compound with the unique environmental conditions and injustices of the northwest quadrant of Salt Lake City. West Salt Lake City is made up of six neighborhoods that were historically redlined and are predominantly working-class, Black, and brown. These neighborhoods are disproportionately impacted by environmental injustices, especially poor air quality. Now, with the relocation of USCF to

14 Stevenson et al., "Utah Prison Relocation Commission: Final Report on the Draper Prison Relocation."

15 Stevenson et al.

16 Landrigan, Rauh, and Galvez, "Environmental Justice and the Health of Children."

17 Pellow, "Struggles for Environmental Justice in US Prisons and Jails."

this area, the reality of the environmental issues faced by those living on the west side are combined with the foundational concerns of incarceration to create compounding injustices.

In 2022-2023, the EPA funded the completion of an environmental justice assessment. The assessment included the six west side neighborhoods in Salt Lake, including the Westpointe neighborhood where USCF is now located. The results of this assessment were damning and confirmed what community members had known for a long time. The assessment showed neighborhoods on the west side of Salt Lake City "have higher instances of pollution and associated health risks and socioeconomic risk factors that exacerbate them."[18] In almost every measure, including asthma burden, cancer risk, and life expectancy, west side residents fared worse than people living on the East side. West side residents also experience higher rates of PM 2.5 (a measure of potential exposure to inhalable particles that are 2.5 micrometers or smaller), ozone, and other harmful pollutants. Salt Lake City's east and west sides are delineated by Interstate 15, which separates historically redlined neighborhoods in the west from wealthier, white neighborhoods in the east.

The people who are incarcerated at USCF live near multiple significant sources of pollution and industrial waste. The west side of Salt Lake City is disproportionately exposed to emissions from multiple oil refineries, the industrial and manufacturing center of the metropolitan area, and the Magcorp Magnesium Chloride Plant. The prison itself is located near the Kennecott Garfield Smelter, Interstate 80, and the Salt Lake City airport. The presence of the airport so near to the prison is especially concerning because it is just nine miles east of the USCF site. Salt Lake City International Airport is undergoing an expansion that will be completed in 2027. Although the expansion includes sustainability goals intended to "reduce criteria air pol-

18 Technical Assistance Services for Communities, "Westside Neighborhoods - Environmental Justice and Air Quality Assessment."

lutants and greenhouse gas emissions to improve public health and reduce environmental impact," the impact of airport emissions and pollution cannot be understated.[19] Incarcerated people at USCF live in direct proximity to these contaminants 24/7 and are unable to escape them.

USCF also lies in the area that is slated to be part of the planned Inland Port in the northwest quadrant of Salt Lake City. While the Utah Inland Port Authority (UIPA), a state corporation, was created in 2018 to lead the process of implementing the northwest quadrant project, its quasi-governmental reach has expanded as it has begun to act "as a development agency of sorts, helping smaller cities and counties develop manufacturing zones along with infrastructure like rail, roads, and utilities."[20] Many of the UIPA's projects, including the northwest quadrant port where USCF is located, are planned for development in critical wetland areas. In a profit-driven system that values land only on its potential profit-making capabilities, wetland areas are only valuable for their future potential profit-making abilities.

Critics of the inland port, including the Stop the Polluting Ports Coalition, state that the so-called environmental outcomes of the UIPA will include drained wetlands and destroyed vital habitat, increased water, light and noise pollution, and disastrous impacts on already precarious air quality.[21] Meanwhile, the predominantly BIPOC, working class, and disproportionately incarcerated people on the west side are the ones who will bear the brunt of the impacts of the Inland Port and they are unlikely to receive much, if any, of the wealth generated from these projects.

Another key concern directly relevant to the lives of those incarcerated at USCF is the looming disaster of the drying Great Salt Lake and the increasing exposure of the lake bed's toxic minerals to open air. As a terminal and saline body of wa-

19 Technical Assistance Services for Communities.

20 Larsen, "'It Seems They're on Hyperdrive' — at Least 9 Utah Communities Have Opened the Door to Inland Port Projects."

21 Stop the Polluting Port Community Coalition, "Stop the Polluting Port."

ter, minerals have accumulated in Great Salt Lake lakebed for millennia.[22] Although the impacts of the toxic dust will affect the entire Salt Lake area, the exposure will be highest for those near the lakebeds. USCF's proximity to Great Salt Lake poses a massive threat to the health of the people who live there: incarcerated people.

This risk of future exposure appears particularly insidious when the same state officials who moved them to this area without their consent are also failing to address the water diversion issue or protect the lake through meaningful legislative action. The state legislature continues to fail to pass meaningful, adequate legislation to save Great Salt Lake. The 2024 legislative session continued to show that the same lack of systemic, large-scale, meaningful action necessary to ensure Great Salt Lake remains at safe levels. This failure to act will continue to have real, harmful and even potentially deadly consequences for the incarcerated people the state is responsible to care for.

Abolition

Environmental factors were not the sole consideration in the siting of the new prison. Other primary factors that the Prison Relocation Commission listed for selecting the USCF site were the ease of access for employees, volunteers, families, and proximity to medical and legal resources for incarcerated prisoners.[23] These foundational rights, access to medical care, legal services, and loved ones are critically important for incarcerated people to live safe, dignified, and just lives. The state claimed that in these areas, the I-80 location was the best option out of those presented. This may seem to present a situation where human rights subsumed environmental and environmental justice concerns. How-

22 Antelope Island State Park, "Great Salt Lake."

23 Stevenson et al., "Final Report of the Prison Relocation Commission: Improving Our Criminal Justice System by Building a Leading-Edge Correctional Facility."

ever, this is not the case. The problem in this situation was not the challenge of balancing environmental and human interests—this is a false binary. People should always have access to loved ones, medical care, legal support, AND safe, just, and protected environments. The reason why these basic rights are put into conflict is not because of the prison's location, but its fundamental existence. A system centered on punishment and enforcement rather than transformation and healing destroys the lives and bodies of humans and ecologies. It is incompatible with environmental justice. Our future must be an abolitionist one to bring true environmental and social justice to our communities.

The one-billion-dollar prison complex is referred to in all official references as a "correctional facility." This euphemistic language covers over what is, in fact, a prison—a place where people are incarcerated—taken out of public view and public consciousness. Deemed incompatible with public life, prisons work to erase people, their lives, and the parts of our society we fail to come to terms with.[24] A prison is still a prison; no matter how "state-of-the-art" it claims to be, it exists to put people in cages for the purpose of punishment, not accountability. Prisons foundationally devalue the lives of those living in them and make them disposable and pollutable. They also harm the spaces and ecologies they occupy through contamination and destructive development.[25]

Abolition is a "political vision with the goal of eliminating imprisonment, policing, and surveillance."[26] Abolition is also a generative strategy. It urges us to work toward the creation of "lasting alternatives to punishment and imprisonment" focused on community care, love, accountability, and support.[27] Critical Resistance, a national grassroots organization leading the work on prison-industrial complex abolition and started by re-

24 Gilmore, Bhandar, and Toscano, *Abolition Geography*.

25 Pellow, "Struggles for Environmental Justice in US Prisons and Jails."

26 Critical Resistance, "What Is the PIC?"

27 Critical Resistance.

nowned abolitionist scholar Ruth Wilson Gilmore, talks about abolition as a practical organizing tool and a long-term vision. They posit that abolition is not only an end goal but a way of living to create the vision of the world we want to see in our everyday lives.[28] Critically, an abolitionist lens does not discount or diminish the severity of the violence that occurs daily in the carceral system and the need for harm reduction. Acknowledging this reality pushes abolitionists to fight for an end to prisons and reject actions that further strengthen the prison-industrial complex, even some types of reforms.

An abolitionist framework allows us to imagine a future that is not constrained by our current reality. Instead of thinking about constructing "nicer" prisons with billions of taxpayer dollars that put the health of our ecosystems and people in danger, it allows us to think about what would actually keep our communities safe and address harm. An abolitionist framework does not pit environmental concerns about the health of the wetlands and its bird populations against the dignity of the lives of those incarcerated. Instead, it helps us see how those lives are inextricable from each other. Abolition challenges the idea that anyone, human or beyond, is disposable.

---

28 Critical Resistance.

Our Lady of Great Salt Lake

Dayna Patterson

"Great Salt Lake is a holy being."
—Malcolm Lehi

the lake is a mother who won't say no
a vessel veined — woven — webbed with blue thread
she unravels till she's a barren bowl

she knows the names of all the birds who home
to her shores — cinnamon teal — avocet
phalarope — pelican — she won't say no

unspooling skein from sky — pooling creek flow
into the refuge of her turquoise bed —
we shallow her blue till barren — her bowl —

saline shroud — dust nimbus — brine fly halo
see her ghosting islands — her spiral tread
the lake is a mother who won't say no

except in arsenic sky — in dwindling snow
in mercury lung — in silent spring — dread
is our garment — how to mend her parched bowl

for her — for the birds — we'll learn to say no
feed her streams — swell her seams — a watershed

gathered to her mending — our mother — we know
she aches to brim — unbrine — to stitch herself whole

her devotion — old pattern — a giving bowl

The Once and Future Lake

Sylvia Torti

Before my son was born, I went often to Great Salt Lake, always to Antelope Island. I'd drive out in the morning, stop along the causeway, and spend a half hour or so seeing who was on the water. Wilson's phalarope, eared grebes, American avocets, black-necked stilts. Then I'd drive onto the island, past the sailboats swaying in the marina, up the curving road and down the back side. In the spring I kept the windows down and listened to western meadowlarks belting out their flutelike songs. Usually, I would spot two or three burrowing owls standing atop their ground nests. At the northwestern side of the island, I'd park and hike out to White Rock Bay where I'd sit on the rocks and eat a sandwich. Looking out at the whitish water and the blue-blue sky, I felt I was on another planet, and I loved that feeling of adventure and weirdness. I did this for many years and then I stopped.

When my son was ten years old, I met Jeff, and he taught me how to raise a boy. How does one do such a thing, I wondered, as raise a son? There's no guidebook. Your parents can't teach you, especially mine, who had three daughters, and everything is changing all the time: you, the child, the world. Jeff knew. In an early conversation, when I expressed my worries, he told me, you just need to stay in the room. Jeff was like that; he made everything sound easy. Jeff is no longer above ground, as he would say, but lately I've been thinking about him, my son, and the lake. Great Salt Lake is shrinking. The son has become a man. The man is dead. Their paths crossing—one living forward, the other backward.

It's called shifting baselines. There is a documentary film about it with regard to climate change, how we, in our generation don't feel loss because we don't know what existed before, and how, in turn, our children can't feel the loss of space or species because they know no difference. A gradual change in the accepted norms for the condition of the natural environment due to a lack of experience, memory and/or knowledge of its past condition. In this sense, what we consider to be a healthy environment now, past generations would consider to be degraded, and what we judge to be degraded now, the next generation will consider to be healthy or normal. According to this academic psychological research, we're doomed.

Jeff had cancer for our entire friendship, for the whole time my son knew him. At first, he didn't talk about it much. He acted so normal it was hard to believe he was sick. He was plump and energetic; he complained about water weight and sweats and joked he was suffering menopause. We laughed and talked often about writing and teaching, but also about my dysfunctional marriage, the desired divorce, fears of how it would affect my son. He invited my son to participate in a yearlong documentary filmmaking course that brought together college students and community members with no formal education. For seven years my son spent every Monday evening with Jeff, and helped to make films about tattoo culture, child prostitution, immigration, meth addiction, and climate change. He learned storytelling, camera work, lighting and editing. He met people from all walks of life. He was often exasperated by Jeff, telling me, "Mom, I ask him questions about what we should do, and his answer is I don't know, what do you think?" Classic Jeff. Empowering the young to figure it out for themselves.

I had always wanted to climb Frary Peak on Antelope Island, and once during the years I was still married and my son was at camp, I convinced my husband to go out with me. I was excited, sure that we'd find the elusive bighorn sheep, and I wanted to see the city from that vantage point. We began to climb, but he got dizzy almost immediately, a newly revealed vertigo. We aborted the effort and drove home. That baseline had shifted irreversibly, but I struggled to accept it.

Years later, I was leaving the university and ran into Jeff as he was going to a student presentation. He pulled me in as well. You've got to be here. It was about gender fluidity, which had just started to be talked about on campus. These kids are teaching me, he said. I have no idea about any of this; all I can do is ask questions and listen. We listened together and then went for an epic dinner. I remember that I told him about what I was missing—a real relationship, time to write, and then I said, "You know, I used to go out to Great Salt Lake all the time and I haven't been there in years." He didn't ask me to do deep introspection into why I hadn't gone, he just said. Go. Take your son. It was like the stay in the room advice. Annoyingly simple. Doable. A mandate.

My son and I drove out to Great Salt Lake. The water was shockingly low, so different from how I remembered it. As we neared Antelope Island, I saw a coyote trotting along the lakebed where years ago there would have been water. The marina was dried up, and all but a couple of decrepit boats were gone. We parked and walked down to the crusty salty edge where the colors were blue and pink and gray and purple. The white soapy water looked like floating clouds. Dead flies and brine shrimp shells had built up into raised circles two feet in diameter in the ground. I scanned the distant water for birds but saw few. My son took close-up photographs of the shoreline and some of the horizon. I took a picture of him squatted down making a video. We agreed we'd return to this spot, to spend more days at the lake.

The years continued. I got the divorce. My son moved through high school as well, I suppose, as any young man can. He continued going to the film class and convinced Jeff to teach him how to cook. There were dinners and shared writing and laughter, events to which my son and I went to celebrate Jeff and his life, his vision, his spirit, his generosity. In time, Jeff began to wither in body. His skin turned crusty, and he called himself a trout, writing a children's book about the man who turned into a trout. He lost his voice at times, but never his spirit. My son and I, as far as I can remember, didn't go back to Great Salt Lake.

In my son's senior year, I had a work conflict and couldn't make it to the documentary film showing. Jeff wrote me the next day. You would have been touched because your son asked if he could make a short speech and it was beautiful. He spoke about you and how, when you suggested joining the class, he wasn't certain he wanted to because the idea came from his mother. (The crowd busted up). And added that "my mom was absolutely right." He went on to talk about how the program has become part of his life. He said he would carry this experience with him to college and wherever he goes after that. Really touching and he was in total command of what he said. You stayed in the room, and it has made all the difference.

The shifting baseline problem comes, I think, from problems of scale and our dependence on lived experience. We live such short lives. Our perceptions are faulty in an irreconcilable way. We adjust and adjust incrementally, and these adjustments add up over our lifetimes and then those of the next and the next generations.

Normal is not static. My son went off to college as Great Salt Lake continued to shrink and then the pandemic took over. I hadn't seen Jeff for months and so I wrote him in late April. My son is here with me, and he's "on fire" as you would say. After years of grunts and half answers, he has ideas, and he wants to hang out and tell me about them. Last week, floating on the Dolores River we saw an otter family, a great blue heron, a black-capped night heron. He knows how to read the water, how to paddle. He told me about the forty days he spent on the Noatak River in the Alaskan arctic (first I've heard of these experiences though they happened two years ago). He talked about the Māori from his time in New Zealand, their values, and the ways they define themselves by the landforms into which they're born. He said, "I'd introduce myself as Mount Olympus, Great Salt Lake, and then my name." He's thinking about power and environment, economy and culture. I need news from you. How's your health?

The next day Jeff wrote back. In retrospect, it was an uncommonly short email. I'm so glad to hear he's in the seam. He's turned into such a fine young man, hard to believe he'll be twenty-one this May. How does that happen? As soon as all this passes, we need a face to face. Until then, I send my love.

Jeff died five weeks later. Great Salt Lake continued shrinking. In May 2022, my son graduated from college, and on July 3, that same year, the level of Great Salt Lake dropped to a historic low.

I now think of Jeff as a Merlin character. In his magical way, he saw into the future, making the raising of my son happen. While no King Arthur, my son represents the best of what I believe is a possible antidote to shifting baselines. He has tired of the cynicism he learned during his college years—the doomsday nature which riddles academic environmental narratives—but he hasn't left the room. He's developed his own personal carbon ethic, carefully deciding where and when he'll travel. He's part of a collective of twenty-somethings who together produce stunning artistic reflections on the place they call home; their latest is focused on Great Salt Lake. He started a business with another group of friends and deep cleans cars using just a few gallons of water, rather than the usual hundred. And, he's leveraging his environmental studies degree toward plant cultivation, believing that the history, art and economics of plants is an honest place to put his energies.

Baselines shift, sometimes quickly and permanently. One day, Jeff was on the other end of my emails, then he was not.

Still, he hasn't left the room. His lessons live on, not just in my son, but in me. His energy has driven this essay, and I'm reminded that not all shifts are permanent. It's a matter of time and scale. This year, the lake is higher than last. This year, there's more determined conversation about the connections between the lake, its ecology and our communal health. The young people are paying attention. They're getting involved.

I hear him. He's saying: Let nostalgia die. Forget academic myopia. Reject doom. Stay in this new room. Find the humor. Listen to what the kids are saying and empower them to figure it out for themselves.

An Invitation to a More Just World

Muskan Walia, as told to Quinn Luthy

I have always loved gardening with my mom in our backyard. I also bird-watch with her. She loves birds, but don't ask me what my favorite one is. I don't know the names like my mom does, I just love to look at them. After all, no bird is better than any other, and there's where we enter into justice, or injustice.

My neighborhood on the Wasatch Front is surrounded by refineries, smokestacks, and highways. For several years, my mom had been developing a nagging, persistent cough. When she went to the doctor about it in the Summer of 2020, she was diagnosed with Chronic Obstructive Pulmonary Disease (COPD). The doctor said it was likely because of the air pollution. The summer she got her diagnosis, I was so angry and upset. It wasn't our fault that our neighborhood was where it was. I didn't get to choose where my home was, but the refineries hurt my mom, nonetheless. I was worried what the air pollution might be doing to my neighbors and to me. That same summer, I was taking an online class at the University of Utah that focused on climate communication and climate change. My high school in Davis School District didn't prioritize teaching about climate change, and so in my mind, it wasn't important. However, one of my teachers taught me about environmental justice, and they said that the impacts of climate change and pollution impacted certain communities more than others, especially here on the Wasatch Front. I was following an Instagram account run by someone who was petitioning their school district to transition to 100 percent renewable energy, and one of their talking points was about air quality and I needed to do the same thing here in Davis County.

So, I launched my own campaign in my local school district. It was bizarre to go from the backyard sustainability of gardening with my mom and having an ethos of sustainability at home to looking at sustainability through a systemic lens. It was a big change. I assembled a youth-led team of students from the same area with similar cultural teachings. We had all been taught to not stir the pot, to not get involved. We worked to build confidence to advocate for resolutions that we wanted to see, including a resolution demanding that our school district pass a commitment to use 100 percent renewable energy by 2040.

After a lot of hard work, our resolutions were adopted by the Davis School District, and in 2017, we received national recognition from the Department of Education and the Department of Energy. We called ourselves Utah Youth Environmental Solutions (UYES) and started reaching out to more young people who wanted to make a difference. With a growing community of supporters and activists, in 2017, UYES worked with legislators to draft the first recognition of climate change by the Utah State Legislature and played a key role in mobilizing public support that led to its passage. At first, we didn't have a toolkit to share with youth or to change systems, and a lot of the youth leadership in the environmental movement dissipates because young people are in very transient stages of life and often move away. We realized that the only way that we would be able to sustain youth leadership in Utah was through education. That's when we connected with the University of Utah Environmental Humanities Graduate Program, and a graduate student there, Maria Archibald, who helped us build a curriculum to equip young people with the tools that they need to advocate for environmental justice.

Our political education is gridlocked by the state, and we wanted to use our platform to overcome that gridlock and provide an environmental justice education to whoever wanted it. That was the start, and we've been working on expanding clean energy campaigns and curricula across the state ever since. By 2024, we had passed a 100 percent clean energy resolution in the Salt Lake School District, and secured student representation on the task force to implement those resolutions. We also passed a 100 percent clean energy resolution in the Park City School District, where UYES students are also playing a formal role leading implementation of these changes. We also have an active campaign in the Granite School District, which was able to get funding from the Inflation Reduction Act to fund a position in the district that could help them transition to 100 percent clean energy. We recently started a campaign in the Canyons School District and are also engaging in conversations around a statewide clean energy campaign.

UYES has been developing a water justice campaign inspired by our own curriculum. We have always used Great Salt Lake as a lens for our students to study environmental justice. We chose to focus on Great Salt Lake in 2020 because we felt that narratives were missing from the conversation on conservation and on preserving recreational access to water, skiing, and hiking. We knew the movement would be more powerful if we included different experiences. We were concerned about Great Salt Lake's potential impacts on the health, safety, and well-being of our communities. We kept reading that Great Salt Lake was going to heighten the air pollution crisis here, and because of that, we thought that we could lead the campaign to save it.

The disappearing Great Salt Lake is often framed as a recreational or an economic issue, so we wanted to jump on and highlight the fate of the lake as a justice issue. People are affected disproportionately by the threats posed to, and by, the lake due to the placement of our homes and our communities. We felt that if we could lead the way forward in terms of protecting Great Salt Lake, it could benefit our own communities as well.

Though it isn't exactly proportional, issues like police brutality, public health (namely, COVID-19), and air pollution impact communities differently based on their socioeconomic status, race, geographical location, etc. Because of these injustices, it is important to create a sustainable response to them. UYES continues to recruit and empower students to demand change in the systems they inhabit. Of course, a lot of different groups have popped up in response to Great Salt Lake's crises and it is reassuring to see so many people who are passionate about the lake. We thought a lot about movement strategy at UYES: What are the gaps within the sustaining of the movement? How are we filling those gaps in a way that doesn't fracture resources? It seems that few groups are focused on offering a deep values-based education. While many organizations are focused on onboarding people who care about the issue and getting them out to do direct action, UYES is focused on deep, intersectional environmental work informed by a justice-oriented approach. We are contextualizing the environmental movement. We are trying to help explain how the environmental movement fits into other social issues which we believe is contributing to a shift in culture and values. Great Salt Lake is one issue, and it is an important issue to mobilize around, but it also offers opportunities to pioneer a culture change in our state and the ways that we interact with resources and with each other.

UYES hosts an Environmental Justice Training Program for students every summer that aims to equip young people with the tools to become environmental leaders in their communities. Our intention is that people who attend the program the tools to bring a justice orientation to any environmental groups that they join as students and beyond. During these workshops, we teach students how to organize for change in their school districts using successful UYES campaigns, how to write op-eds, what environmental justice is, and how to plan direct actions for the environment. We organize regular direct actions for Great Salt Lake both at the lake and the Utah State Capitol. UYES has gotten a lot of attention for its "die-ins" at dried sections of Great Salt Lake's lakebed and the Capitol, but we also attend vigils with Save Our Great Salt Lake and the Making Waves Artist Collective, and paint countdown clocks all over to signal the imminent disappearance of Great Salt Lake. Because we are young people, we want lawmakers and advocacy groups to recognize the entanglements between our futures and the future of Great Salt Lake. We have published op-eds addressed to lawmakers and the public and try to take up space in magazines, newspapers, blogs, etc.

A few years ago, we worked with a group of lake-facing organizations to advocate for Great Salt Lake as a sovereign legal entity that would have human rights. This kind of legal framework would match the urgency of the crises facing the lake. One of our alums, Lola Maldonado, sued the state of Utah on behalf of future generations alongside six other young people. That case (Natalie R. v. State of Utah) argues that petrochemical development in the state "infringes residents' rights to life, liberty, and property under Utah's due process clause." These direct actions, coupled with protests, educations, and cooperation with other groups are at the core of UYES' strategy to center environmental justice in relation to Great Salt Lake.

We have to be intentional and strategic about the way that we operate. The other thing that is unique about the ways that we're engaging with the lake is our vision. By working with students, and by being very slow and methodical about our strategies, we want to prioritize working outside of the political system to change what is politically possible. Our tactics aim to change the narrative and disrupt business as usual and the status quo so that what is currently politically impossible, becomes possible.

But what is environmental justice? For me, and my communities, environmental justice is the idea that environmental and social issues are inextricably connected. We can't solve an environmental problem without looking at the social systems that caused it. As one UYES slogan goes, "environmentalism without class struggle is just gardening." Environmental justice advocates for peoples' rights to a safe and healthy life. Everybody deserves justice and the right to organize and care in the ways that they want to.

Right now, the current narrative about the disappearing Great Salt Lake from our legislators, and some organizers, is centered on economics. We're focused on the idea that we need to "just get water to the lake." However, if we explored this issue as a symptom of something bigger, as a symptom of a colonial, racist, classist history, we could create just futures for everyone here. Everybody who lives by the lake will tell you a different, but specific way that Great Sale Lake disappearing affects their lives. If we are able to commit to a justice-oriented approach to saving the lake, it will lay the groundwork for our approach to future environmental and political concerns. If we're trying to find solutions to the problem, we have to ask, who are we doing this for? The solutions need to enact justice for everyone, not just certain groups. The effects of disappearing Great Salt Lake on brine shrimpers deserve our consideration, but so too do the effects on people who are incarcerated, people of color, people who live near the lake, disabled people, etc.

Threats to Great Salt Lake presents us an opportunity to care for everyone. If we just water it down to a piece of legislation and "getting water to the lake" because it is good for the economy, we lose a huge opportunity to change how we approach other environmental justice issues in the state. The issue is actually a transformative opportunity if we take advantage of it. Imagine a transformed future, where all Utahns have the right to clean air, and get to have meaningful work.

But it is even more transformative than that. We could remove movement policing from social movements here so that people could advocate for themselves and their communities. It takes a diversity of tactics and levers to change a system and a culture, and right now we have an opportunity to do just that. In this moment, we can shift how we relate to the environment and to each other. That sort of fundamental change is a necessary toolkit for our future social questions that we need to deal with. The way that we respond to the crisis of a disappearing Great Salt Lake can lay the foundation for a revolution.

We can't continue to think of individual issues as disconnected from each other, in silos, instead, you have to ask: How does this issue, this specific issue, tie into the bigger picture of social change? In fact, we are all working towards saving Great Salt Lake if we are all working towards justice. If you're fighting against gentrification, you're fighting for Great Salt Lake. If you're fighting against the genocide in Palestine, you're fighting for Great Salt Lake. If you're fighting against police brutality, you're fighting for Great Salt Lake. So, whether or not you know every statistic, economic policy, water usage law, it doesn't matter. You don't need to know any of that, you can still make a meaningful difference, and that is how we build power within the movement. We must intentionally include people who don't know everything. That's what builds power. That's what leads to cultural change.

Even though Great Salt Lake lies in an endorheic basin, it is connected to all of us and impacted by the environmental damage that our species has caused around the planet. Even if we pass comprehensive legislation addressing the disappearing Lake now, that legislation will still have been crafted in an unjust system. Any legislation passed in an unjust, capitalistic system will be inherently unjust and capitalistic, that's why it is so important to support people using diverse tactics. When we work outside the system to shift what is politically possible, we are altering the system, not just perpetuating it.

Ghazal for Great Salt Lake

After May Timbimboo Perry, After Darren Parry

Willy Palomo

After a Shoshone hunter brought down a great kill, he called
his village to gift a feast to the bellies of his brothers.

You should have stored it for your family, a mountain man
chided, as if we could cheat the bellies of our brothers.

The mountain man was confused when the hunter
responded, I store the meat in the belly of my brother.

The heavens gave us snow. Mountains gave us a river.
The river gave us life sweet for the bellies of our brothers.

If the heavens, the mountains and rivers did not give so freely,
know no blood would beat in the belly of my brother.

From gull to microbial, all are whole through the Lake.
For millennia, life was replete in the belly of our mother.

There is more than enough if we only take what we need.
There is no need to compete in the belly of our mother.

With women as with nature, they delight in what they can
take. That is the way they treat the bellies of their mothers.

From the red rock to the great and spacious building
on the hill, our destinies meet in the belly of our mother.

We share this feast with the grebes, nestled in her hair.
Both bird and man have seats in the belly of our mother.

We share this feast with the bison, thundering down the ridge.
We both stamped our feet down the belly of our mother.

When our lives are at stake and the Lake calls our names,
know we always find peace in the belly of our mother.

Abide

Karin Anderson

When I was twenty-two, I worked as a recreation helper at a care center near my hometown. Dreaming up ways to while away long geriatric hours allowed me to be a humanities type in a medical setting. We made frosted cookies for family visits. We flew kites on the front lawn. We recorded personal narratives, which is how I learned that sin has always been rampant in American Fork, Utah.

I had a hometown friend named Fred Forman, a dirty old man who badgered my sister and me for kisses. "A sexy one. None of that simpy grandpa stuff." Fred had explained to me how to make hard mountain cider: Fill a wooden keg with pressed apple mash, load it onto a packhorse, carry it above the canyon intake, and set it in a stony hiding place. Go back up come spring with an augur and spigot, catch two-hundred proof alcohol in your canteen.

"Let the horse do the thinking on the way down," he advised.

Fred and his saner brother Roby had played in a jazz quartet when they were young. They gigged church dances and makeshift nightclubs. I asked Fred if they could still make tunes. "You betcha," he said, so I invited them to play for the folks at the care center.

"You got to give me a kiss for it," he said.

"I'll bet you come even if I don't," I answered, and I was correct.

They pulled up in a van, four old men in snazzy shirts and

bolo ties. Fred uncased his tenor sax. Roby sat down to test the piano keys. The "boys" set up drums and plugged in a pearly F-hole guitar.

Fred bellowed, "This is for all you kids use to dance out to Saltair," and Roby murmured "One, two, three, four. . ."

First measure of "In the Mood" shocked the room. Sleepy old folks sat up straight. Comatose droolers lifted their heads. Wanda Rivers stood up to shimmy like the flapper she must have been. Holden Malmstrom, past a hundred and perfectly lucid, called out requests: "There is a Tavern in the Town," "Sweet Georgia Brown," "When it's Springtime in the Rockies," and the band answered, effortless.

The room was transported to a place I'd never been. Joyful, but also overtaken by melancholy, each listener drawn into a timeless dimension. Wanda was crying uncontrollably. "How will I ever tell my Daddy? He'll kill us both!"

Fred was sweating, plumb wore out. Roby looked like he could jam on into the night. Aides wheeled delirious residents out toward dinner. The energy was haunting.

Holden ambled over, suave. "It's just that we're all remembering nights at Great Salt Lake," he explained. "Saltair all lit up like a sultan's palace. The dance floor had springs under it, so it gave a little under the rhythms, lifted when we all jumped together. My god those were the days."

I'd heard of Saltair, seen pictures, but I'd never understood the communal passion. The old resort was by then burned down and defunct. The popular devotion to Great Salt Lake had dried up.

"We'd go out to the decks for a breather, sometimes to sip a little—well, you know," Holden went on. "The stars were so bright out there above the islands. They reflected perfect in the water. Not so many lights in the city as now. We felt like the only people on the planet, just this one palace set on the lapping water. Us boys thought we were Kubla Khan.

"Anyway, that music brought it all back. Funny how time comes atcha, ain't it."

■ ■ ■

Great Salt Lake now is largely unknown and unknowable to regular citizens like me. Much of the shoreline—most of the north and west perimeter—is closed off by ranches and private industries: livestock, salt, magnesium, Sea Monkeys. The compelling landforms along the west face of Stansbury Island are marked by stern prohibitions; the graded gravel road is only a begrudging corridor to the north end where rough hiking trails open to guide a wanderer nervously east.

Besides the marvelous Antelope Island State Park (and, now, remarkably a newly accessible Frémont Island), most of the angular islands are privately owned and verboten. Only a few people with professional credentials are allowed to visit Egg Island—and I get it, as it's a crucial avian nesting site. But the restrictions lend an authoritarian mystique to the lake and its phantasmagoric hues. It can be hard for "regular" Utahns to feel the passionate bond we need to love and defend our defining regional feature. Most of us catch a semi-encompassing view as we gaze out the constricted window of a jet, musing over marbled-paper marshlands as we're going away or coming back. We can't discern what's water and what's mirage as we jam across I-80 toward Nevada. We point out glittering salt piled outside the Morton plant. We read travelers' runic blessings and curses written with rocks on hardened salt along the shoulders.

The lake makes us who we are, in so many ways and so completely, we forget to notice. We've been taught to understand it as wasteland, as wasted water.

We must go there, again and again—and again, despite natural and unnatural prohibitions: step out of the car, squish across cracked saline silt, bash a shin on the rocks. Get cold or very hot. Swallow bugs, absorb throat-grabbing scents, hear the talky lilt of shorebirds.

Great Salt Lake is unimaginably beautiful. It answers to no preconception.

▪ ▪ ▪

Or: We ought to be able to live in its timeless presence without having to think about it much at all. The lake should simply be here, unthreatened by our irrelevant lives, carrying on with its own cycles of expansion and retreat, beckoning to pelicans and seagulls, loons, avocets, dowitchers and godwits, catching and transforming cloud compositions, delivering sustenance to the mountain peaks and valley floor.

It doesn't matter how much I love or don't love this lake, how representative I am or am not, what reasons I or anyone else might furnish to plead its cause: the lake belongs to itself, its reasons none of our affair.

▪ ▪ ▪

The Wasatch Front lakes—Utah and Great Salt—remained mythic for non-Indigenous travelers well after most of the American West was "discovered." Near the high boundary of Spanish (and then Mexican) territories, mysterious waters lapped just beyond permissible sightlines for mountain men who knew incursion could mean death. Jim Bridger took a solid first gander of Great Salt Lake (at least the Bear River floodplain) in 1824 from what is now Idaho's southern border. Virtuous, bear-bitten Jedediah Smith illegally led a group of explorers south of the lake to locate the Spanish Trail to California in 1826. Ordered to leave San Diego and return to American territory, he and his men clawed across (up and down) hundreds of miles of arid Basin and Range. He cried for joy when he perceived the west shoreline of Great Salt Lake—the first discernible landmark of return.

In 1841, five years before the Donners, Reeds, and their unlucky collaborators were conned into taking Lansford Hastings "shortcut" to California below the south shore of Great Salt Lake, the Bidwell-Bartleson group made the first Anglo emigrant attempt to cross the West with wagons. An eighteen-year-old mother named Nancy Kelsey, the sole woman among the brash punks who bushwhacked a route to forbidden California, was the first white woman to see Great Salt Lake.

The group traversed the north shoreline, angling southwest toward the future Wendover cowboy. Standing at Bidwell Pass offers a good idea of the terrain they were up against. They bailed on their wagons near the Ruby Range, I'd guess at least two basins overdue. Nancy rode a horse the rest of the way with her one-year-old daughter in front of her. Some accounts say she was pregnant as well, which sounds all intrepid until we recall how many Shoshone women were also pregnant and caring for children at the time in the same region. Also, until we follow the Kelseys forward in history to learn of their career brutality toward the Elem and Pomo people in the pretty places we now tour on wine trains: ruthless land and cattle theft, enslavement, rape, protracted starvation, and torture.

Spanish explorers and soldiers, familiar with long-settled territories further south, were forbidden to indulge in extra-military travel, and despite Spanish "ownership," the Wasatch valleys that cradled the lakes at hand were firmly inhabited by Ute, Paiute, and Shoshone peoples. In 1776, Dominguez and Escalante made a journey of incomprehensible visions from Santa Fe, New Mexico, to the south rim of Utah Valley, wondering all the way when they'd zero in on Monterey, California.

I've read that the Catholics promised grateful, happy Ute people they'd return to convert all to truth and glory, but at the moment the fathers were tired and needed to go home. I've heard that others burned grass from the south shores of Utah Lake all the way down to the mouth of Spanish Fork Canyon, making northward travel impossible—something like closing all the gas stations, I guess. I've read that Escalante took an escorted trip to taste the salt of the lake, what he believed was an inlet of the Pacific, but that version is an outlier. All accounts report that the priests and their party dinked along the Nebo foothills for several perplexing weeks and decided to return to Santa Fe, reassuring themselves that a river to California simply had to exist just a little farther on, likely spilling from the great mythic inland sea, providing an easy future route to the Pacific.

■ ■ ■

I grew up in Utah Valley, an ardently conservative region that most of my academic Salt Lake City friends won't approach unless they're blazing through to California. The damaged lake visible from my childhood bedroom window was Utah Lake, a huge, shallow freshwater body that draines north, via the Jordan River, into the drainless Great Salt Lake.

I didn't know until a few years ago, after I talked to a ninety-two-year-old farmer near my home below Mount Olympus, that the industrially polluted (yet gradually recovering) water from Utah Lake has been diverted this way from the outlet for over a century, pumped uphill and sideways across Salt Lake Valley in trade for the fresh mountain runoff of the canyon creeks. Old pioneer irrigation claims took too much from the culinary needs of a booming Salt Lake City population, so the powers that be arranged a swap. The scale of appeasement engineering—canals, headgates, pump stations—is astonishing now that I've learned to perceive it.

More astonishing: A crucial original mountain feed for Utah Lake was the hefty Provo River, long ago dammed and diverted beyond capacity. An early "solution" was to dig a six-mile tunnel, straight through hard-rock Uinta mountains from an unrelated watershed. Constructed in the 1950s, the marvel of the Duchesne Tunnel was quickly deemed inadequate. By now Utah Valley extracts water again from the same flow, downstream, diverting from Strawberry Reservoir (in the process of significant enlargement) to replenish Utah Lake via the Spanish Fork River. The new flow eroded the original riverbed so violently that a whole network of pipelines now redefines Fifth Water hot springs, further down.

Transport below the massive Jordanelle dam in Wasatch County jackknifes Provo River water down Provo Canyon and back north to other side of the Wasatch Range, to the upper Utah and lower Salt Lake valleys before it ever reaches Utah Lake.

Etcetera.

This information isn't obscure. It's easy to track the water and acrimony on the internet. It's even easier to scratch at the illusion of plenitude and ignite something quick as wildfire among saints and citizens. I understand, but as denizens of a cyclically lush-arid cultural region we need to rehearse the wizardry behind the blossoming of lawns and roses. Alfalfa. Somehow when we see water, put our hands in it, dive in, take a drink, we just want to believe.

But, summary: The Salt Lake Valley (bottomed out by Great Salt Lake) can't sustain its voracious habits and therefore pumps water from Utah Valley. Utah Valley can't sustain its voracious habits and so diverts water from the Wasatch and Duchesne Valleys. You'd have to take a long four-wheel-drive odyssey to internalize a glimmer of the scale: Transforming the densely populated Wasatch Front into a continuous green fever dream requires breathlessly unnatural engineering.

It's impressive, for sure, to stand at the high-altitude reservoir in the rugged Uinta gash where the headwaters of the Duchesne River are tunneled into the Provo. The ancient bed of once-rowdy cascades now trickles like a rivulet, exposing eons of whitewater erosion, cabin-sized boulders tumbled to jewel tones, deep churnholes below defunct surges. Water destined by geography for the Green River, and then Colorado, now rushes beneath a mountain range to merge with the Provo River, en-route to Jordanelle and Deer Creek reservoirs, enroute to Utah Lake—enroute to Great Salt Lake.

Except almost none of it arrives. Even with all that engineering, all that cheating and re-feeding, Great Salt Lake is sucking in its sides and dying of thirst. And the Green River, flowing to the great and diminishing Colorado, cannot sustain its "obligations" even as Upper Basin states squabble for their share that is legally, if not actually, more than enough to green-light hundreds of new subdivisions, startups, and densely-packed condo units sprawling the outskirts of every city on the Wasatch Front.

▪ ▪ ▪

A culture founded on prophecies of destruction will eventually tire of waiting and start fulfilling. The colonized state of Utah is built on a paradigm of environmental destruction decreed as prerequisite to renewal. Mortals consume a tenuous desert ecosystem so God can return to lift up the faithful as the wicked die of dust, heat, crickets, earthquakes, maggots, misery and empty grocery shelves—purging the earth of sin before it can be divinely cleansed of litter, toxic algae, ozone, poison particulates.

▪ ▪ ▪

When Canada geese migrate in the spring and fall, I hear them conversing like a happy contentious family a mile off and a mile beyond. They fly directly over my house, sometimes so low I can see their webbed and tucked-back feet, almost count their pointy toes. They stop at the creek beyond, then lift again still chattering, traveling to rest (or reside) at Great Salt Lake.

When the strange, stinky air of the (Great Salt) Lake effect rises spinning from the ancient bed, finds its atmospheric bearings, and gales like a locomotive toward the massive, tilting, tiered stone of Storm Mountain, I can watch it approach and pass directly above my roofline. The smell is choking, unforgettable, rich with life. The top skin of lake water lifts into sky, to cloud, to mountain, to running stream. To return.

We don't live near Great Salt Lake. We live in it. Everything is churning.

▪ ▪ ▪

Great Salt Lake water reclines in a bed more like a dinner plate than a cereal bowl. Photographs of my once-midsized children at White Rock Bay on a stifling day fifteen years ago show them a quarter mile out in transparent water, still only ankle deep. The light is surreal.

At or near the lake's historic level, a single wet season can extend the circumference by several miles in every direction. Howard Stansbury, commissioned by the US government to survey the lake in 1849, wrote "We had a hearty laugh at the circumstance of the anchor of the yaul being above water." When the wind blew east, all the water went with it, leaving the boats mired in mud until the lake rolled back to lift them.

Stansbury measured the greatest depth of the lake at thirty-three feet, between Hat and Frémont Islands. Dale Morgan reports: "Usually, they found the lake only five or six feet deep, and sometimes only a few inches." This means that a reduction of only an inch or two can suck in the lake's land coverage to an almost unrecognizable degree. The lake doesn't "drop" so much as pull in on itself, exposing thousands of acres of salt-saturated sediments where birds, insects, and bratty kids might otherwise frolic in harshly crystalline water, where winds can no longer spin the putrid thrilling lake effect toward the Wasatch summits to unload cotton candy powder.

It means that a drop of several feet congeals something barely waterish into the deepest pockets of the terminal lakebed, so salty even the hyper-adapted brine shrimp can't survive. When the shrimp die, the bugs and birds vacate or die. The valley bakes, the poison winds churn, the mountains burn.

■ ■ ■

I'm not a scientist. Not a poet, not an artist. I bring no unique wisdom to a communal plea to rescue an ecosystem. I just live here.

It's my home, however ill-got by fanatic ancestors, and I hope to live here, gently. I've spent my adult life searching for home, even though I've lived right here forever. An obnoxious rejoinder in my state: Well, if you don't like it here, why don't you move somewhere else?

I love this damaged place. I can gripe if I want to.

This is my home.

I know the planet changes beneath us. One of the most beautiful places on the planet is the Silver Island Range just north of Wendover, straddling the Utah / Nevada border. The region is a moonscape—deadly dry and geologically wrenched. Sit at the mouth of any one of the natural caves above the old Bonneville waterline and everything transforms: a memory of lake, lake, lake all the way east to the distant Wasatch Front, all the way north and south to vanishing horizons. Mammoths and short-tooth bears and huge scary cats bellow in the distances. Family fires signal from one canyon ridge to the next. Children float stick boats and rounded leaves, sending them to unknowable destinations. Mothers make pliant shoes, soften cave floors for bedding, weave totem creatures from twigs and straw. Fathers do whatever hard-traveling cave dads do.

Stars shine upward, as bright in the endless, bottomless water as they are in the sky.

Those people have evaporated, although their powdered, petrified poop still yields layer-by-layer clues to their evolving diets and the climate-constrained vegetation. Their tools and firebeds and fragments of basketry speak to their vivid lives. The water they knew is gone but for Great Salt Lake, for Utah Lake, murmuring desert remnants.

■ ■ ■

Whatever the fate of Great Salt Lake, I'll soon be extinct as the people who lived on the shores of Bonneville. As extinct as the room full of people at the care center, mooning after old dance refrains. I can't believe in immortality, and the main reason I'm sorry about that is that I want to watch my weird corner of the planet move forward into the eons. I want to witness the collisions of mountain ranges. I want to see red sandstone erode and break and rise and reform. I want to watch water rush from the Pacific to refill the Great Basin, spread and spill into the Humboldt and Snake rivers, wash out highways and wagon tracks, beckon sturgeon and cutthroat trout, summon mutant creatures to drink at the shores.

Short of that, I want to live here in this valley, despite the mess and the crowd and the politics, despite the heritage I can't come to terms with, the cultural smugness and blithe political screw-ups and the hard personal history and the stupid, stupid mistakes I've made in this place. I want home, with its strange water and salt and turbulent basin air, to abide.

I want it so direly I've let myself dip into crazy. I picture myself hunkered down in a boarded-up back room, waiting out the latest arsenic storm slamming against the brittle bricks in 110 degree Santa Ana winds. I pretend there will be water enough to carry in buckets to and from the vestige of Big Cottonwood

Creek a quarter mile off. I'll hand-water my precious shade tree until it shelters my whole roof. I'll set my grown children in the garage, in tents in the back yard, under the covered porch if they come. Home.

Hell, we'll eat Mormon crickets.

I'm fully launched into my seventh decade, but still I imagine surviving—in the same delusional ways that buoyed my Latter-Day Saint ancestors—the very people who girded their loins with prophecies of the desert blossoming as the rose even as the wicked (like me) meet their apocalyptic fate.

I'll say what I'm able to say: I do not wish to depart.

What I wish more: I want Great Salt Lake to be.

Spiraling Toward Yes

Hanna Saltzman

Three months after my son's birth, I took my Brooklynite cousin, Ilanna, to meet Great Salt Lake. We parked at a favorite spot that, when I first visited almost twenty years ago, was mere steps from the water: the artist Robert Smithson's *Spiral Jetty*, a 1,500-foot-long counterclockwise corkscrew of rock that once spun into a vast inland sea. In April 1970, Smithson moved half the weight of the Eiffel Tower of black basalt and mud from the shore into the lake, where water whirled through the spiral's giant rings. Then the lake rose and submerged the sculpture for decades before receding again. Now, Ilanna and I climbed onto dry volcanic boulders under a fierce August sun. We squinted toward where water should be but saw only sand and salt. The jetty coiled like a snakeskin and unfurled like a question mark.

This day was to be my first full day away from my baby, a trial run before returning to my job as a pediatric resident physician, when I'd resume eighty-hour work weeks in the children's hospital. In a few days, I was supposed to leave my own baby to care for other people's babies. My baby, who lived in the home of my body for nine and a half months. My baby, whose body feels like home.

Ilanna, eight months older and my lifelong soul sister, sensed my distress and hopped on a plane to help me remember a version of myself that did not involve wearing a Baby Bjorn. She had one request as temperatures soared into triple digits: do something besides hike. Our car bumped along the gravel road up to the *Spiral Jetty*, breast pump balanced on my lap, milk sloshing out of plastic nipple cups. I wanted my cousin to witness this lake that gave the name for the city I call home. This lake that gifts us snow and green glittering aspens but also pollution and dust. This lake that—or perhaps, who—is both a mother nurturing all beings in this valley and an existential threat to all she has nurtured.

Ilanna had heard about Great Salt Lake earlier that summer, when The New York Times described Utah's "environmental nuclear bomb," a incendiary political phrase that reflects a dire truth: the threat of an unthinkable amount of potentially toxic dust turned airborne. Water misuse coupled with climate change and the megadrought have led the largest saline lake in the Western Hemisphere to lose more than half of its water. Scientists have predicted that it could dry entirely in the next few years. When human water diversion led Owens Lake in Southern California to dry up in 1926, it became the single largest source of dust pollution in the United States and held that title for almost a century. Great Salt Lake is more than ten times bigger than Owens Lake. And because water flows into Great Salt Lake but not out, toxins from industries such as agriculture and mining accumulate on the lakebed. Water and salt keep these pollutants in the ground. But when wind rustles dry lakebed, toxins can rise as dust.

What pediatricians know: Air pollution can hurt children starting in the womb and increase risk for health concerns including premature birth, asthma, neurodevelopmental problems, and childhood cancers. Even small amounts of heavy metals like arsenic and lead can potentially harm children's delicate bodies and brains.

What mothers know: There is nothing we want more than for our children to be healthy and safe.

When Ilanna read about the environmental nuclear bomb, she'd called me in a soft panic. I answered the phone while pushing my son's stroller along a tree-lined urban creek that offered shade in the June heat. Her questions: Is it true? Is it as bad as it sounds? Are you going to move?

I swallowed and looked down at my baby. Asleep, his eyes danced behind pale lids with their lacy lilac veins. His tiny nostrils fluttered in and out nearly as fast as a fit adult's heartbeat. Babies' fast breathing makes them even more vulnerable to particulate matter, those tiny invisible particles of pollution that matter deeply to climate change and human health. My own breath became shallow. I wondered whether my baby was, at this very moment, breathing invisible trails of lake dust.

"I don't know," I said into the phone. I slipped my finger into the depths of my son's sleeping fist. He squeezed back in that newborn reflex that is also a profound connection of body to body.

Now, Ilanna and I were walking past the *Spiral Jetty* under a cloudless summer sky. Our sandals crunched on salt crystals sharp as shards of broken bone. Their textures reminded me of a bleached deer carcass, pale vertebrae crumbling at the edges, vertebral discs pressed with bumps like the print of a thumb or the folds of a brain, angular spinal joints molded by flesh long gone. The jetty became a dot in the distance. Still no water.

Ilanna gave me a look. I could tell she was thinking about when I'd asked her to come on a "little walk" in the foothills and we wandered for miles, and when I took her hiking in the Tetons and promptly lost the bear spray, and when I dragged her up a muggy mountain in the Berkshires to show her a weather station whose view was obscured by clouds. And here we were on our "not-hiking" activity, trekking through salt fields under a blazing sun without a clear destination, our Nalgenes already empty.

Then, suddenly, we saw it: water. Water turned pink by algae and bacteria, water all the way to the horizon.

"A pink lake in the middle of mountains!" Ilanna said, her mouth parted in wonder. "Is this a fairytale?"

I squeezed her hand and pulled us forward into the cherry blossom water. Foam of salt and air swirled up our calves. When the water reached our thighs, we lay back and floated, held by each other's hands and some of the saltiest water on Earth. Held by the hope that this lake again will rise. The hope that this lake, this valley, this planet can be saved. The hope that we, too, can be saved.

"Spiritual," my cousin later named the experience. She said it was one of the first times she had ever used that word to describe a personal memory.

■ ■ ■

I went back to work, and soon the children's hospital became the busiest in its hundred-year history, slammed by a tripledemic of COVID, flu, and RSV. Babies' lungs filled with waters of infection and inflammation. Medical teams strapped oxygen masks on small faces, shoved breathing tubes down tiny throats. As the hospital ran out of beds, babies spilled into the hallways of the emergency department, while others double bunked and gasped together for air. Doctors, nurses, and respiratory therapists ran from room to room, yanking disposable masks over our N-95s, flinging yellow single-use gowns on and off at each door. I stuffed my overflowing patient list into the pocket of my scrubs and tried to keep the patients straight, tried to find time to pump milk for my baby, tried to breathe.

Meanwhile, my infant was boycotting nighttime sleep. My husband, Nate, and I stayed up for much of each night then rushed to early morning hospital shifts. From before dawn until after dusk, I led teams of junior doctors through the tripledemic, eventually dragging my cooler of breastmilk home in the dark. I hoped that my milk's antibodies would protect my son from becoming a patient. Months smeared together in a delirium of exhaustion and spirals of fear, punctuated by my child's remarkable changes: his moments of learning to babble, giggle, and crawl that as a pediatrician I measured in milestones but as a parent I witnessed with wild, immeasurable wonder.

In January, our water bill was high, which we chalked up to a leaky toilet. We fixed the toilet. I published an op-ed about how the drying of Great Salt Lake hurts kids' health and we desperately need to conserve water. In February, the city left a note on our front door announcing high water use. We called an indoor plumber, who couldn't find a problem and recommended asking an outdoor plumber. The outdoor plumber waved a device over snow and ice in our small urban yard, then shook his head. "Have to wait till the thaw to figure this out," he said, brushing snow off his truck.

Meanwhile, the bills kept coming. Invisible water was leaking from our historic home through a hole we could not find or fix. The broken pipe did not care that we took care to plant desert shrubs instead of grass. The water escaping the pipe would be diverted long before it reached Great Salt Lake.

Spring brought floods from the snowiest winter in recent history—a La Niña anomaly that gave the lake a little more time. The plumber returned and found the location of the leak, but couldn't fix it for a few more weeks. On a warm May morning, the leaky pipe suddenly burst. In a flash, the silent, sightless trickle became a flood. We turned off our water and vacated our home.

The pipe, it turned out, was a hundred years old and made of lead, which we learned also filled our soil. When the pipe broke, it lost the protective coating that kept the lead in place. Unbeknownst to us, for months the unprotected lead had been contaminating our drinking water. Leaded water had been filling my son's sippy cup that he proudly thrust toward ours—with "Cheers!" —and the tall glasses I guzzled while nursing him, and the breastmilk my body made for my baby from that same water.

A week later, I sat in my son's pediatrician's office for his one-year-old checkup. I had walked to the appointment from the pediatric ICU, where that morning, my toddler patient died. His father cradled his child's cold body. His mother stared at the wall, silent as salt. I stood at the doorway, hands shaking, unsure how to stay, unsure how to leave.

My son wriggled on my lap while I undressed him for his vaccines. I tried to focus, but my thoughts were back in the ICU. The medical assistant squeezed a drop of blood from my baby's toe. He yelped and nuzzled into my chest. After a few minutes, his pediatrician entered the room. She gently told me that my son had lead in his blood.

"It's barely elevated," she said. "We should confirm it." I tried to stay calm, but her news broke the levee of me. I sobbed into my son's hair. No safe level of lead: words I intimately knew from my work in pediatrics and environmental health, words I had shared in that op-ed about risks of the drying Great Salt Lake. Lead is the one heavy metal that pediatricians routinely test. When children breathe leaded dust, the lead can enter their blood even more easily than if they eat or drink it. Perhaps lead levels will become a proxy for other less-easily-testable dangers of the drying lake like arsenic and uranium, a sign of lake dust becoming part of children's blood and flesh and brains.

Nate and I briefly entertained the idea of buying a new house. We talked, too, about leaving Salt Lake City, leaving Utah. But we couldn't just buy a new home. More than the can't, was the won't. We told ourselves that the sleep deprivation was making us neurotic. We stopped talking about moving. What would it take for us to choose to leave?

We fixed the pipe, installed a water filter, and replanted the garden, where penstemons and phlox took the place of herbs and began to flourish in the leaded soil. My son's blood lead level, which fortunately wasn't ever highly elevated, dropped over the next few months. With each blood draw, the blue rubber band squeezed his arm while his eyes filled with tears and betrayal, the way my patients must also look when they get lab tests that I order to assess risk of things unseen. When children breathe or ingest lead, some exits the body in urine and stool. The rest flows through the bloodstream until it settles in bones and teeth, liver and spleen. The worst place for the metal to land is the brain. When lead settles in tissues such as bone, it hibernates, but in times of physiologic stress, it can leach back into the blood and again reach the brain.

Because my son's lead level was not that high, I knew his brain would probably be fine. Yet even small exposures impart a risk of neurologic damage. I lay awake at night imagining lead depositing in the weave of my son's bones, the sponge of his kidneys, the folds of his brain: the neuron-packed tissue that led him to shout "Hello," gape at how an ant can hoist a leaf, and wave with both hands at the gorgeous, glittering moon.

■ ■ ■

When I leave work each evening, I always look out across the city from the hospital's perch high in the hills, past twinkling car lights and a cluster of skyscrapers, toward overlapping layers of mountains, until my eyes find Great Salt Lake. On clear evenings, the lake is a shimmering silver stripe that brings a primordial sense of calm. On dusty or smoggy days, haze obscures the water. Those sunsets are unfairly beautiful, the sky painted bubblegum and sherbet by light scattered through polluted air. On those nights, my mind swirls with health angst and thoughts about the meaning of home: what it means to call a place home, what it takes to choose to leave your home. What it takes to dig in and stay.

The Salt Lake Valley, in some ways, is a magnifying glass for global environmental threats. When our mountain-wrapped skies fill with smog trapped in the bowl of the valley, we must inhale what we pollute. We see, taste, and breathe the effects of the way we choose to live on this Earth. Eventually, with the right combination of warmth and wind and changes in pressure, the pollution diffuses, and we rejoice at breathing clean air. But those particles of pollution are not gone. Wildfire smoke from Canada enters children's lungs in New York. The Amazon rainforest would not be so lush without dust from the Sahara. Particulate matter: particles that matter.

The Salt Lake Valley is also a magnifying glass for mind-bending timelines of human destruction. Great Salt Lake could dry before my child starts elementary school. We likely have only a few years—before my son starts high school—to avert worse-case climate scenarios. And per the Institute of European Environmental Policy, more than half of global carbon dioxide emissions have occurred since 1990, the year of my birth.

I struggle to comprehend these staggering timelines. It is like standing by a roaring river while gazing up at a towering cliff, then hiking to the top of the cliff and seeing the river transformed into a delicate thread. The two worlds seem impossible to reconcile, even after traveling between them.

The winter after we fixed our water pipe and moved back into our home, our family attended the second annual "Save the Great Salt Lake" rally. It was an unusually warm Saturday in January. My patients were suffering severe illnesses without clear solutions, my conversations with their parents sticky with grief. I wanted to spend the weekend on the couch, but our toddler whizzed around the house, so we walked to the Utah Capitol, rolling up our sleeves while sparrows chirped with spring. At the rally, my son darted between legs and giggled at costumes of brine shrimp and eared grebes. We sang and listened to poetry. The vibe was respectful, loving, almost sacred. But a big brown sign announced the catastrophe we're careening towards: "No to Toxic Dust Bowl."

Yet unlike some of my patients' illnesses, and unlike most situations in the climate crisis, this emergency does have a clear, attainable solution. Keep the lake wet. My other hope is this:

Our climate grief, I believe, comes not only from fear and despair about self-preservation, but also from an ancient, wild wonder and love for the living world—one that children effortlessly embody. If we can remember and reclaim this cellular, earth-facing awe as the compass that guides our choices, maybe we will have a chance.

When the rally ended, it started to rain. Drops became puddles that looked as big as lakes to my son. He squealed and ran toward the water, arms stretched wide, in the posture of people greeting the beings they love most in the world. He beamed like I do when I come home from work and he rushes toward me, healthy and safe. He beamed like Ilanna and me as we floated with outstretched arms and let water saltier than the sea lift us toward the sun.

My son's open-arm, giggly sprint seemed to invoke a poem that Joel Long, a poet and longtime friend, wrote when Nate and I got married, an epithalamium about the *Spiral Jetty* and Great Salt Lake:

> It is no wonder but wonder that the artist / chose this place… If you kneel down in the water, half your body submerged / … you know that this lifting is pleasure, / so with your whole body you smile with all the water beneath you and all the water for one hundred miles, a compass of joy, revealing what it's like to be held, to be raised by something / we cannot understand but with pleasure, with love, the water sound lapping against your ears, and this other sound coming / from your mouth that everything on earth knows means yes.

An artist moved half the Eiffel Tower's worth of volcanic rock into an oceanic lake to construct a sculpture intended to render impermanence. A poet transformed that image into words to bless the wedding of lovers who created a lake-loving child born into a world that glitters and quakes.

My chest aches when I think about how someday my son will step outside and realize all there is to grieve, how he will grow to understand the stakes of the choices of those who came before him. I want to float with him in fairytale pink water with amazement alongside sorrow, and show this lake, this Earth, this home that we mean Yes.

in human time

Lisa Bickmore

not dimensional and not
in my mind spacious

for so long the lake was
a blank with only a book
full of floating Mormons to fill it

meaning it was a lacuna
news to me its population of
flies and microfauna

although a man I knew once
had a boat   was a brine shrimp
fisherman who fancied himself
a captain   fancied himself rough
and ready and more than that
raised Mormon but an emphatic renouncer

A good captain always shares
the catch with his crew
he told me   as if
naming a foundational ethic
of the lake

the lake was fuller then I think
perhaps stretching our capacity

for understanding
for a century or more enough
of us took water as a right
refusing to know that water
taken as a right
eventually punishes

in the last three years we've gone twice
and each time it felt more
like a dream   pink and foamy
at the recessive shore
from which my husband picked up
armfuls of foam shore-bloom
knee-high barely wet but surely salty

■ ■ ■

years before
along the eastern shore
of another inland sea
the Salton its diffuse horizons
miraging as we stopped
to look across

the towns we drove through
someone's idea of future resorts
ending in hard-pan failure

and still someone some ones
live there somewhere besides
in the houses taken down
to the studs

abandon hope all ye who enter

scrawled in spray paint
by a literalist on one wall
buried alive on another

at the south end
a wild bird refuge
at dusk numberless water birds
aloft   the sun burning
to its conclusion

at that shore we saw
dead birds too   and dead fish
despite its refuge
the sea shrinking and toxic

I don't want to say *harbinger*

■ ■ ■

when we went to the salt lake
the first time   of course
we went to see the jetty
as we drove   the signs
both indicated and confused
it glittered   all of it
a dead long-necked bird
curved into a half-heart
diamantine in salt

is this a story that will help?

that first time was three weeks
before my father died
the second three months

after my sister

the spiral like a tattoo
a spiral like time unfurling
not geologic time because it is
human scale   made by a man
with earth movers and ideas
human scale and therefore
containing the seed of loss

longer than a single life though

intended to be that intended to
undo very slowly   be undone
only by erosion by waves and time
itself

                        and in that like the lake
also made by the earth moving

by ancient waters' changes

the next time I am there
I want to be there
when it rains   to watch snow
melt into its salt I want to mark

no further anniversaries
I want to witness water
having its own way

CONTRIBUTORS

KARIN ANDERSON is the author of the novels *Before Us Like a Land of Dreams*, *What Falls Away*, and *Things I Didn't Do*, and co-editor of *Blossom as the Cliffrose* and *Utah Lake Stories*. She lives in Salt Lake City, Utah.

LISA BICKMORE is the author of three books of poems, *flicker*, *Ephemerist*, and *Haste*. She is the founder/publisher of the new independent nonprofit Lightscatter Press. She lives in West Jordan, Utah.

AYJA BOUNOUS is a Salt Lake City–based writer. She is the author of *Junior Bounous and the Joys of Skiing* and *Shaped by Snow: Defending the Future of Winter*, and a contributor to *Alta and Little Cottonwood: Jewel of the Wasatch Mountains*. Bounous holds a MA in Environmental Humanities from the University of Utah and hosts *Snow + Salt*, a podcast exploring seasonal rhythms in the Wasatch.

ALEX (ALISSANDRU) CALDIERO: Sonosopher, poet, polyartist, and scholar of humanities and intermedia. Caldiero was born in the ancient town of Licodia Eubea, Sicily. He immigrated to the United States at age nine, and was raised in Manhattan and Brooklyn. Caldiero is the author of numerous publications, including *Sonosuono*, *Some Love*, his work is anthologized in *Text-Sound Texts*, (*Dictionary of the Avant-Gardes*, *ORIGINS*, and *Fire in the Pasture*). Caldiero is Sr. Artist-in-Residence at Utah Valley University.

ROB CARNEY is the author of *Accidental Gardens: New and Revised* and nine books of poems, most recently *The Book of Drought*. He has written a featured series called "Old Roads, New Stories" for Terrain.org. He is a Professor of English at Utah Valley University and lives in Salt Lake City, Utah.

KATHARINE COLES'S fourteen books include her poetry collections *Time and Chance* and *Ghost Apples*; a collection of essays, *The Stranger I Become*; and her memoir, *Look Both Ways*. A Distinguished Professor at the University of Utah, she has received awards from The Guggenheim Foundation, the US National Science Foundation's Antarctic Artists and Writer Program, the National Endowment for the Arts, and the National Endowment for the Humanities. She lives in Salt Lake City, Utah.

STAR COULBROOKE is the author of several chapbooks, notably Walking the Bear, and three poetry collections, *Thin Spines of Memory*, *Both Sides from the Middle*, and *City of Poetry*, and edited the *Helicon West Anthology*. Coulbrooke served as the inaugural Poet Laureate for the City of Logan and directed the Utah State University Writing Center until her retirement in 2020. She lives in Smithfield, Utah.

ADAM O. DAVIS is the author of *Index of Haunted Houses*. His work has appeared widely in journals and anthologies, including *AGNI*, *The Believer*, *The Best American Poetry*, *The Paris Review*, and *ZYZZYVA*. He lives in San Diego, California, where he teaches English literature at The Bishop's School.

LYNN DE FREITAS began her involvement with FRIENDS of Great Salt Lake shortly after it was founded in 1994. She has experience working with federal, state, and local stakeholders on developing policies that address the unique role and characteristics of the Great Salt Lake ecosystem. She has a bachelors in biology from

Montclair State College and a Masters of Education in Educational Systems and Learning Resources from the University of Utah. She lives in Salt Lake City, Utah.

DANIELLE BEAZER DUBRASKY is the author of *Drift Migration.* Several journals have published her poems, including *Chiron Review, Ninth Letter, South Dakota Review,* and *Sugar House Review.* Her other publications include *Invisible Shores* and *Blossom as the Cliffrose: Mormon Legacies and the Beckoning Wild.* She is a professor of creative writing at Southern Utah University, and currently resides in Cedar City, Utah.

JUSTIN EVANS was born and raised in Central, Utah. After high school he joined the army. Since graduating from Southern Utah University, Evans lives on the Utah-Nevada border with his wife and sons. He published eleven chapbooks and full-length collections of poetry, including his most recent book, *Cenotaph.*

SARAH FOX is a Seattle-based historian drawn to the stories we tell about places, bodies, and the relationships between them. Fox is the author of *Downwind: A People's History of the Nuclear West* and is currently completing the manuscript for her second book project, *At Home in the Plume: Unruly Waste and Reckoning in the Pacific Northwest.* Fox holds a PhD in History from University of British Columbia. She is a member of the Core PhD faculty in Sustainability Education at Prescott College.

TERI HARMAN is a writer, scholar, and nature photographer. She holds an master's degree in environmental humanities from the University of Utah. She serves as a content specialist for the UVU Museum of Art and volunteers with Conserve Utah Valley. Teri lives in Saratoga Springs, Utah, with her partner and three children.

ANDY HOFFMAN is a writer, teacher, and publisher. He is the author of *At the Edge and End of Water*, and his work has appeared in over thirty national literary journals. From 2001 to 2024, Hoffman edited and published Elik Press, and he has received awards for both fiction and nonfiction from the Utah Arts Council and the Utah Humanities Council. A resident of Salt Lake City, Utah, he loves the landscape, characters, and his life.

BROOKE LARSEN is a journalist at *The Salt Lake Tribune*. Her reporting covers water, land, climate, the energy transition, labor and communities across the West, and has appeared in *High Country News*, *Sierra*, *Salt Lake City Weekly*, *Undark*, and more. Larsen co-edited the anthology *New World Coming* and co-produces the podcast and multimedia storytelling project Stay Salty: Lakefacing Stories. She holds an MA in environmental humanities from the University of Utah and lives in Salt Lake City.

JOEL LONG has a forthcoming book of essays titled *Watershed*. He has published chapbooks called *The Onaqui Horses of the West Desert*, *Chopin's Preludes*, and *Saffron Beneath Every Frost*. His books include *Winged Insects*, *Lessons in Disappearance*, and *Knowing Time by Light*. His poems and essays have appeared in various publications. He lives in Salt Lake City, Utah.

QUINN LUTHY (they/them) is a writer and editor usually based in Seattle, Washington, on the unceded and stolen land of the Coast Salish peoples. Their work creates queer ecologies and is centered around queer responses to the climate crisis. Quinn holds a bachelor's degree from the New School and received an MA in environmental humanities from the University of Utah.

SARAH MAY is a queer Salvadoreña artist, poet, organizer, facilitator, and bruja. She graduated from the University of Utah with a bachelor's in fine art in photography and digital imaging and earned a master's in community leadership from Westminster

University. May has long called Pia Appaa, Great Salt Lake, home. May is the co-founder of Making Waves Artist Collaborative.

ELI MCCANN is a writer, humorist, and lawyer based out of Salt Lake City. He is the author of *We're Thankful for the Moisture* and the forthcoming novel *Stitched*. McCann is a columnist for *The Salt Lake Tribune* and produces a storytelling podcast and live storytelling show called *Strangerville*. His writing and storytelling have been featured in publications including *The Washington Post*, *BBC*, *Newsweek*, and others.

MICHAEL MCLANE is a poet, editor and essayist. He holds a PhD in creative writing from Victoria University, a master's of science in environmental humanities from the University of Utah, and a master's of fine arts from Colorado State University. McLane is the author of two chapbooks—*Trace Elements* and *Fume*. He is an editor with *Sugar House Review* and *Dark Mountain*, and was a founding editor of *saltfront*. His work has appeared in numerous journals. Born and raised in Salt Lake City, Utah, McLane resides in Martinborough, Aotearoa/New Zealand.

SCOTT MORRIS is an environmental historian and writer. He earned a master's of fine arts in creative writing from Goddard College and a PhD in American history from the University of Utah. A book on the economic and environmental history of the Great Salt Lake Basin is forthcoming from the University of Utah Press. Scott lives with his wife, son, three dogs, and nine chickens in the foothills of Wyoming's Wind River Range.

WILLY PALOMO (he/they/she) is the author of *Mercury in Reggaetón* and *Wake the Others*. In November 2024, Palomo's Spanish-to-English translation of *Tres Tercas Trincheras* by Marielos Oliva was published in Europe. A veteran of the Salt Lake City poetry slam scene, he has performed in 160+ public engagements. He is the son of two refugees from El Salvador.

DARREN PARRY is the former Chairman of the Northwestern Band of the Shoshone Nation. He is the author of *Tending the Sacred: How Indigenous Wisdom will Save the World* and *The Bear River Massacre: A Shoshone History*. Parry attended the University of Utah and Weber State University and received his Bachelor's Degree in Education. In 2024, he received an Honorary PhD in Education from Utah State University. He lives in Paradise, Utah.

DAYNA PATTERSON is the author of *O Lady, Speak Again* and *If Mother Braids a Waterfall*. She collaborated to produce *A Spiritual Thread*, a poetry collection of interwoven poems. Two of her poems appear in *Best Spiritual Literature*, 2023. She lives in Bellingham, Washington.

ALYSSA QUINN is the author of the novel *Habilis* and is an assistant professor of creative writing at Kenyon College. Originally from Utah, they now reside in Knox County, Ohio.

PAISLEY REKDAL is the author of four books of nonfiction and seven collections of poetry, including *West: A Translation*, which was longlisted for the 2023 National Book Award in Poetry and won the 2024 Kingsley Tufts Prize and the Reading the West Book Award for Poetry. Her poems and essays have appeared in *The New Yorker*, *The New York Times Magazine*, *Poetry*, *The New Republic*, and on National Public Radio, among others. Rekdal is a Distinguished Professor at the University of Utah, where she teaches in the Creative Writing Program and directs the American West Center. Between 2017-2022, she served as Utah's Poet Laureate. She lives in Salt Lake City, Utah.

KYLAN RICE is the author of *An Image Not a Book* and co-author of *Primer*. His poems and creative prose can be found in *Colorado*

Review, Denver Quarterly, Kenyon Review Online, Oxford Poetry, Tupelo Quarterly, and *West Branch*. He is an assistant professor of English at Utah State University and co-editor of Thirdhand Books.

HANNA SALTZMAN writes about health, nature, parenting. Her essays, flash nonfiction, and poetry appear in *River Teeth, The Sun, Terrain.org, Intima*, and *JAMA*. She lives in Salt Lake City, where she works as a pediatrician.

NAN SEYMOUR is a poet and advocate who weaves words to cast spells on Great Salt Lake's behalf. Her story "Lake Woman Leaving" was awarded the 2022 Alfred Lambourne Prize from Friends of Great Salt Lake. Seymour is the founder of the River Writing Collective and author of *prayers not meant for heaven* and *irreplaceable: a collective praise poem for Great Salt Lake*. A long-time Utahn, she now lives in Tucson, Arizona.

HOLLY SIMONSEN lives in Salt Lake City, Utah. Simonsen holds a master's of fine arts from Vermont College of Fine Arts. Her work can be found in *Hayden's Ferry Review, Copper Nickel, Ecotone*, and elsewhere. Simonsen serves as Programs Director for FRIENDS of Great Salt Lake.

MADI SUDWEEKS was born and raised in the Salt Lake Valley on occupied Shoshone, Goshute, and Ute lands. After graduating from the University of Utah with degrees in history and social work, she worked at a local organization focusing on advancing grassroots leadership and racial equity in education. Sudweeks also completed the environmental humanities program at the University of Utah.

SYLVIA TORTI is an ecologist and writer and currently serving as President of College of the Atlantic, Bar Harbor, Maine. She holds a PhD in biology from the University of Utah. She is a creative writer who published *The Scorpion's Tail* and *Cages*. Her short stories and essays have been published in numerous magazines and edited volumes.

CLAIRE WAHMANHOLM is the author of *Wilder*, *Redmouth*, and, most recently, *Meltwater*. She lives in the Twin Cities, Minnesota.

MUSKAN WALIA is a lead organizer with Utah Youth Environmental Solutions, where she supports youth-led campaigns around environmental justice education, water justice, and clean energy. She resides in Bountiful, Utah.

NICOLE WALKER is the author of several books including *Processed Meats: Essays on Food, Flesh and Navigating Disaster*. She has written several essays for *The New York Times* and is a noted author in several editions of *Best American Essays*. She edits the Crux series of nonfiction at the University of Georgia press. She lives in Flagstaff, Arizona, where she teaches creative writing at Northern Arizona University.

CHARLES WAUGH is the co-editor and co-translator of four books of Vietnamese environmental fiction: *Dương Hướng's No Man River* and *Tạ Duy Anh's The Termite Queen* with Quan Manh Ha, and the story collections *Wild Mustard* with Văn Giá and Nguyễn Lien, and *Family of Fallen Leaves: Stories of Agent Orange* with Nguyen Lien. He teaches writing at Utah State University, and is the Associate Editor for Fiction at *ISLE*. He lives in Logan, Utah.

RACHEL WHITE makes poems to praise the living earth and question the social relations destroying it. She is co-founder and publisher of *THE NOMAD*, a nonprofit literary magazine dedicated to writers. Her poetry chapbook, *The Velvet Earth after Rain*, was honored as a 2025 Utah Book Awards Notable Read. White received an MFA in Poetry from the University of Utah. She lives in downtown Salt Lake City, Utah.

BROOKE WILLIAMS writes about evolution, consciousness, and his own adventures exploring both the inner and outer wilderness. His books include *Open Midnight—Where Wilderness and Ancestors Meet*, *Mary Jane Wild—Two Walks and a Rant*, and *Encountering Dragonfly—Notes on the Practice of Re-enchantment.* He lives with the writer, Terry Tempest Williams and their two cats near Moab, Utah.

TERRY TEMPEST WILLIAMS is the award-winning author of seventeen books of creative nonfiction, including the environmental classic *Refuge*, *The Hour of Land*, *Erosion*, and *The Glorians.* She is a member of the American Academy of Arts & Letters and is currently the writer-in-residence at the Harvard Divinity School. She divides her time between Cambridge, Massachusetts and Castle Valley, Utah.

NATALIE PADILLA YOUNG is a co-founder and editor in chief of the poetry magazine *Sugar House Review.* She is half Puerto Rican and half Brigham Young, working as an art director for a Salt Lake City ad agency. She published *All of This Was Once Under Water.* Natalie's poetry has appeared in *swamp pink, Green Mountains Review, Tampa Review, Rattle, South Dakota Review, Los Angeles Times, Tar River Poetry, Terrain.org*, and elsewhere. She lives in Cedar City, Utah, with the poet Nano Taggart and two dogs.

FROM THE EDITOR

Alex Caldiero passed on February 9, 2026, just a short time before this anthology went to press.

Alex was the Sonosopher, the Word Shaker, the "sonal wise guy," and he was someone I felt hugely fortunate to call a friend. In the same way that Great Salt Lake is an ecotone, a space of transitions and convergence, Alex was a literary and spiritual ecotone. He was a performer and sonic archaeologist, Mormon and shaman, dad and dadaist. He was a generous teacher as well. Like the lake, he was complex, brooding, capable of creating his own weather at times (both in a classroom and on a stage). I first saw him perform in the basement of a Lutheran church in Salt Lake City when I was fifteen years old. I was fascinated and smitten and terrified all at once. Over the years, I found that I was far from the only one to experience that potent reaction. He brought people to poetry who may not have cared to find their way otherwise, through alleyways guttural and oneiric and often hilarious. He knew, beyond all else, that "Poetry is wanted here!" I will miss him and I regret that he will not see this text or join us at the lake for a celebration of just the kind of strange, wondrous, and liminal space that he inhabited. But I do know that he's out there with us in some form, where he wanted to be: "where the sound goes, after the bell stops ringing."

—**MICHAEL MCLANE**

NOTES

A longer version of Katharine Coles' essay "Naming Creatures" was originally published as a chapter in the book *Writing Landscape and Setting in the Anthropocene: Britain and Beyond*, published by Palgrave Macmillan.

Sarah May's poems "5. Appearance of Beak," "7. Feathers tracts seen," and "13. Covered in Feathers" appear in her chapbook *Our stories are our bodies*, which was published by Glass Spider Publishing.

An earlier version of Nicole Walker's essay "Everyone Wants to be a Brine Shrimp" was published by *Terrain.org*.

ABOUT TORREY HOUSE PRESS

Torrey House Press exists at the intersection of the literary arts and environmental advocacy. THP publishes books that elevate diverse perspectives, explore relationships with place, and deepen our connections to the natural world and to each other. THP inspires ideas, conversation, and action on issues that link the American West to the past, present, and future of the ever-changing Earth.

We believe that lively, contemporary literature is at the cutting edge of social change. We seek to inform, expand, and reshape the dialogue on environmental justice and stewardship for the natural world by elevating literary excellence from diverse voices.

Torrey House Press is a 501(c)(3) nonprofit publisher. Our work is made possible by generous donations from readers like you.

Visit www.torreyhouse.org for reading group discussion guides, author interviews, and more.

SPECIAL THANKS

Torrey House Press is supported by Back of Beyond Books, Bright Side Bookshop, The King's English Bookshop, Maria's Bookshop, the Ballantine Family Fund, the Jeffrey S. & Helen H. Cardon Foundation, the Lawrence T. Dee & Janet T. Dee Foundation, the McMullan/O'Connor Family Fund, the Palladium Foundation, the Stewart Family Foundation, the Barker Foundation, Karin Anderson, Kif Augustine & Stirling Adams, Diana Allison, Richard Baker, Karey Barker, Patti Baynham & Owen Baynham, Matt Bean, Klaus Bielefeldt, Joe Breddan, JB Brett & Jeff Grathwohl, Karen Buchi & Kenneth Buchi, Betty Clark & Gary Clark, Rose Chilcoat & Mark Franklin, Linc Cornell & Lois Cornell, Teow Lim Goh, Susan Cushman & Charlie Quimby, Lynn de Freitas & Patrick de Freitas, Pert Eilers, Ed Erwin, Sally Glaser & David Bower, Laurie Hilyer, Phyllis Hockett, Mabelle Hueston & John Hueston, Kirtly Parker Jones, Emily Klass, Rick Klass, Jen Lawton & John Thomas, Kaitlyn Mahoney, Susan Markley, Leigh Meigs & Stephen Meigs, Mark Meloy, Kathleen Metcalf, Donaree Neville & Douglas Neville, Marion S. Robinson, Danny Rosen, Jack Schmidt, Linnea Spears-Lebrun, Jennifer Speers, Molly Swonger, Rachel White, the National Endowment for the Humanities, the National Endowment for the Arts, the Utah Division of Arts & Museums, Utah Humanities, the Salt Lake City Arts Council, and Salt Lake County Zoo, Arts & Parks. Our thanks to individual donors, members, and the Torrey House Press board of directors for their valued support.

www.ingramcontent.com/pod-product-compliance
Lightning Source LLC
Jackson TN
JSHW021411150326
99271JS00001B/288

* 9 7 9 8 8 9 0 9 2 0 0 9 6 *